W9-ANK-438

FANTASTIC FOUR VOL. 3: BACK IN BLUE. Contains material originally published in magazine form as FANTASTIC FOUR #11-14 and ANNUAL #1. First printing 2015. ISBN# 978-0-7851-9220-6. Published by MARVEL WORLD-, INC., a subsidiary of MARVEL ENTERTAINMENT, LLC. OFFICE OF PUBLICATION: 135 West 50th Street, New York, NY 10020. Copyright © 2014 and 2015 Marvel Characters, Inc. All rights reserved. All characters featured s issue and the distinctive names and likenesses thereof, and all related indicia are trademarks of Marvel Characters, Inc. No similarity between any of the names, characters, persons, and/or institutions in this magazine those of any living or dead person or institution is intended, and any such similarity which may exist is purely coincidental. Printed in Canada. ALAN FINE, EVP - Office of the President, Marvel Worldwide, Inc. and EVP & Marvel Characters B.V.; DAN BUCKLEY, Publisher & President - Print, Animation & Digital Divisions; JOE QUESADA, Chief Creative Officer; TOM BREVOORT, SVP of Publishing; DAVID BOGART, SVP of Operations & Procure-. Publishing; C.B. CEBULSKI, SVP of Creator & Content Development; DAVID GABRIEL, SVP Print, Sales & Marketing; JIM O'KEEFE, VP of Operations & Logistics; DAN CARR, Executive Director of Publishing Technology; N CRESPI, Editorial Operations Manager; ALEX MORALES, Publishing Operations Manager; STAN LEE, Chairman Emeritus. For information regarding advertising in Marvel Comics or on Marvel.com, please contact Niza. Director of Marvel Partnerships, at ndisla@marvel.com. For Marvel subscription inquiries, please call 800-217-9158. Manufactured between 2/20/2015 and 3/30/2015 by SOLISCO PRINTERS, SCOTT, QC, CANADA.

8 7 6 5 4 3 2 1

BACK IN BLUE

WRITER: JAMES ROBINSON
PENCILERS: LEONARD KIRK (#11-13 & #14 PRESENT)
WITH MARC LAMING (#14 FLASHBACKS) & TOM GRUMMETT (ANNUAL #1)
INKERS: KARL KESEL (#11-13 & #14 PRESENT), MARC LAMING (#14 FLASHBACKS)
& TOM PALMER (ANNUAL #1)
COLORISTS: JESUS ABURTOV (#11-13 & #14 PRESENT) WITH
TAMRA BONVILLAIN (#14 PRESENT) & LOVERN KINDZIERSKI (#14 FLASHBACKS) AND
JIM CHARALAMPIDIS (ANNUAL #1)
LETTERER: VC'S CLAYTON COWLES
COVER ART: LEONARD KIRK & JESUS ABURTOV (#11-14); AND
GREG LAND, JAY LEISTEN & NOLAN WOODARD (ANNUAL #1)
ASSISTANT EDITOR: EMILY SHAW
EDITOR: MARK PANICCIA

COLLECTION EDITOR: SARAH BRUNSTAD
ASSOCIATE MANAGING EDITOR: ALEX STARBUCK
EDITORS, SPECIAL PROJECTS: JENNIFER GRÜNWALD & MARK D. BEAZLEY
SENIOR EDITOR, SPECIAL PROJECTS: JEFF YOUNGQUIST
BOOK DESIGNER: NELSON RIBEIRO
SVP PRINT, SALES & MARKETING: DAVID GABRIEL

EDITOR IN CHIEF: AXEL ALONSO
CHIEF CREATIVE OFFICER: JOE QUESADA
PUBLISHER: DAN BUCKLEY
EXECUTIVE PRODUCER: ALAN FINE

FANTASTIC FOUR CREATED BY STAN LEE & JACK KIRBY

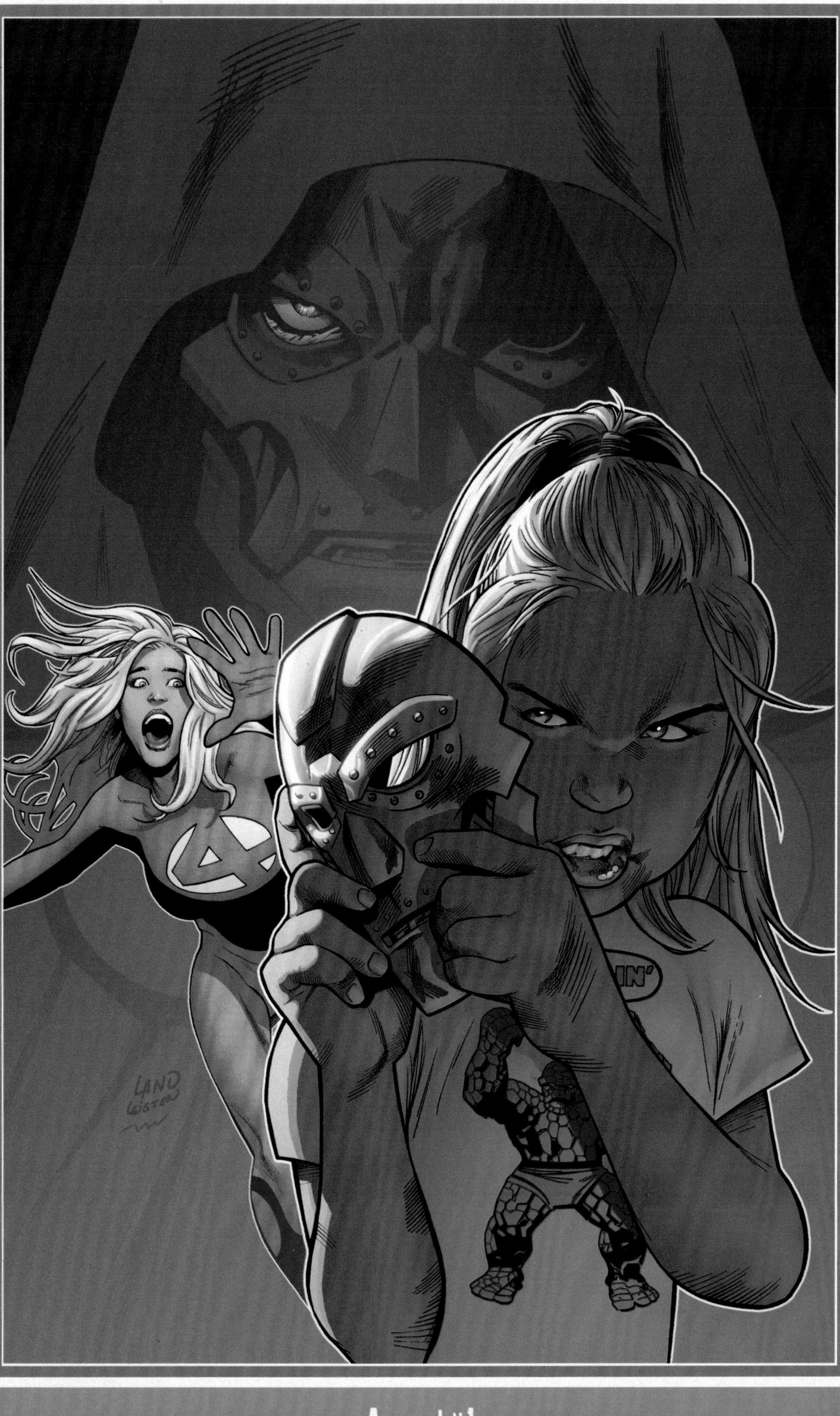

Annual #1

FANTASTIC 4

The once great family, the **FANTASTIC FOUR**, has fallen apart.

After an inter dimensional attack on the city was blamed on the **FANTASTIC FOUR**, problen
continued to mount: **JOHNNY** sacrificed his powers during the invasion; a court ruled th
the FF had to vacate the **BAXTER BUILDING**; the children of the **FUTURE FOUNDATIC**
were taken into S.H.I.E.L.D. custody for their safety, leaving **SUE** and **REED** heartbrok
and alone; **BEN** was framed for the murder of **PUPPET MASTER**.

Johnny isolated himself further from the family, drowning himself in a 24/7 pa
world while old friend **WYATT WINGFOOT** tried unsuccessfully to talk him out of h
downward spiral.

Ben discovered old flame/woman scorned **SHARON VENTURA, AKA SHE-THING,**
running the super villain prison yard.

And Reed, now working for futurist **JOHN EDEN**'S scientific utopia, was pulled into anoth
battle with the **WIZARD**—this time backed by members of the dark magic team, **SALE**
SEVEN. Reed sent out an S.O.S., and fortunately **SCARLET WITCH** answered.

Reed and Sue's extraordinarily intelligent daughter, **VALERIA**, broke her mothe
heart when she ran away from home to live in the country of **LATVERIA** with her "uncl
VICTOR VON DOOM. The child disapproved of Reed and Sue's ways and is determin
to make Latveria's dictator into a force for pure good in the world.

But Sue's been through enough loss. She wants to bring her daughter home…

Even if she has to face the world's most powerful monarch on her own.

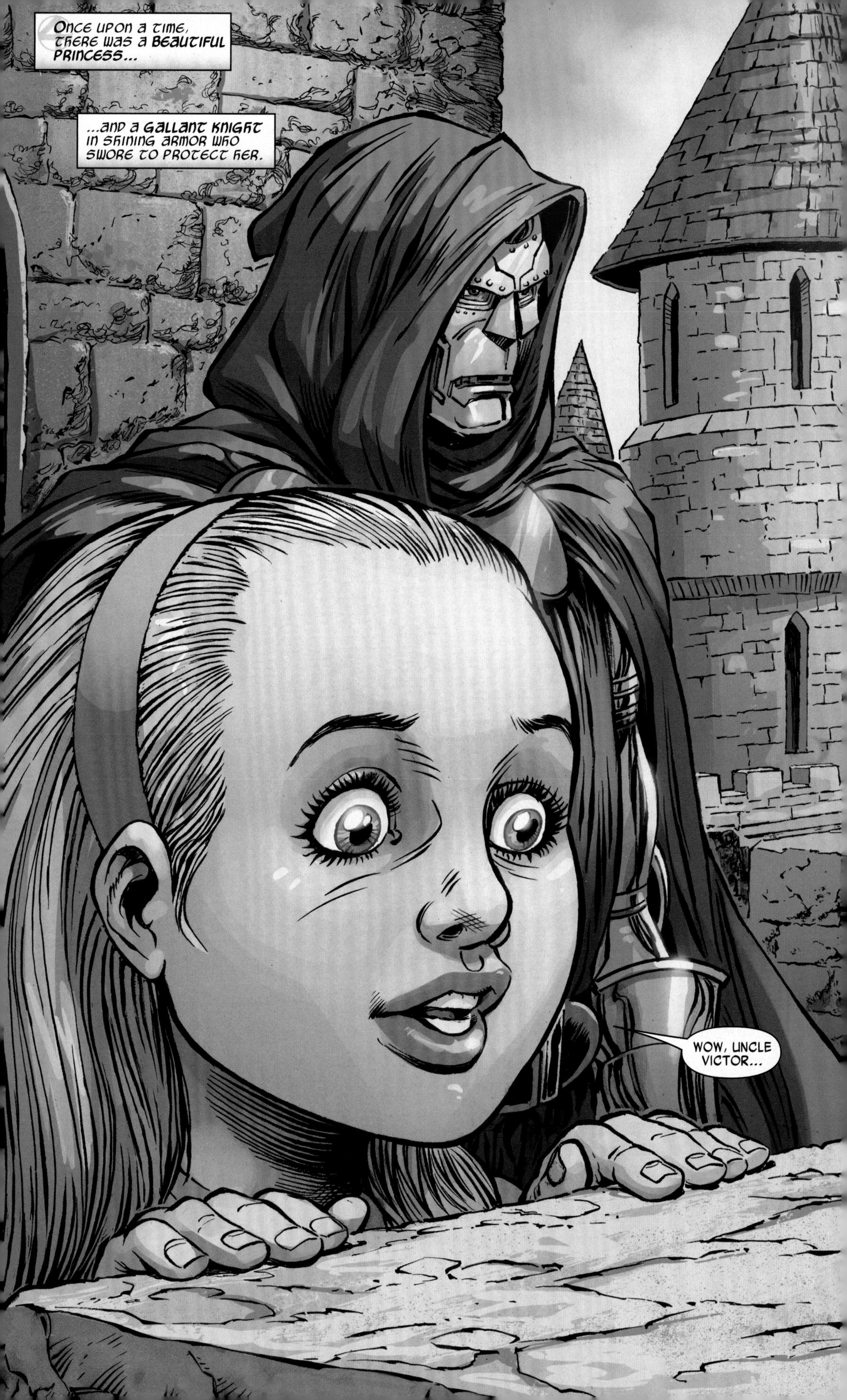
ONCE UPON A TIME, THERE WAS A BEAUTIFUL PRINCESS...
...AND A GALLANT KNIGHT IN SHINING ARMOR WHO SWORE TO PROTECT HER.
WOW, UNCLE VICTOR...

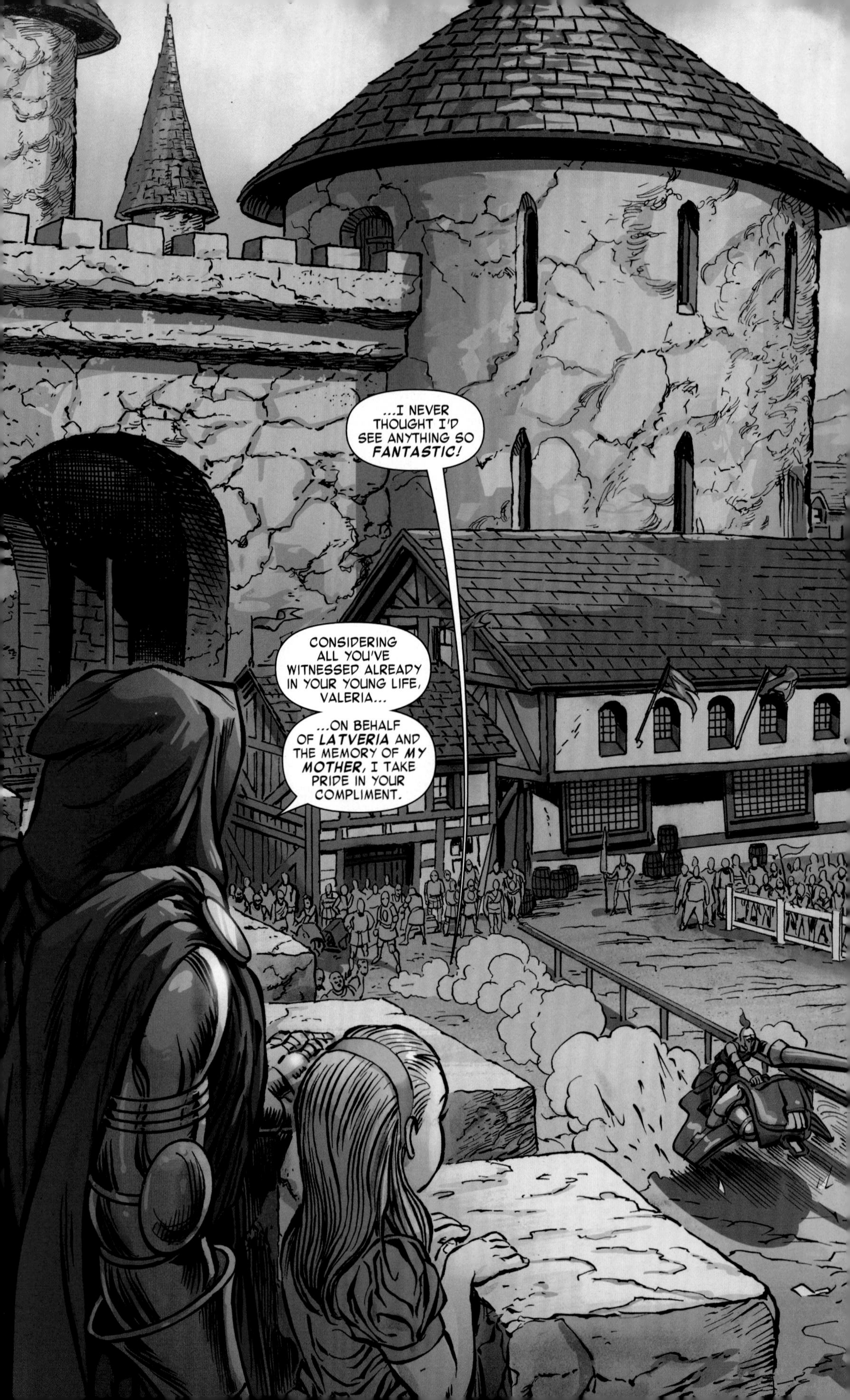
...I NEVER THOUGHT I'D SEE ANYTHING SO FANTASTIC!
CONSIDERING ALL YOU'VE WITNESSED ALREADY IN YOUR YOUNG LIFE, VALERIA...
...ON BEHALF OF LATVERIA AND THE MEMORY OF MY MOTHER, I TAKE PRIDE IN YOUR COMPLIMENT.

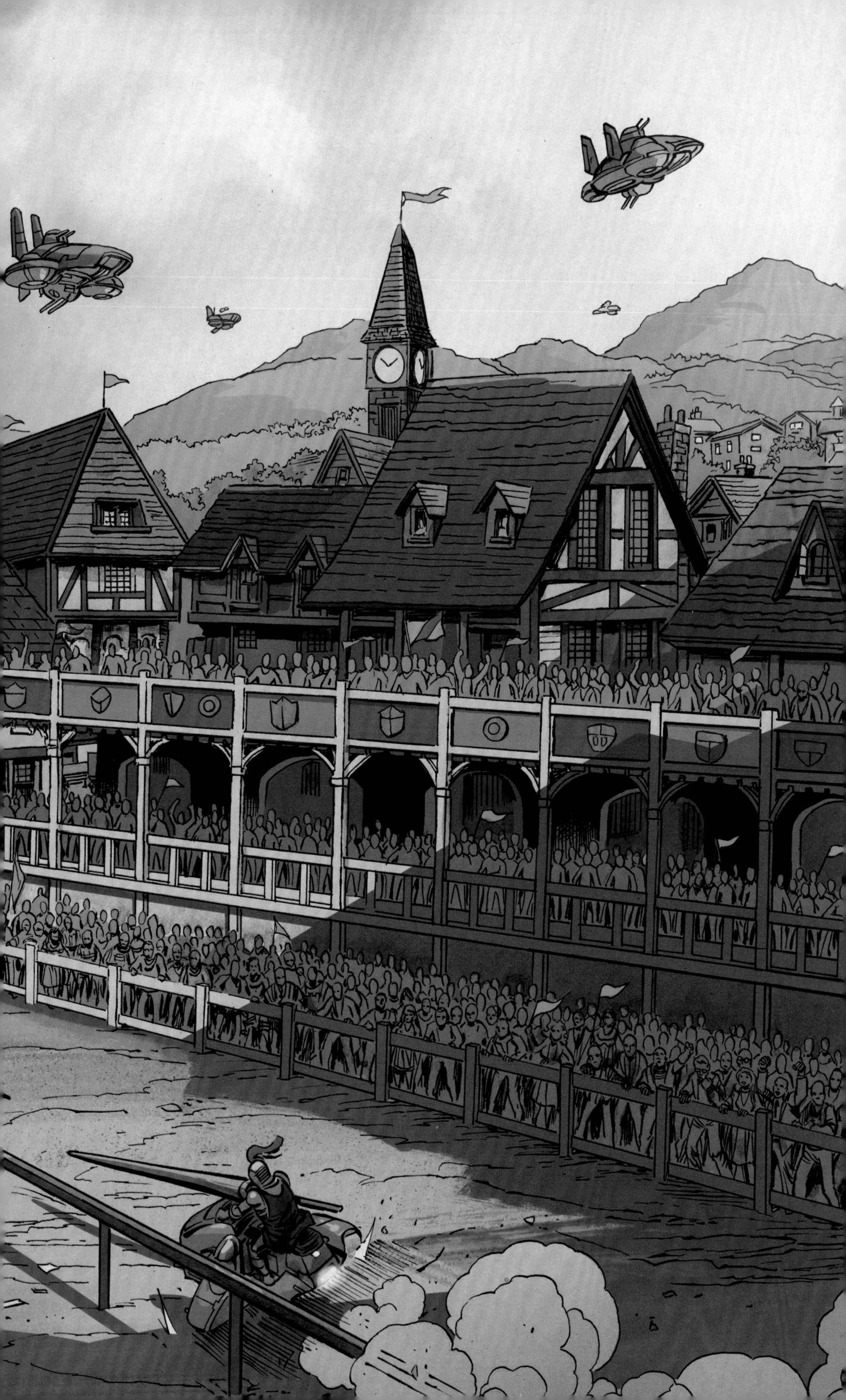

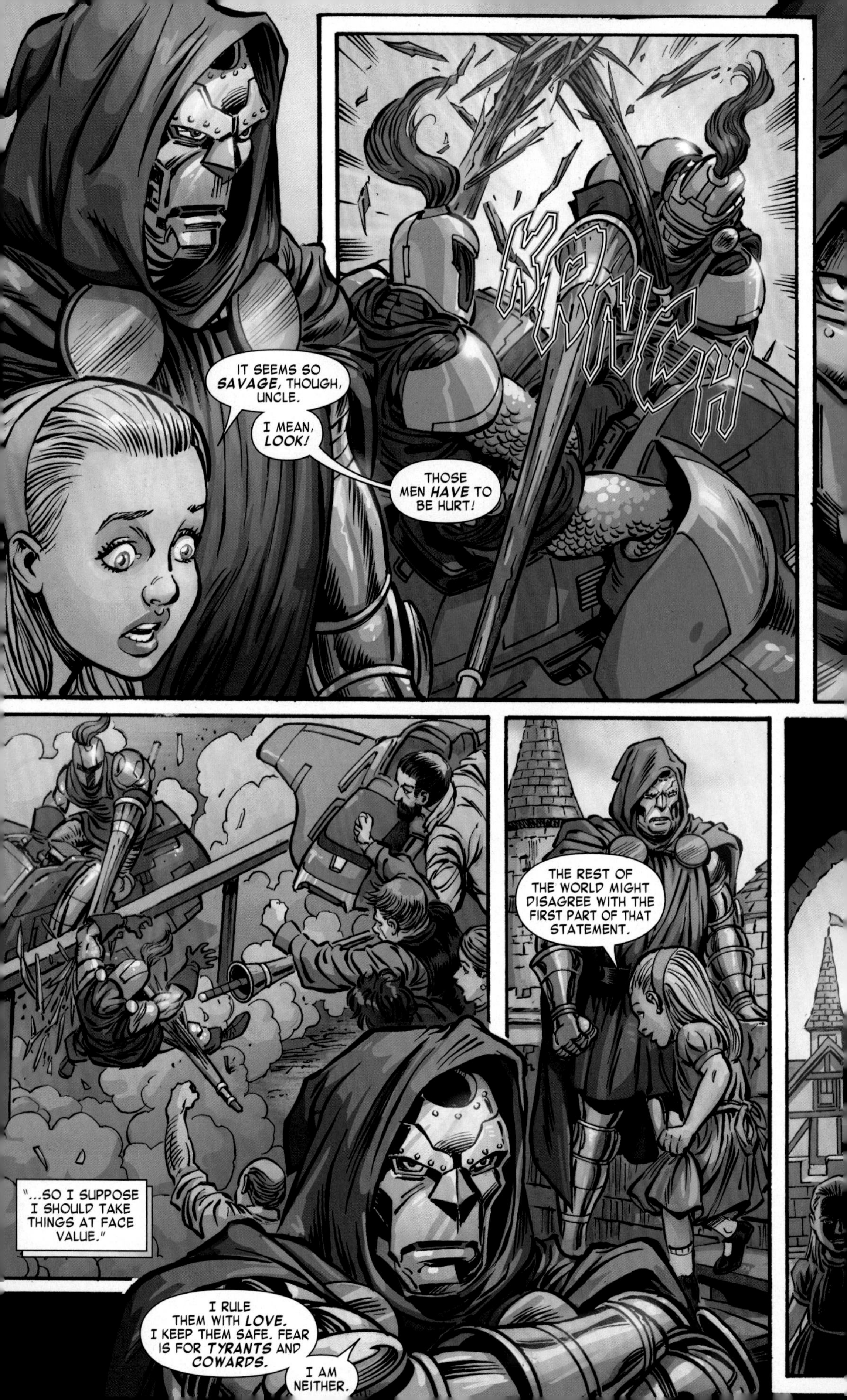

KRNCH
IT SEEMS SO SAVAGE, THOUGH, UNCLE.
I MEAN, LOOK!
THOSE MEN HAVE TO BE HURT!
THE REST OF THE WORLD MIGHT DISAGREE WITH THE FIRST PART OF THAT STATEMENT.
"...SO I SUPPOSE I SHOULD TAKE THINGS AT FACE VALUE."
I RULE THEM WITH LOVE. I KEEP THEM SAFE. FEAR IS FOR TYRANTS AND COWARDS.
I AM NEITHER.

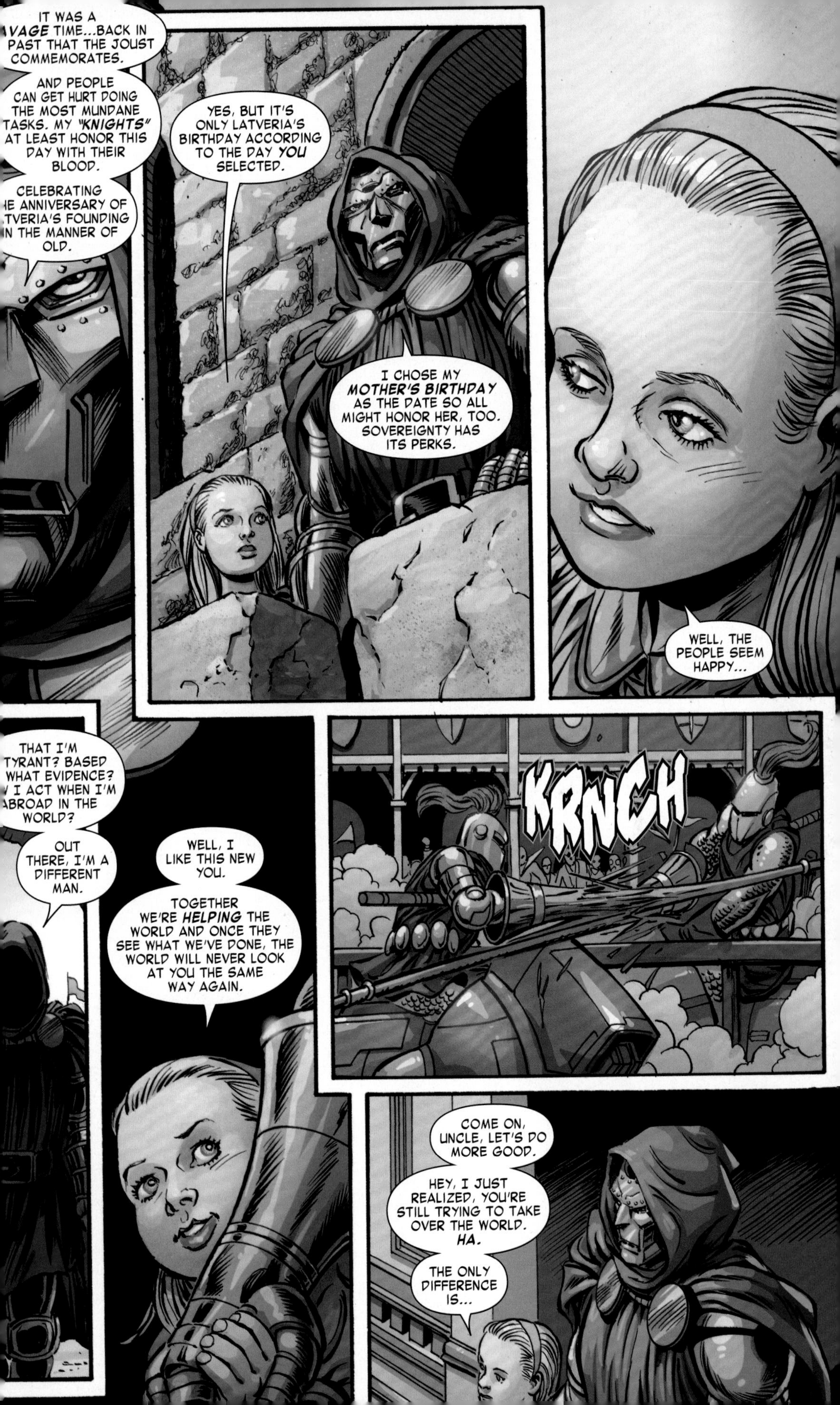

IT WAS A VAGE TIME...BACK IN PAST THAT THE JOUST COMMEMORATES.
AND PEOPLE CAN GET HURT DOING THE MOST MUNDANE TASKS. MY "KNIGHTS" AT LEAST HONOR THIS DAY WITH THEIR BLOOD.
CELEBRATING HE ANNIVERSARY OF TVERIA'S FOUNDING IN THE MANNER OF OLD.
YES, BUT IT'S ONLY LATVERIA'S BIRTHDAY ACCORDING TO THE DAY YOU SELECTED.
I CHOSE MY MOTHER'S BIRTHDAY AS THE DATE SO ALL MIGHT HONOR HER, TOO. SOVEREIGNTY HAS ITS PERKS.
WELL, THE PEOPLE SEEM HAPPY...
THAT I'M TYRANT? BASED WHAT EVIDENCE? I ACT WHEN I'M ABROAD IN THE WORLD?
OUT THERE, I'M A DIFFERENT MAN.
WELL, I LIKE THIS NEW YOU.
TOGETHER WE'RE HELPING THE WORLD AND ONCE THEY SEE WHAT WE'VE DONE, THE WORLD WILL NEVER LOOK AT YOU THE SAME WAY AGAIN.
KRNCH
COME ON, UNCLE, LET'S DO MORE GOOD.
HEY, I JUST REALIZED, YOU'RE STILL TRYING TO TAKE OVER THE WORLD. HA.
THE ONLY DIFFERENCE IS...

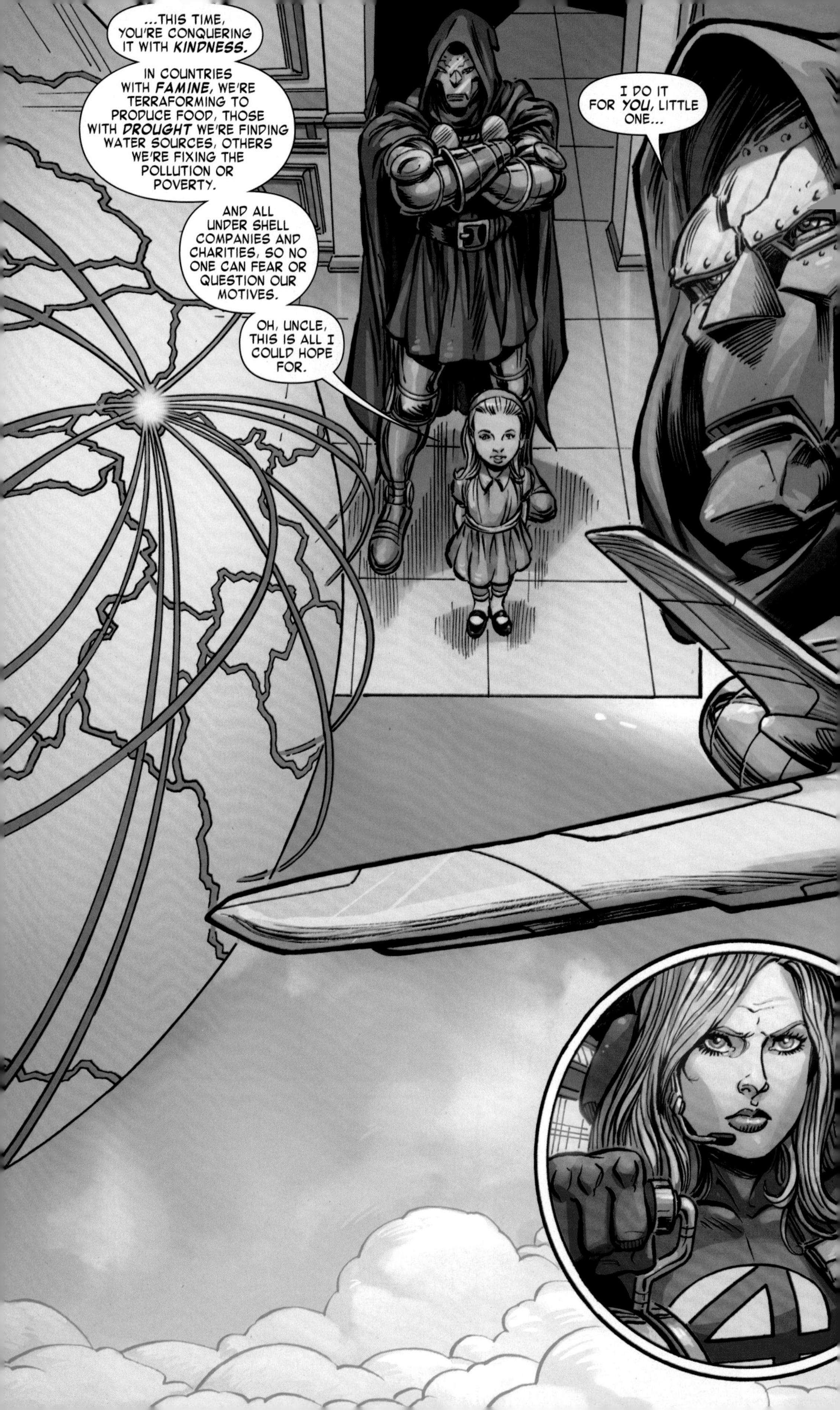
...THIS TIME, YOU'RE CONQUERING IT WITH KINDNESS.
IN COUNTRIES WITH FAMINE, WE'RE TERRAFORMING TO PRODUCE FOOD, THOSE WITH DROUGHT WE'RE FINDING WATER SOURCES, OTHERS WE'RE FIXING THE POLLUTION OR POVERTY.
AND ALL UNDER SHELL COMPANIES AND CHARITIES, SO NO ONE CAN FEAR OR QUESTION OUR MOTIVES.
OH, UNCLE, THIS IS ALL I COULD HOPE FOR.
I DO IT FOR YOU, LITTLE ONE...

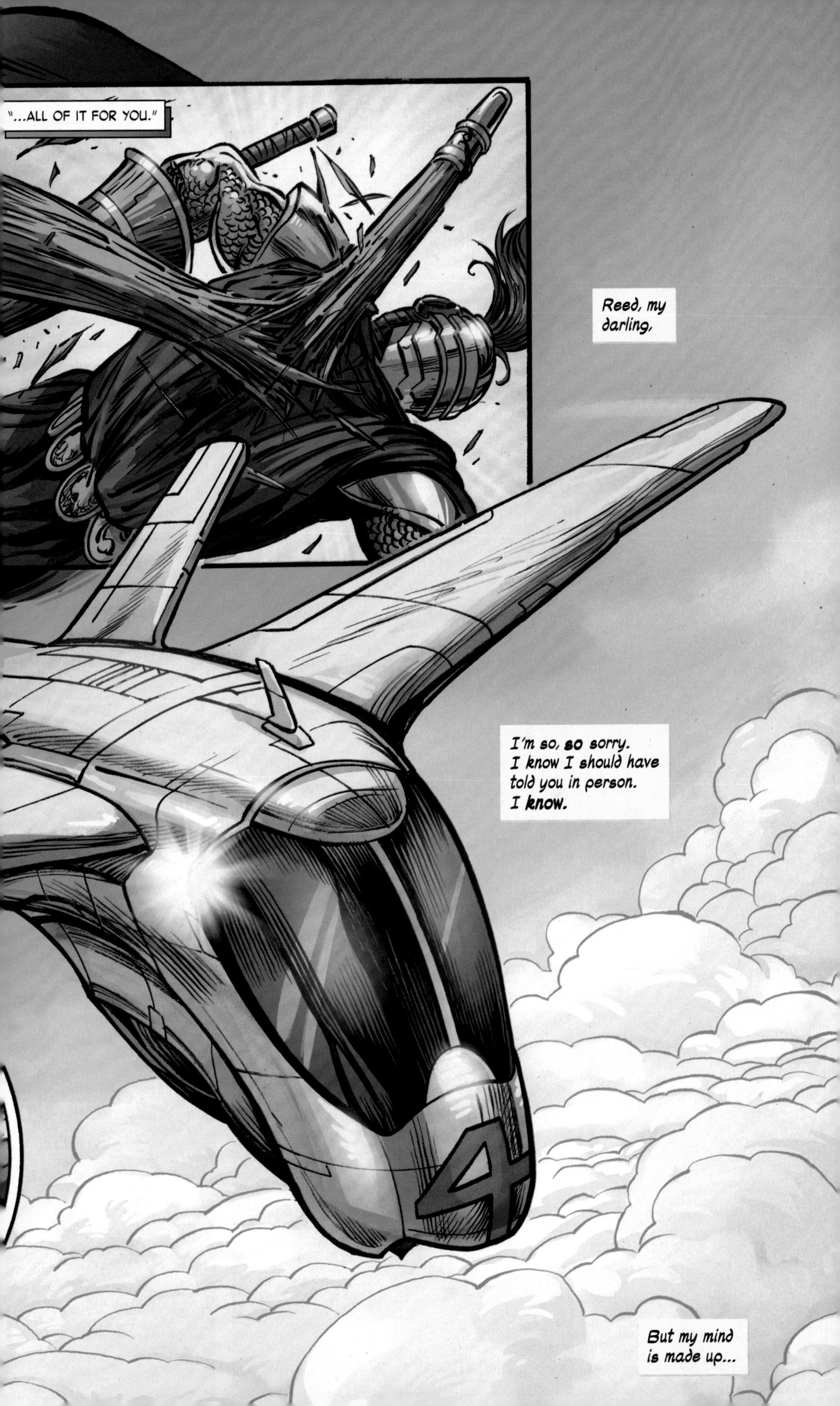
"...ALL OF IT FOR YOU."
Reed, my darling,
I'm so, **so** sorry. I know I should have told you in person. I **know.**
But my mind is made up...

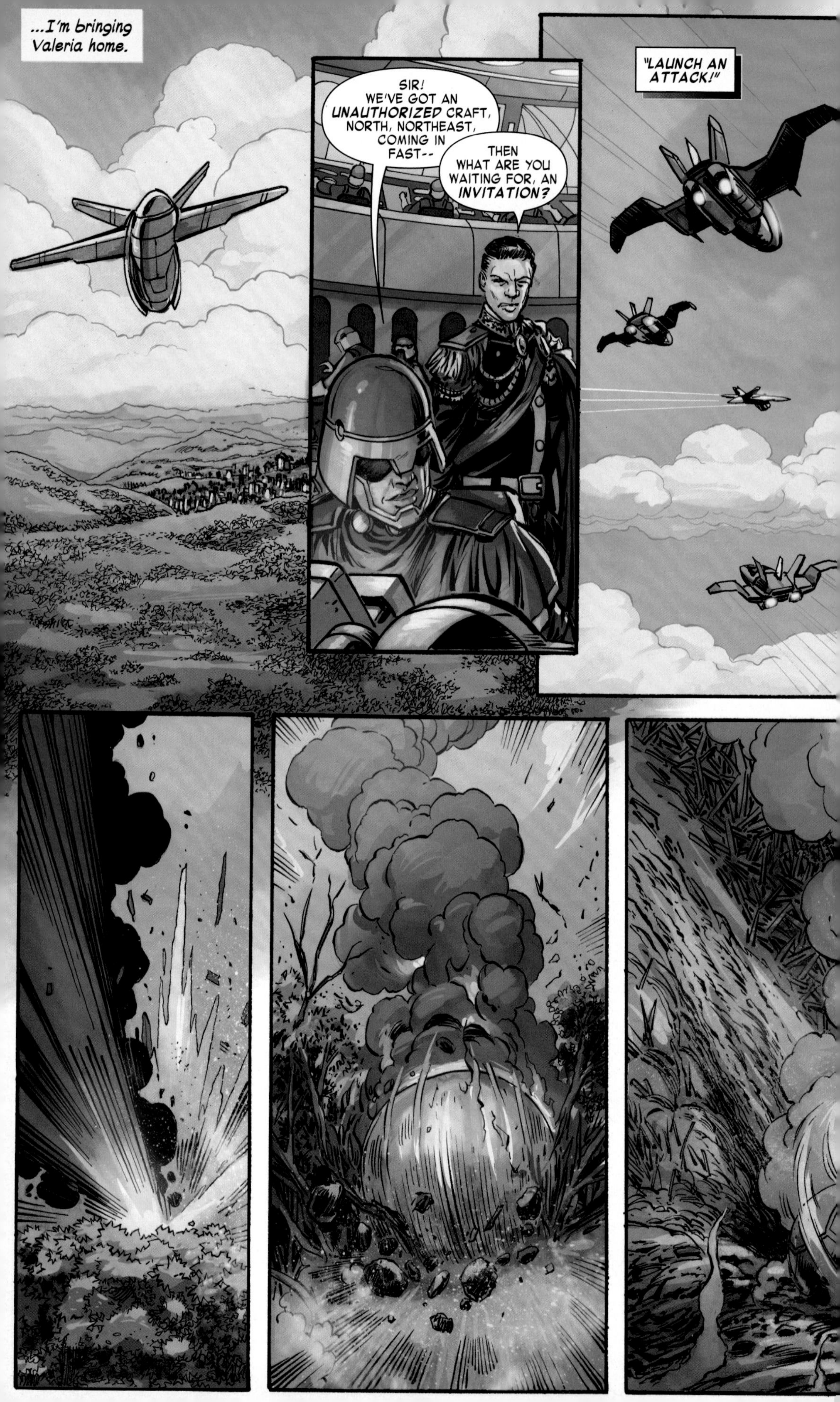

...I'm bringing Valeria home.
SIR! WE'VE GOT AN UNAUTHORIZED CRAFT, NORTH, NORTHEAST, COMING IN FAST--
THEN WHAT ARE YOU WAITING FOR, AN INVITATION?
"LAUNCH AN ATTACK!"

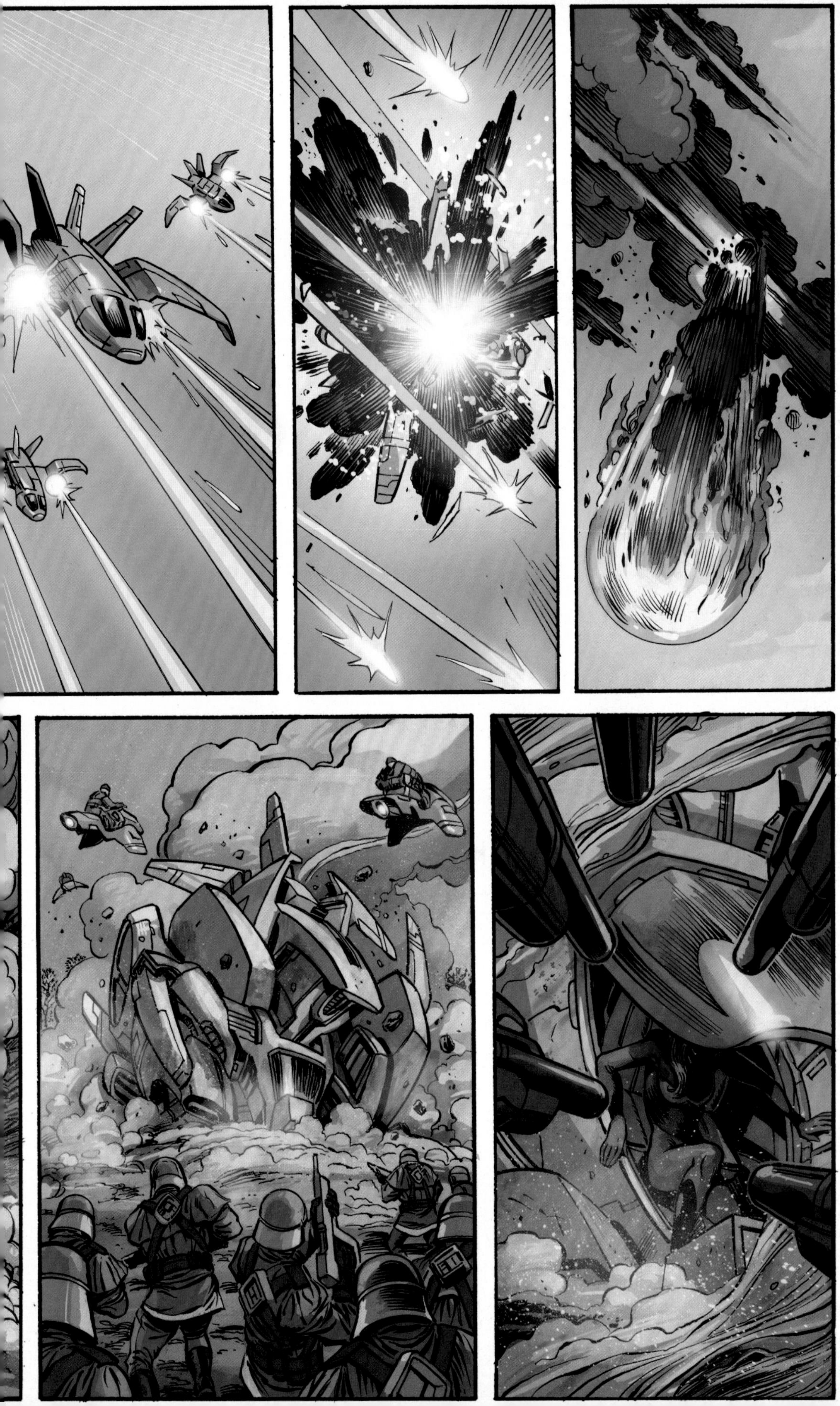

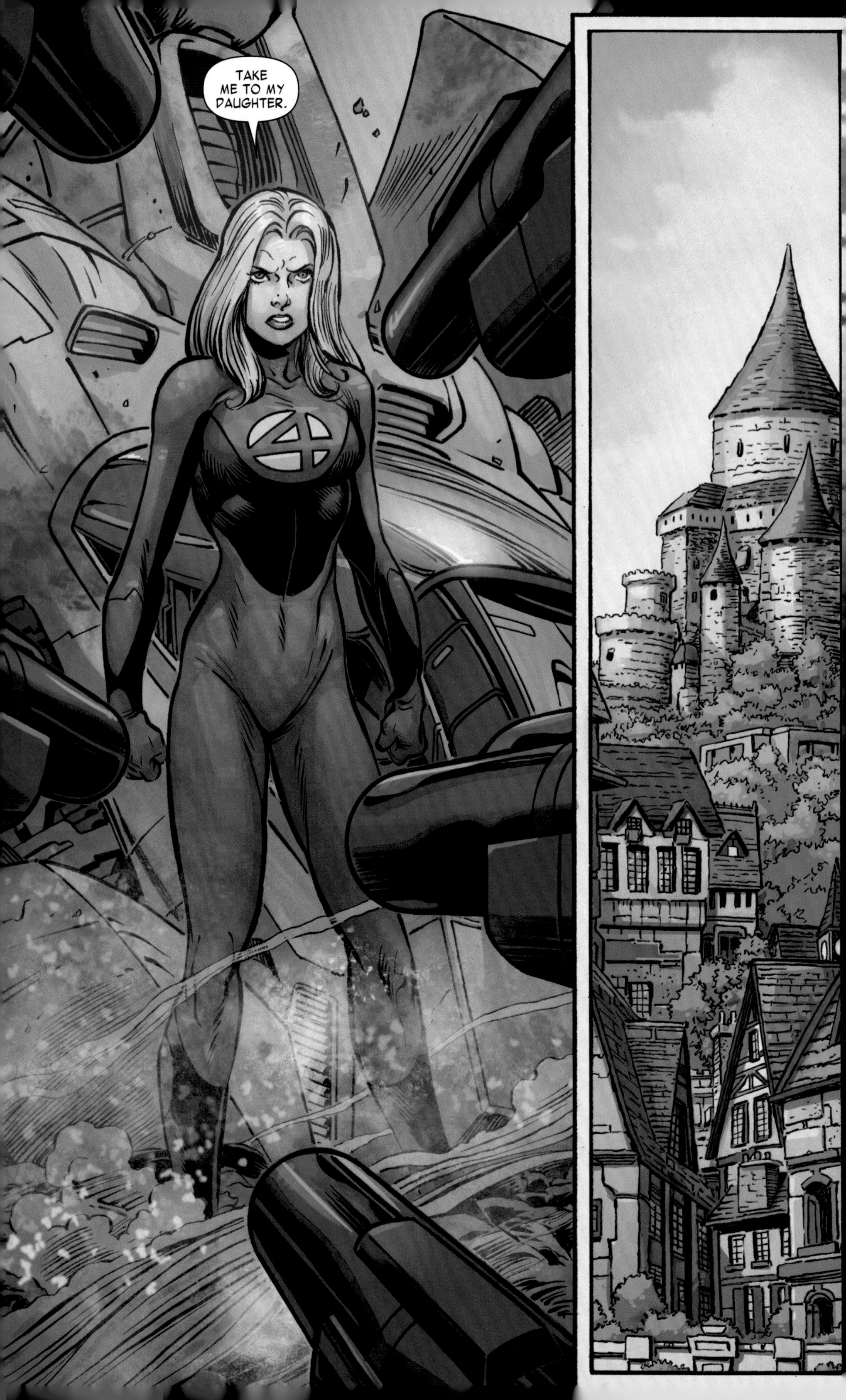
TAKE ME TO MY DAUGHTER.

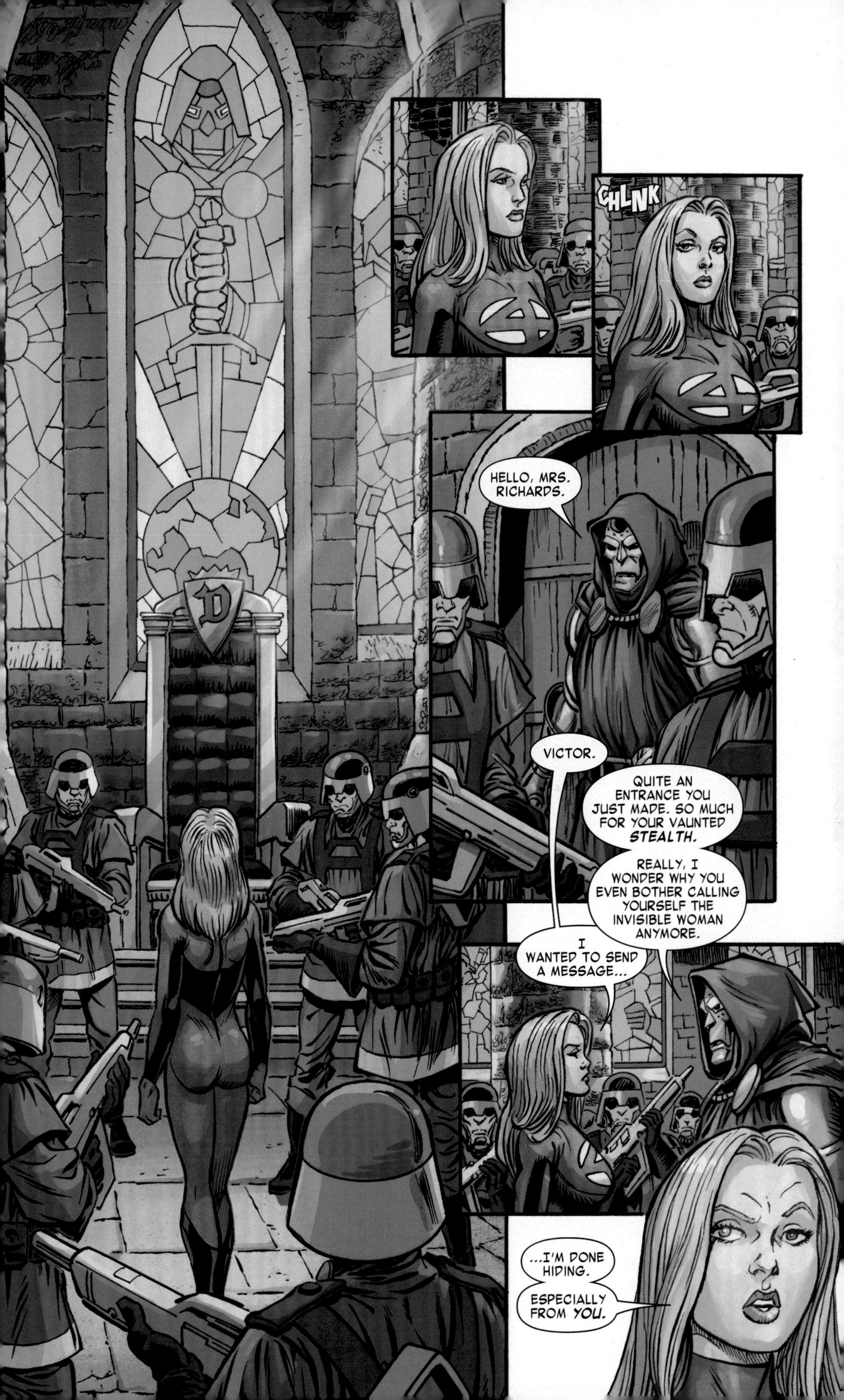
CHLNK
HELLO, MRS. RICHARDS.
VICTOR.
QUITE AN ENTRANCE YOU JUST MADE. SO MUCH FOR YOUR VAUNTED STEALTH.
REALLY, I WONDER WHY YOU EVEN BOTHER CALLING YOURSELF THE INVISIBLE WOMAN ANYMORE.
I WANTED TO SEND A MESSAGE...
...I'M DONE HIDING.
ESPECIALLY FROM YOU.

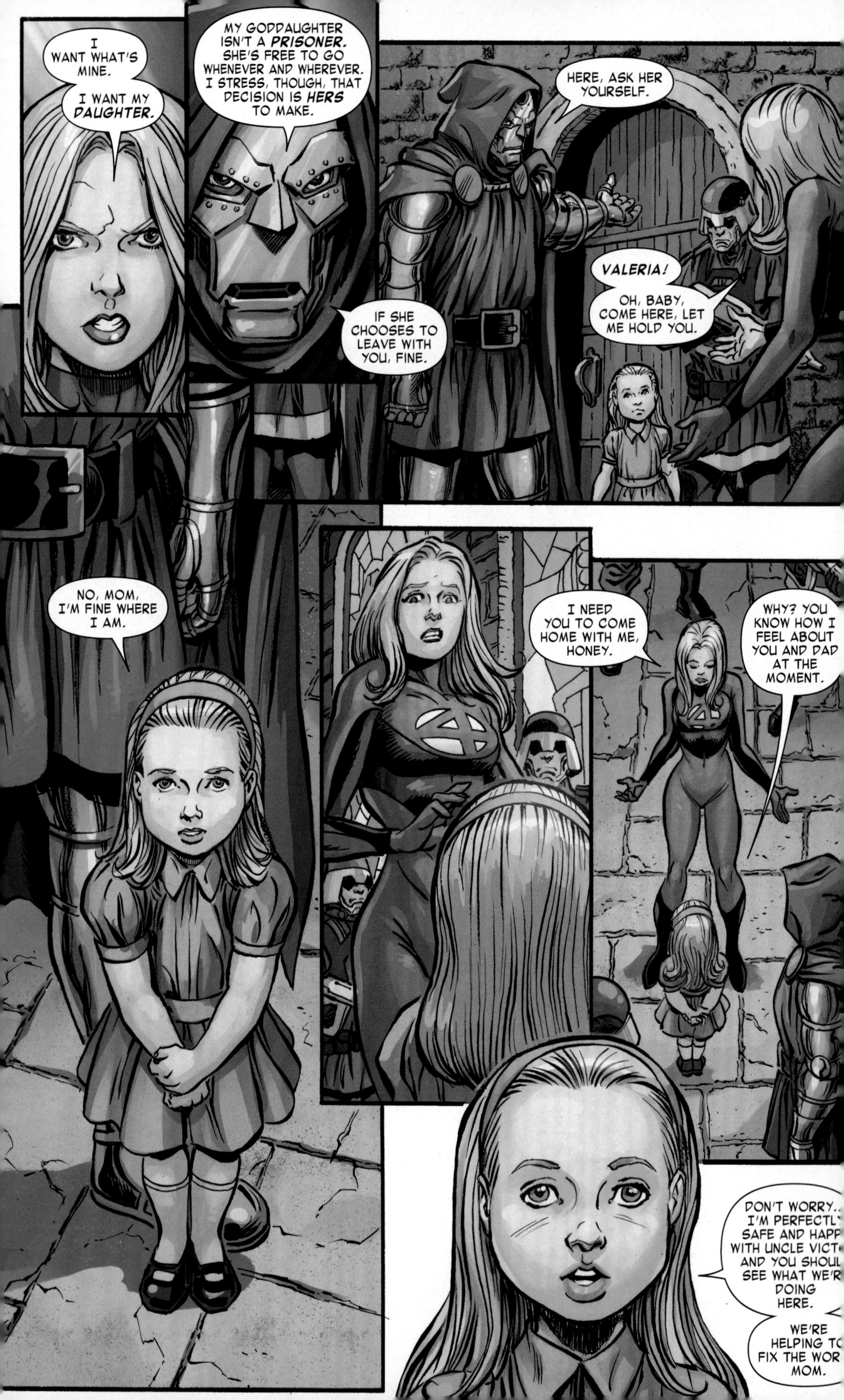

I WANT WHAT'S MINE.
I WANT MY DAUGHTER.
MY GODDAUGHTER ISN'T A PRISONER. SHE'S FREE TO GO WHENEVER AND WHEREVER. I STRESS, THOUGH, THAT DECISION IS HERS TO MAKE.
IF SHE CHOOSES TO LEAVE WITH YOU, FINE.
HERE, ASK HER YOURSELF.
VALERIA!
OH, BABY, COME HERE, LET ME HOLD YOU.
NO, MOM, I'M FINE WHERE I AM.
I NEED YOU TO COME HOME WITH ME, HONEY.
WHY? YOU KNOW HOW I FEEL ABOUT YOU AND DAD AT THE MOMENT.
DON'T WORRY... I'M PERFECTL SAFE AND HAPP WITH UNCLE VICT AND YOU SHOUL SEE WHAT WE'R DOING HERE.
WE'RE HELPING T FIX THE WOR MOM.

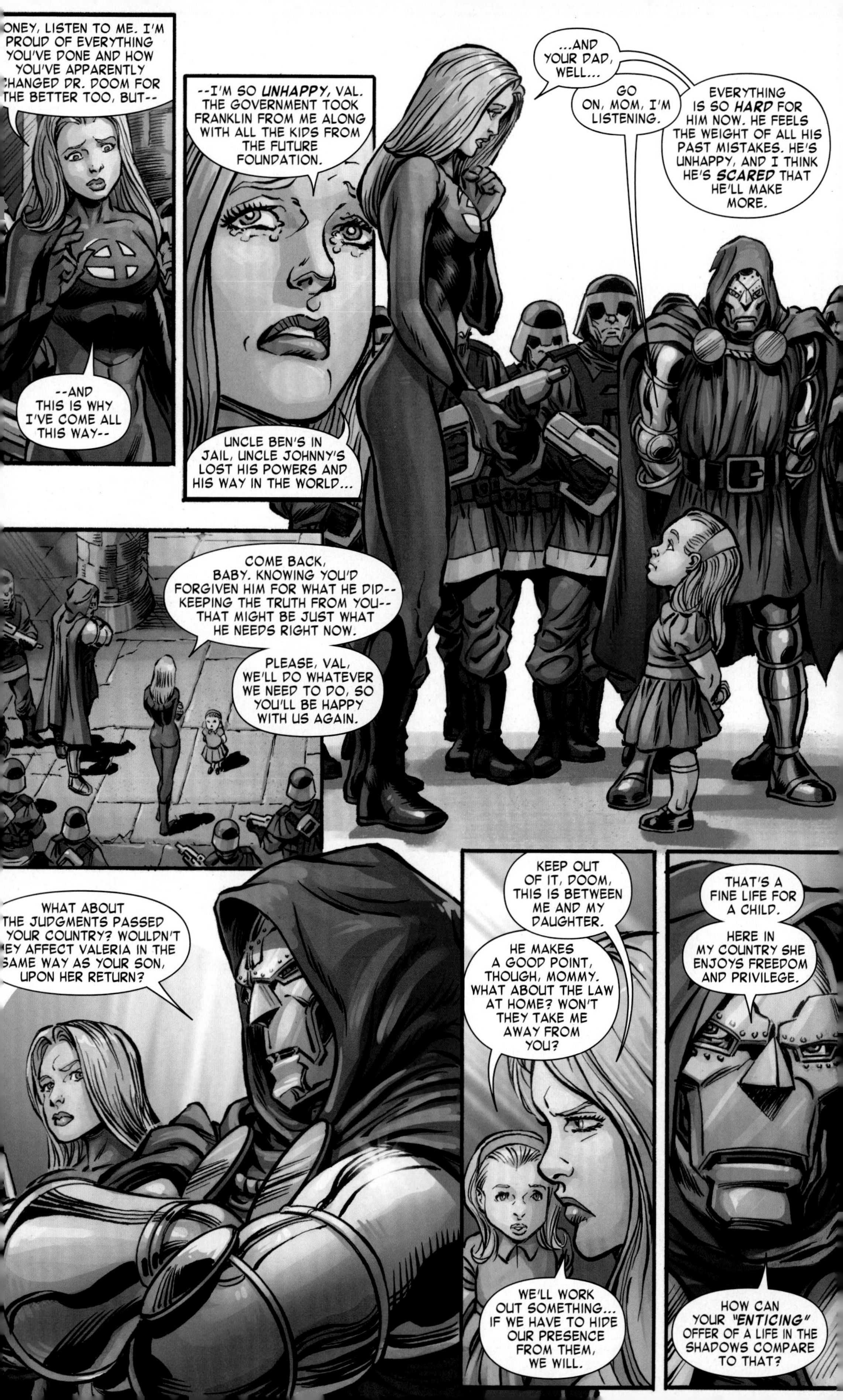
ONEY, LISTEN TO ME. I'M PROUD OF EVERYTHING YOU'VE DONE AND HOW YOU'VE APPARENTLY CHANGED DR. DOOM FOR THE BETTER TOO, BUT--
--AND THIS IS WHY I'VE COME ALL THIS WAY--
--I'M SO UNHAPPY, VAL. THE GOVERNMENT TOOK FRANKLIN FROM ME ALONG WITH ALL THE KIDS FROM THE FUTURE FOUNDATION.
UNCLE BEN'S IN JAIL, UNCLE JOHNNY'S LOST HIS POWERS AND HIS WAY IN THE WORLD...
...AND YOUR DAD, WELL...
GO ON, MOM, I'M LISTENING.
EVERYTHING IS SO HARD FOR HIM NOW. HE FEELS THE WEIGHT OF ALL HIS PAST MISTAKES. HE'S UNHAPPY, AND I THINK HE'S SCARED THAT HE'LL MAKE MORE.
COME BACK, BABY. KNOWING YOU'D FORGIVEN HIM FOR WHAT HE DID-- KEEPING THE TRUTH FROM YOU-- THAT MIGHT BE JUST WHAT HE NEEDS RIGHT NOW.
PLEASE, VAL, WE'LL DO WHATEVER WE NEED TO DO, SO YOU'LL BE HAPPY WITH US AGAIN.
WHAT ABOUT THE JUDGMENTS PASSED YOUR COUNTRY? WOULDN'T EY AFFECT VALERIA IN THE SAME WAY AS YOUR SON, UPON HER RETURN?
KEEP OUT OF IT, DOOM, THIS IS BETWEEN ME AND MY DAUGHTER.
HE MAKES A GOOD POINT, THOUGH, MOMMY. WHAT ABOUT THE LAW AT HOME? WON'T THEY TAKE ME AWAY FROM YOU?
WE'LL WORK OUT SOMETHING... IF WE HAVE TO HIDE OUR PRESENCE FROM THEM, WE WILL.
THAT'S A FINE LIFE FOR A CHILD.
HERE IN MY COUNTRY SHE ENJOYS FREEDOM AND PRIVILEGE.
HOW CAN YOUR "ENTICING" OFFER OF A LIFE IN THE SHADOWS COMPARE TO THAT?

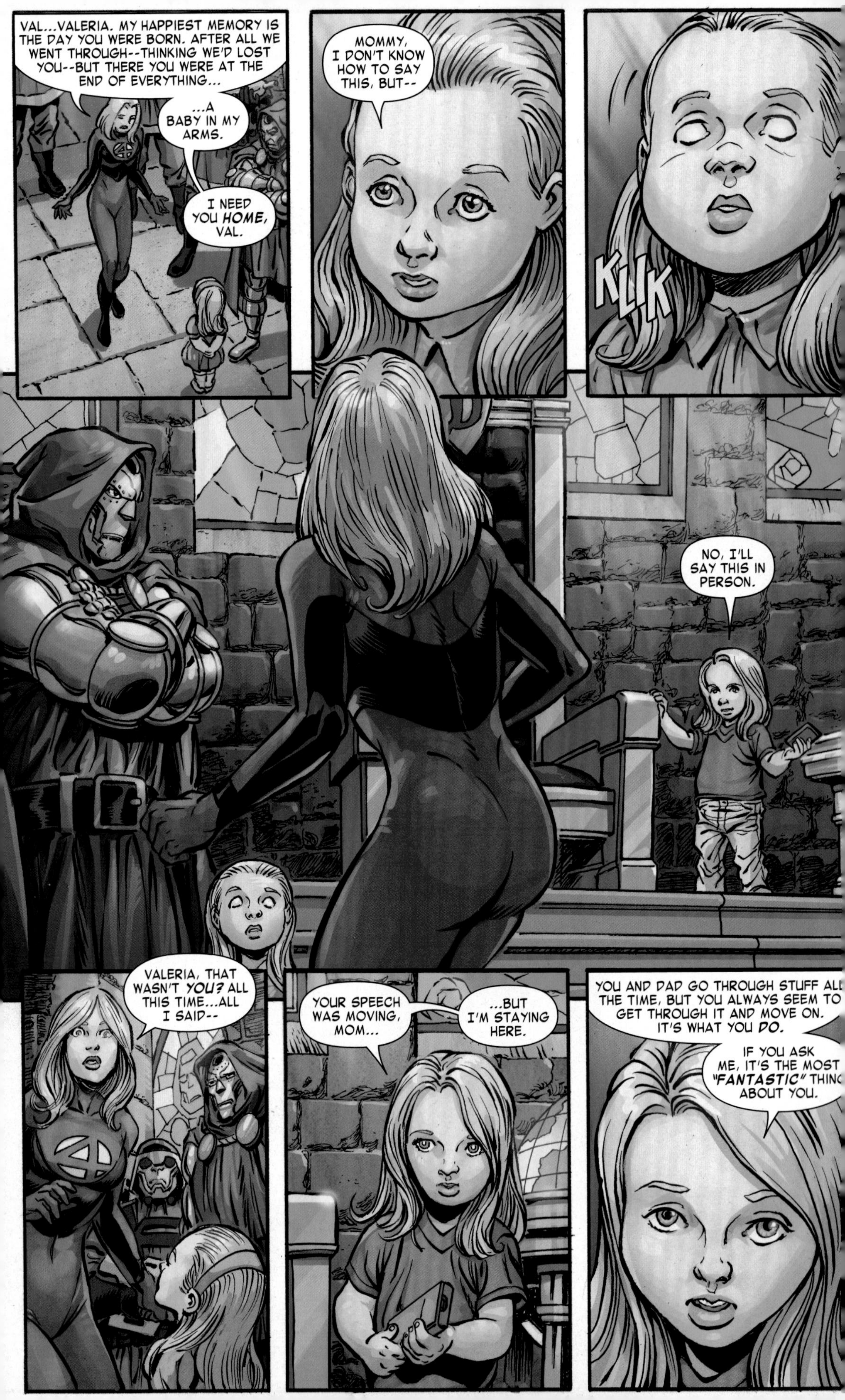
VAL...VALERIA. MY HAPPIEST MEMORY IS THE DAY YOU WERE BORN. AFTER ALL WE WENT THROUGH--THINKING WE'D LOST YOU--BUT THERE YOU WERE AT THE END OF EVERYTHING...
...A BABY IN MY ARMS.
I NEED YOU HOME, VAL.
MOMMY, I DON'T KNOW HOW TO SAY THIS, BUT--
KLIK
NO, I'LL SAY THIS IN PERSON.
VALERIA, THAT WASN'T YOU? ALL THIS TIME...ALL I SAID--
YOUR SPEECH WAS MOVING, MOM...
...BUT I'M STAYING HERE.
YOU AND DAD GO THROUGH STUFF ALL THE TIME, BUT YOU ALWAYS SEEM TO GET THROUGH IT AND MOVE ON. IT'S WHAT YOU DO.
IF YOU ASK ME, IT'S THE MOST "FANTASTIC" THING ABOUT YOU.

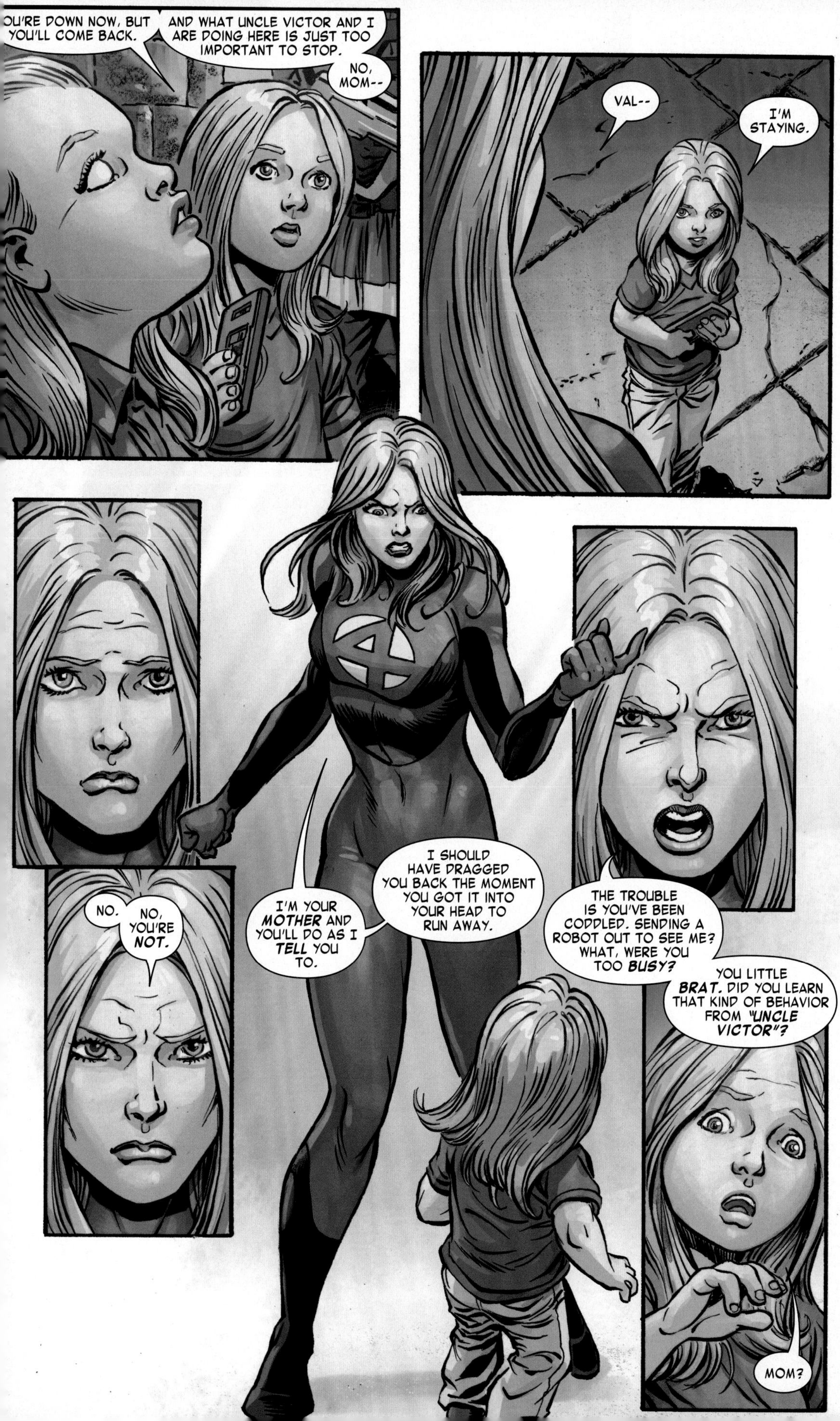

OU'RE DOWN NOW, BUT YOU'LL COME BACK.
AND WHAT UNCLE VICTOR AND I ARE DOING HERE IS JUST TOO IMPORTANT TO STOP.
NO, MOM--
VAL--
I'M STAYING.
I'M YOUR MOTHER AND YOU'LL DO AS I TELL YOU TO.
I SHOULD HAVE DRAGGED YOU BACK THE MOMENT YOU GOT IT INTO YOUR HEAD TO RUN AWAY.
NO.
NO, YOU'RE NOT.
THE TROUBLE IS YOU'VE BEEN CODDLED. SENDING A ROBOT OUT TO SEE ME? WHAT, WERE YOU TOO BUSY?
YOU LITTLE BRAT. DID YOU LEARN THAT KIND OF BEHAVIOR FROM "UNCLE VICTOR"?
MOM?

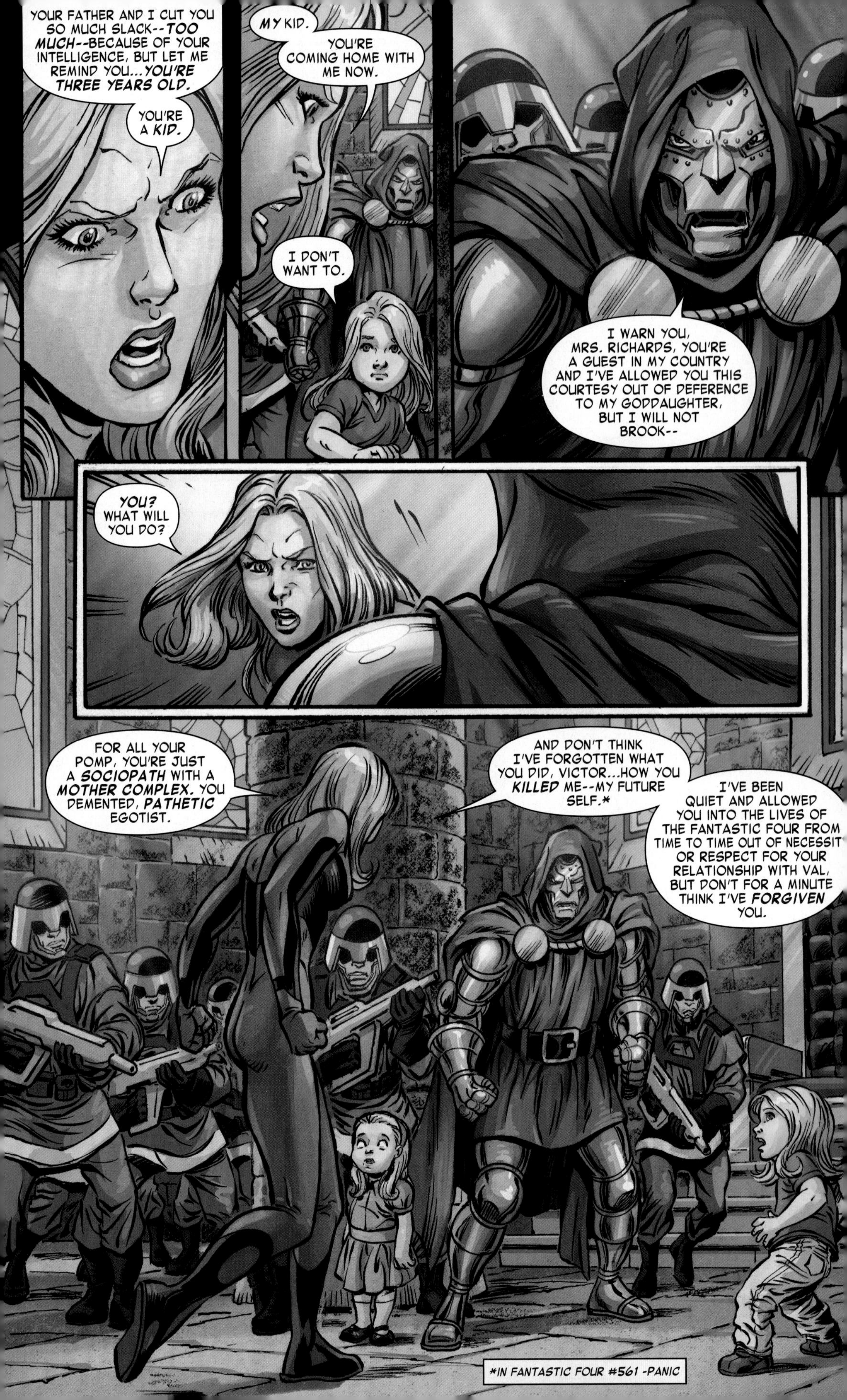
YOUR FATHER AND I CUT YOU SO MUCH SLACK--TOO MUCH--BECAUSE OF YOUR INTELLIGENCE, BUT LET ME REMIND YOU...YOU'RE THREE YEARS OLD.
YOU'RE A KID.
MY KID.
YOU'RE COMING HOME WITH ME NOW.
I DON'T WANT TO.
I WARN YOU, MRS. RICHARDS, YOU'RE A GUEST IN MY COUNTRY AND I'VE ALLOWED YOU THIS COURTESY OUT OF DEFERENCE TO MY GODDAUGHTER, BUT I WILL NOT BROOK--
YOU? WHAT WILL YOU DO?
FOR ALL YOUR POMP, YOU'RE JUST A SOCIOPATH WITH A MOTHER COMPLEX. YOU DEMENTED, PATHETIC EGOTIST.
AND DON'T THINK I'VE FORGOTTEN WHAT YOU DID, VICTOR...HOW YOU KILLED ME--MY FUTURE SELF.*
I'VE BEEN QUIET AND ALLOWED YOU INTO THE LIVES OF THE FANTASTIC FOUR FROM TIME TO TIME OUT OF NECESSIT OR RESPECT FOR YOUR RELATIONSHIP WITH VAL, BUT DON'T FOR A MINUTE THINK I'VE FORGIVEN YOU.
*IN FANTASTIC FOUR #561 -PANIC

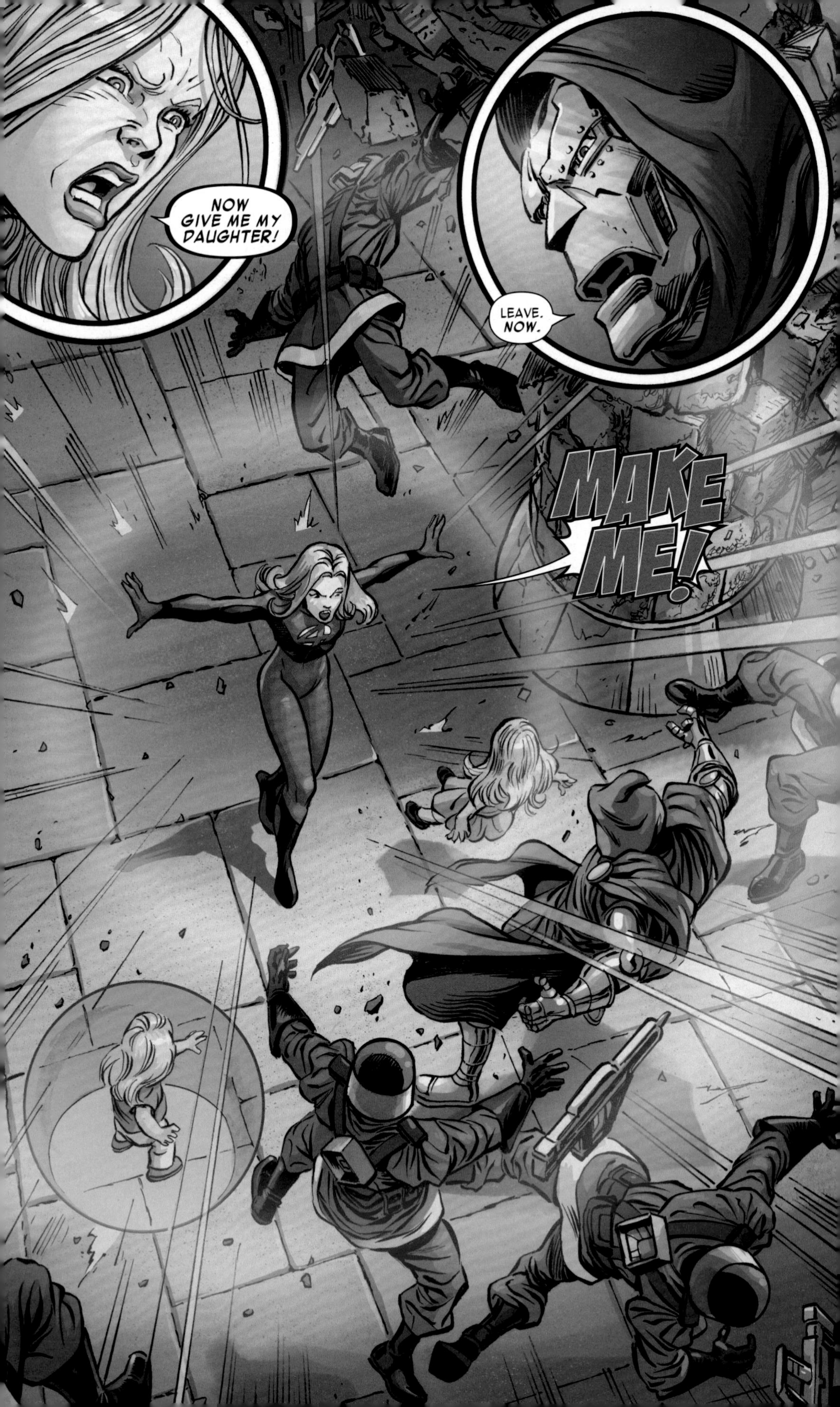
NOW GIVE ME MY DAUGHTER!
LEAVE. NOW.
MAKE ME!

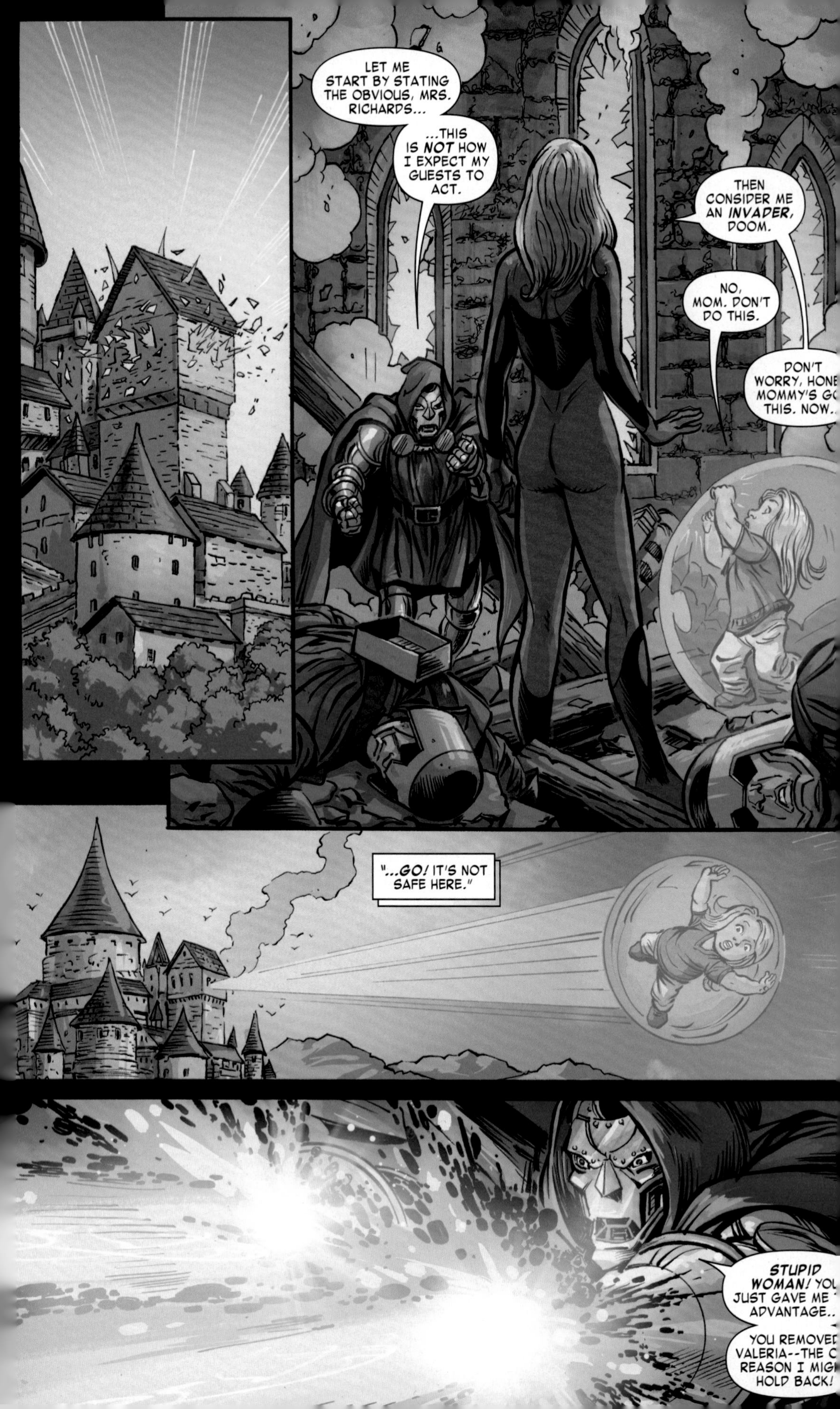
LET ME START BY STATING THE OBVIOUS, MRS. RICHARDS...
...THIS IS NOT HOW I EXPECT MY GUESTS TO ACT.
THEN CONSIDER ME AN INVADER, DOOM.
NO, MOM. DON'T DO THIS.
DON'T WORRY, HONE MOMMY'S GO THIS. NOW...
"...GO! IT'S NOT SAFE HERE."
STUPID WOMAN! YOU JUST GAVE ME ADVANTAGE...
YOU REMOVED VALERIA--THE REASON I MIG HOLD BACK!

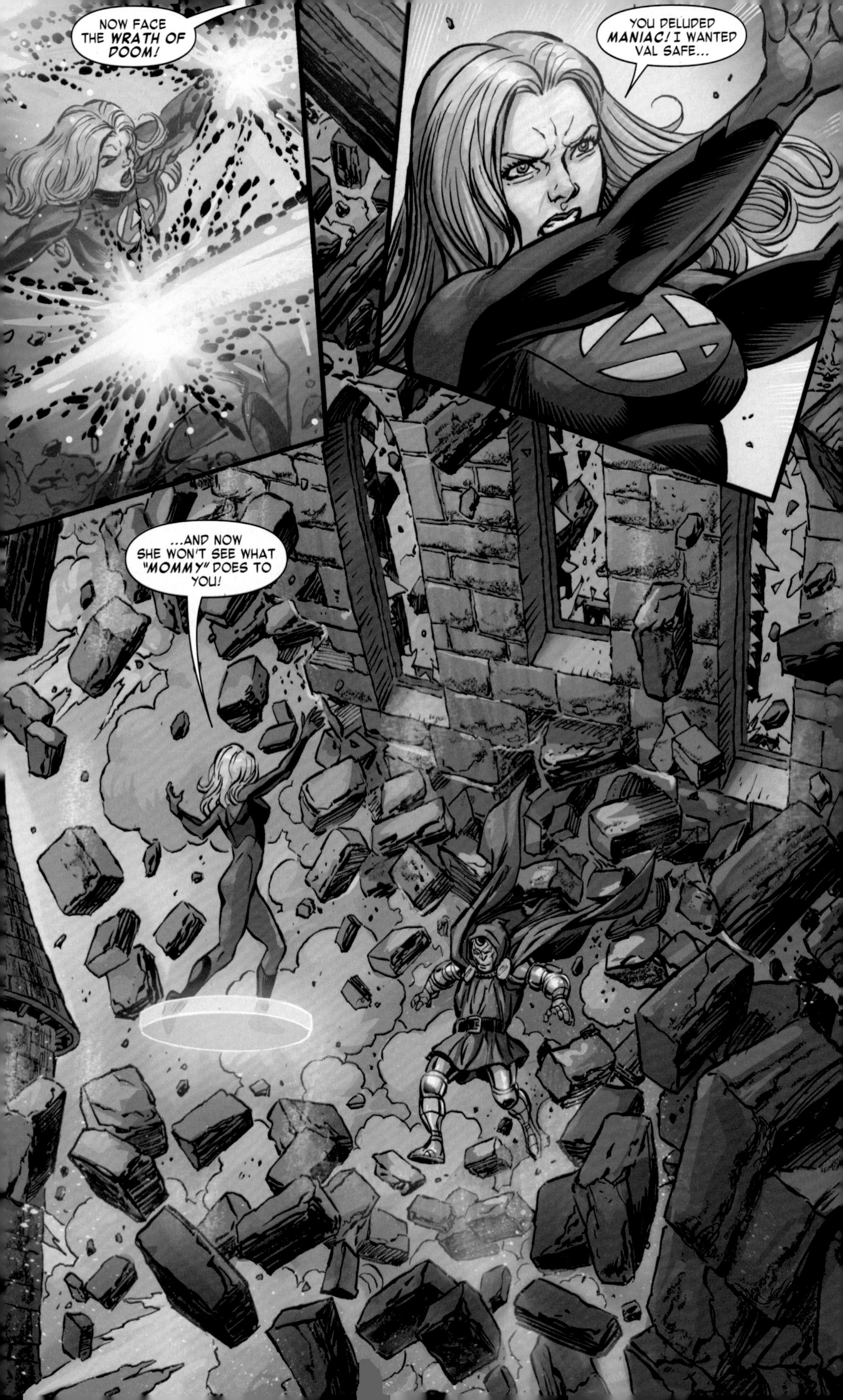
NOW FACE THE WRATH OF DOOM!
YOU DELUDED MANIAC! I WANTED VAL SAFE...
...AND NOW SHE WON'T SEE WHAT "MOMMY" DOES TO YOU!

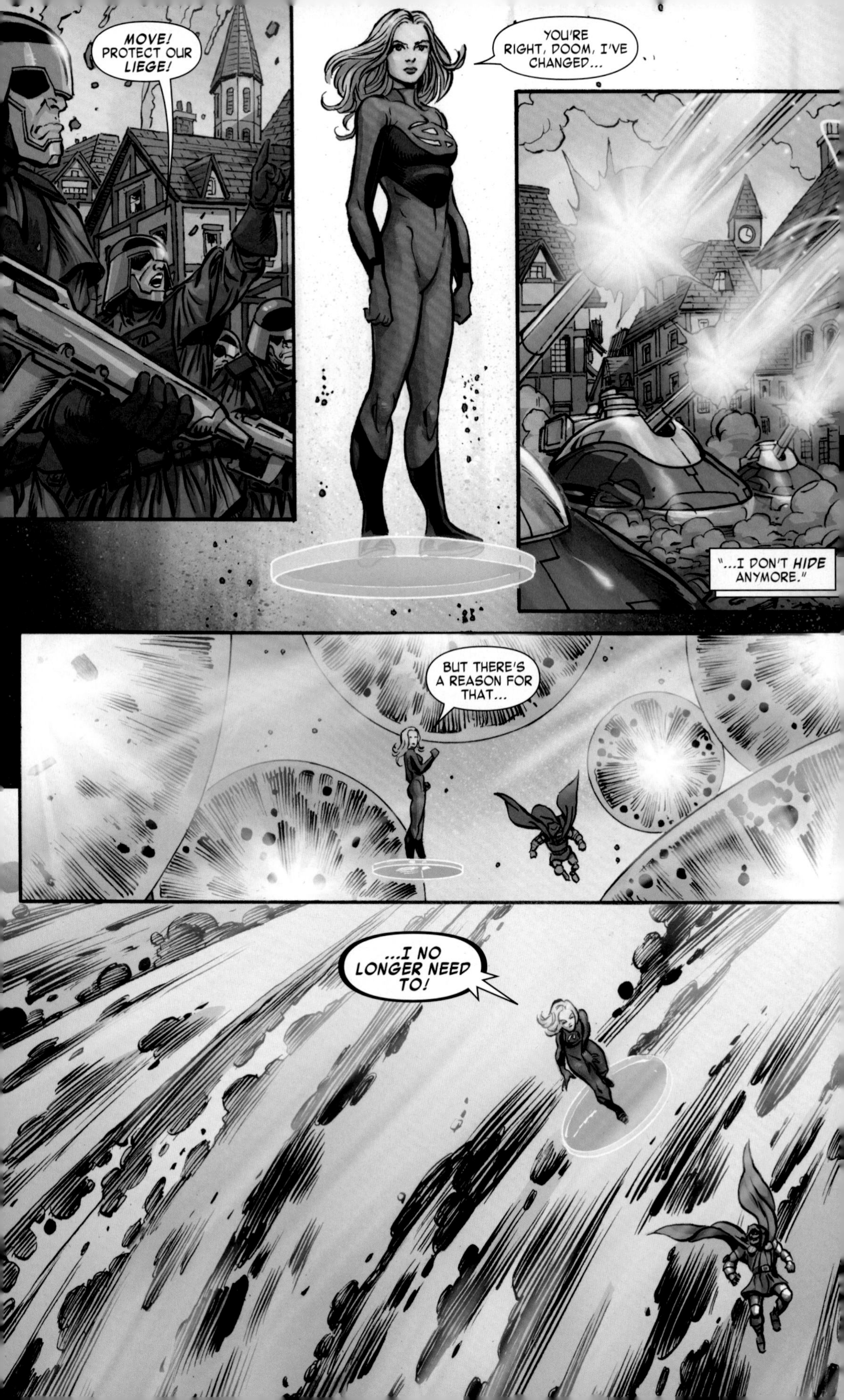
MOVE! PROTECT OUR LIEGE!
YOU'RE RIGHT, DOOM, I'VE CHANGED...
"...I DON'T HIDE ANYMORE."
BUT THERE'S A REASON FOR THAT...
...I NO LONGER NEED TO!

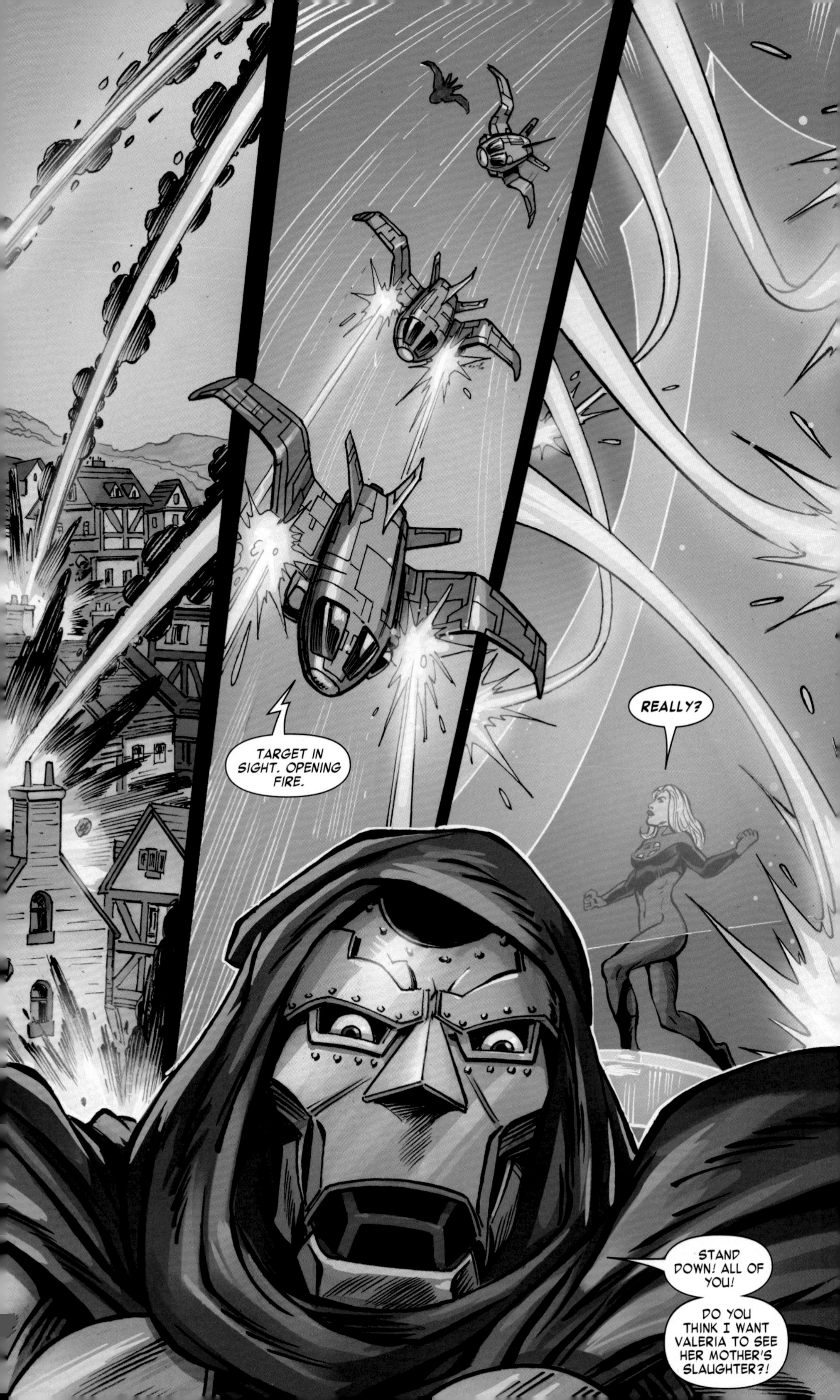
TARGET IN SIGHT. OPENING FIRE.
REALLY?
STAND DOWN! ALL OF YOU!
DO YOU THINK I WANT VALERIA TO SEE HER MOTHER'S SLAUGHTER?!

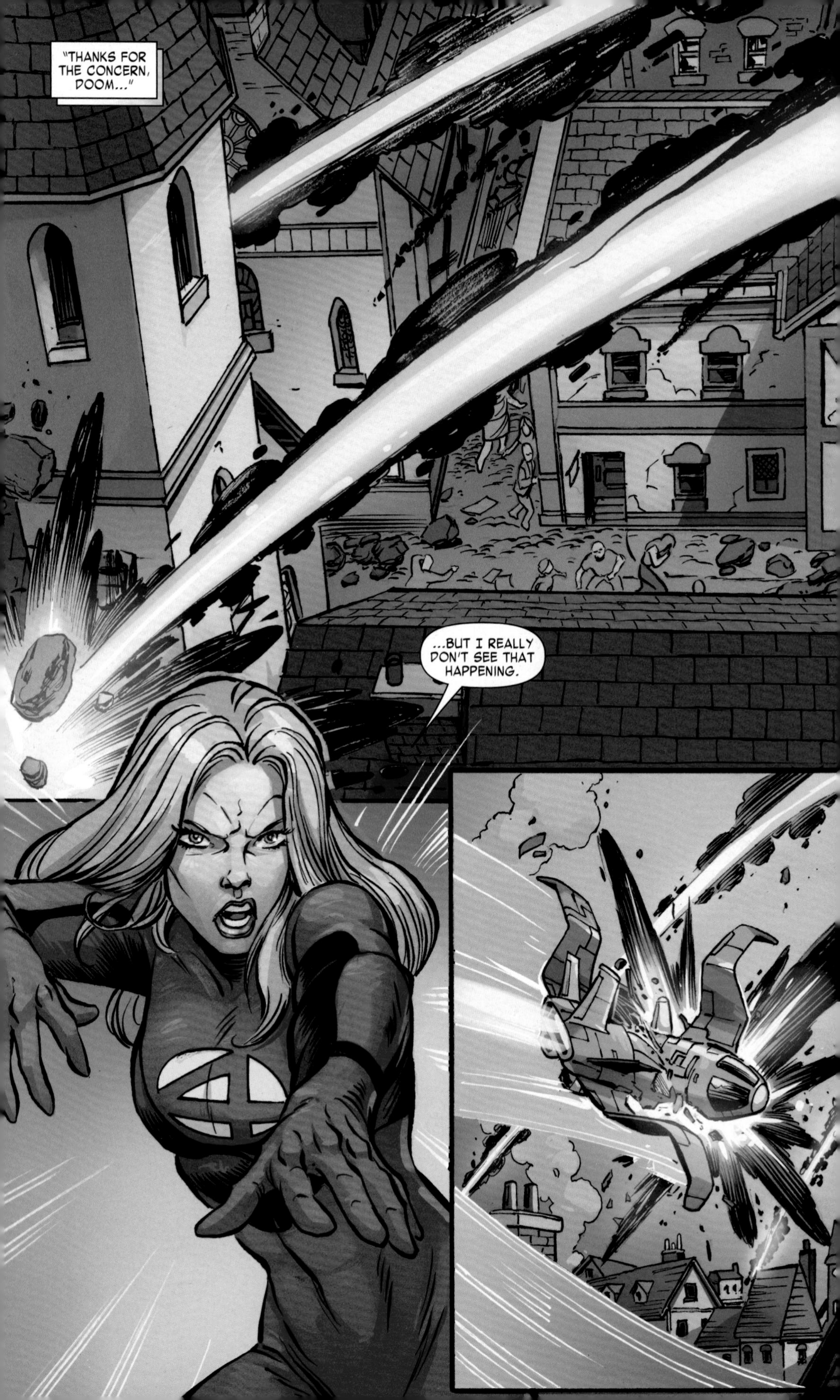
"THANKS FOR THE CONCERN, DOOM..."
...BUT I REALLY DON'T SEE THAT HAPPENING.

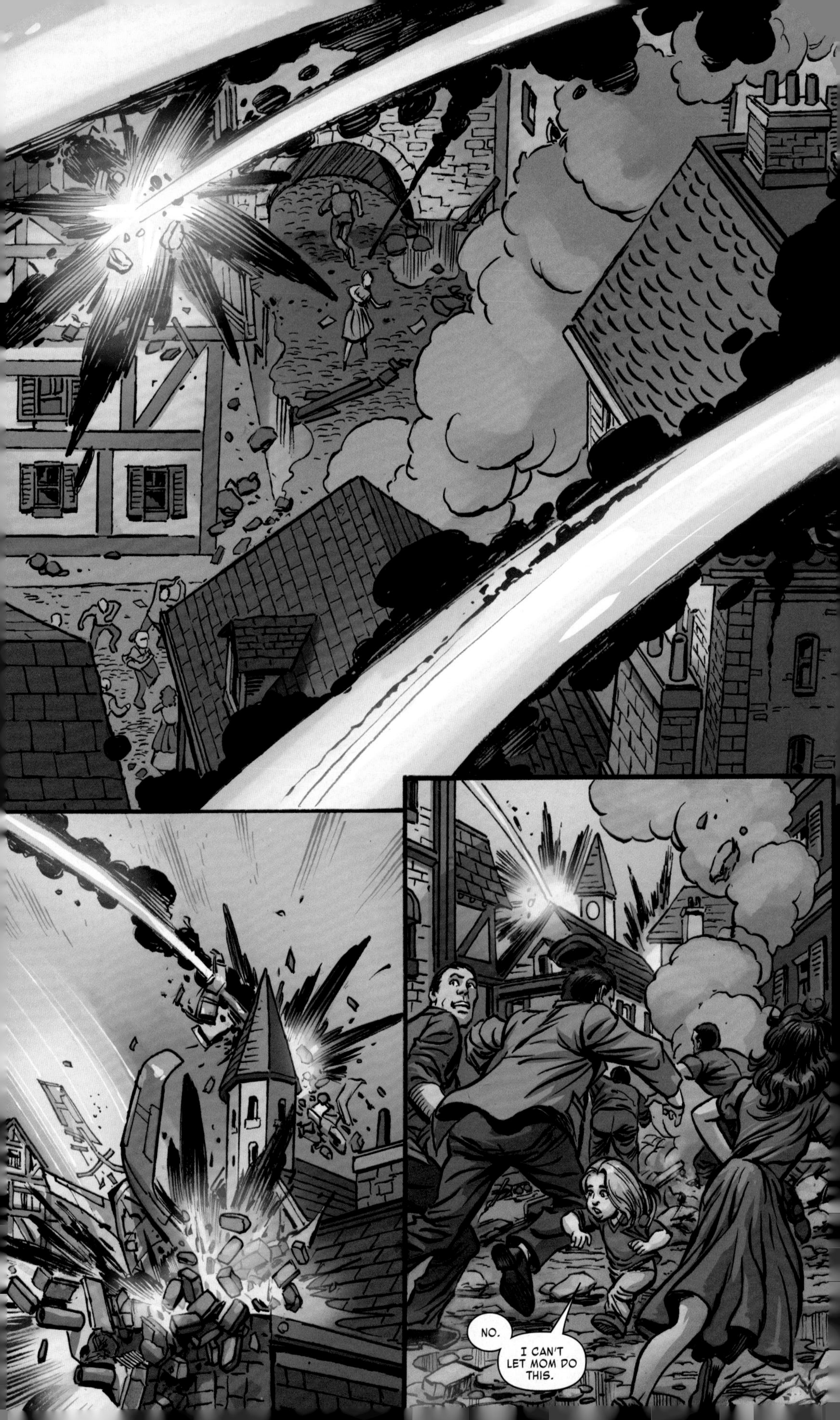
NO.
I CAN'T LET MOM DO THIS.

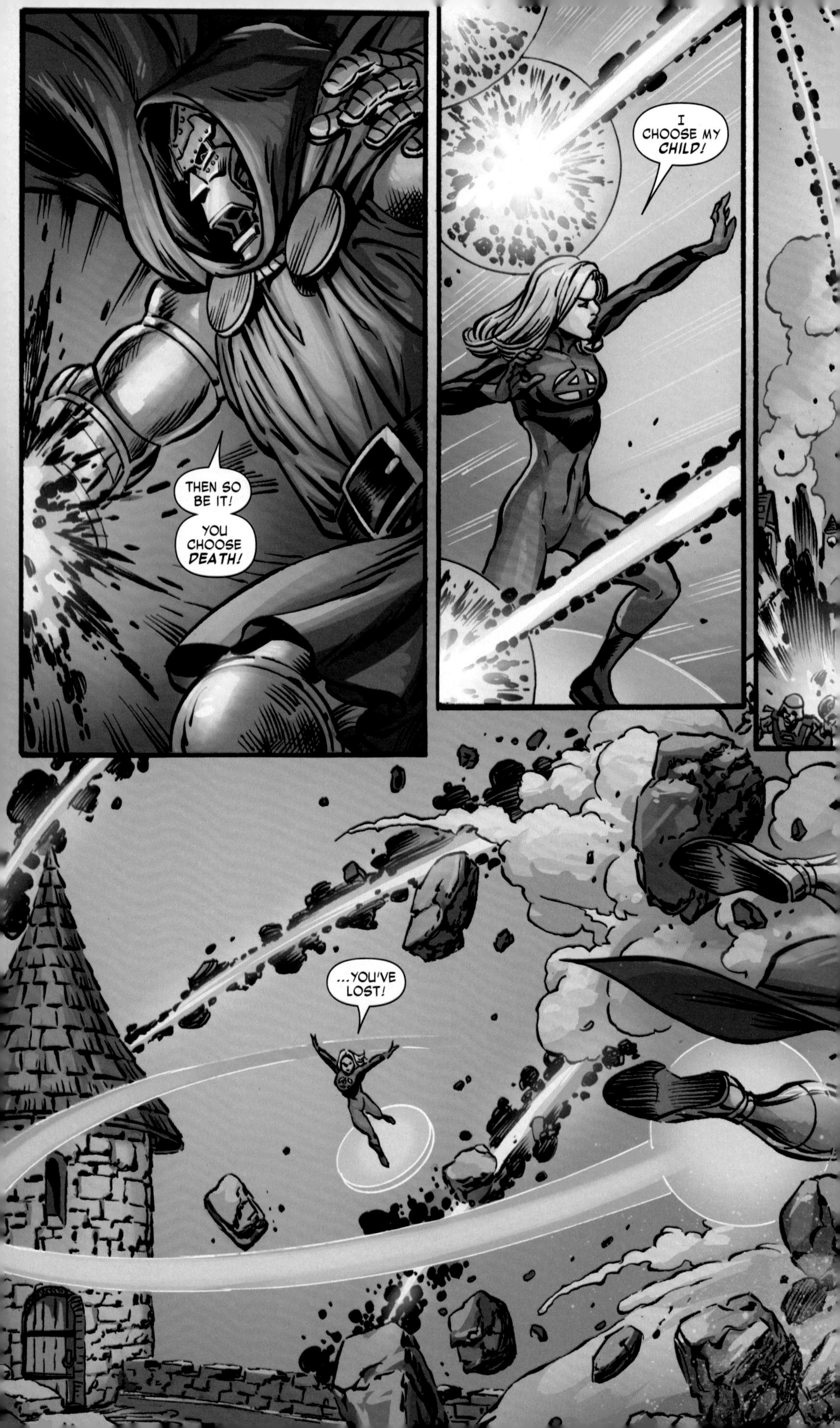
THEN SO BE IT!
YOU CHOOSE DEATH!
I CHOOSE MY CHILD!
...YOU'VE LOST!

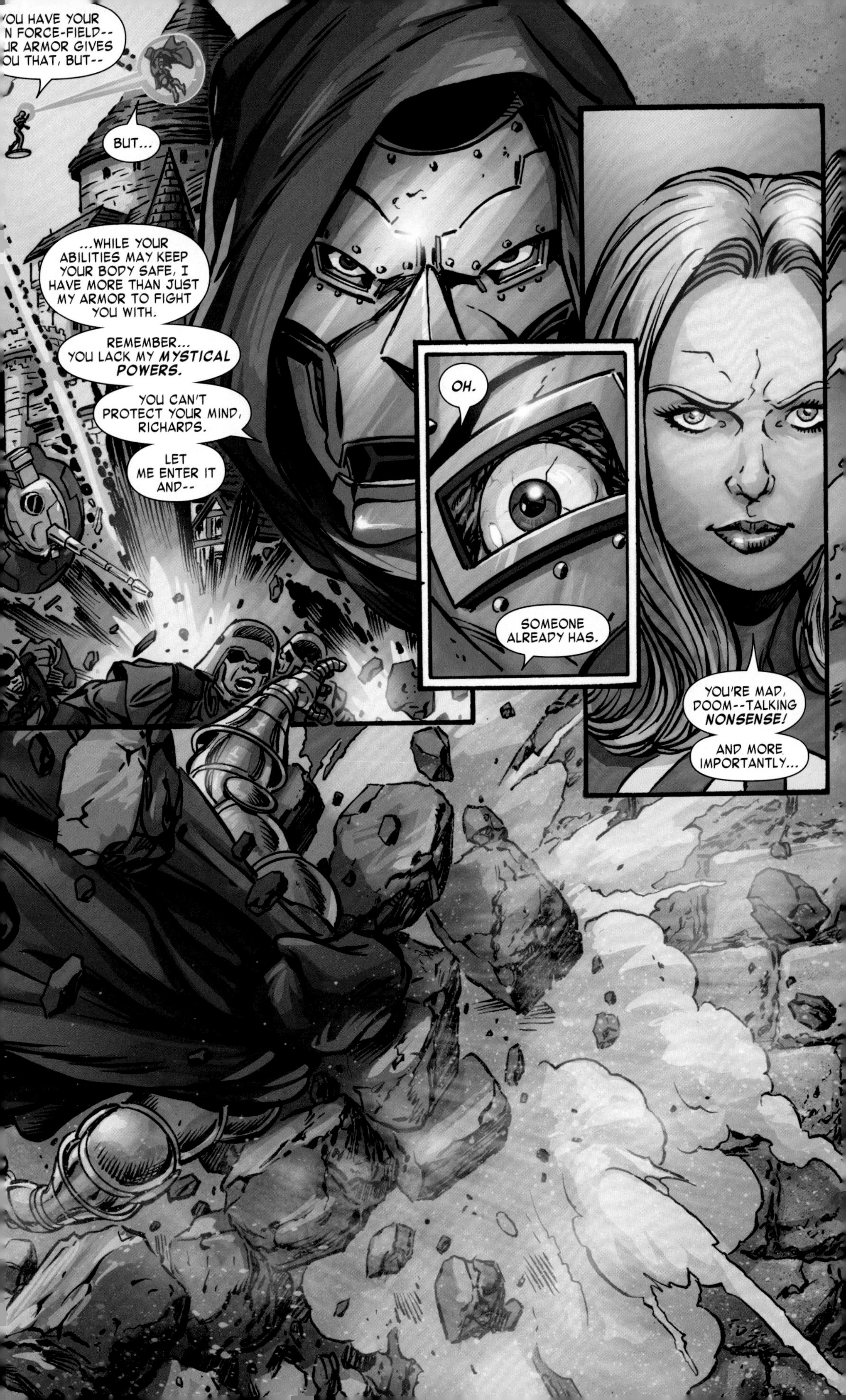
YOU HAVE YOUR
N FORCE-FIELD--
UR ARMOR GIVES
OU THAT, BUT--
BUT...
...WHILE YOUR ABILITIES MAY KEEP YOUR BODY SAFE, I HAVE MORE THAN JUST MY ARMOR TO FIGHT YOU WITH.
REMEMBER... YOU LACK MY MYSTICAL POWERS.
YOU CAN'T PROTECT YOUR MIND, RICHARDS.
LET ME ENTER IT AND--
OH.
SOMEONE ALREADY HAS.
YOU'RE MAD, DOOM--TALKING NONSENSE!
AND MORE IMPORTANTLY...

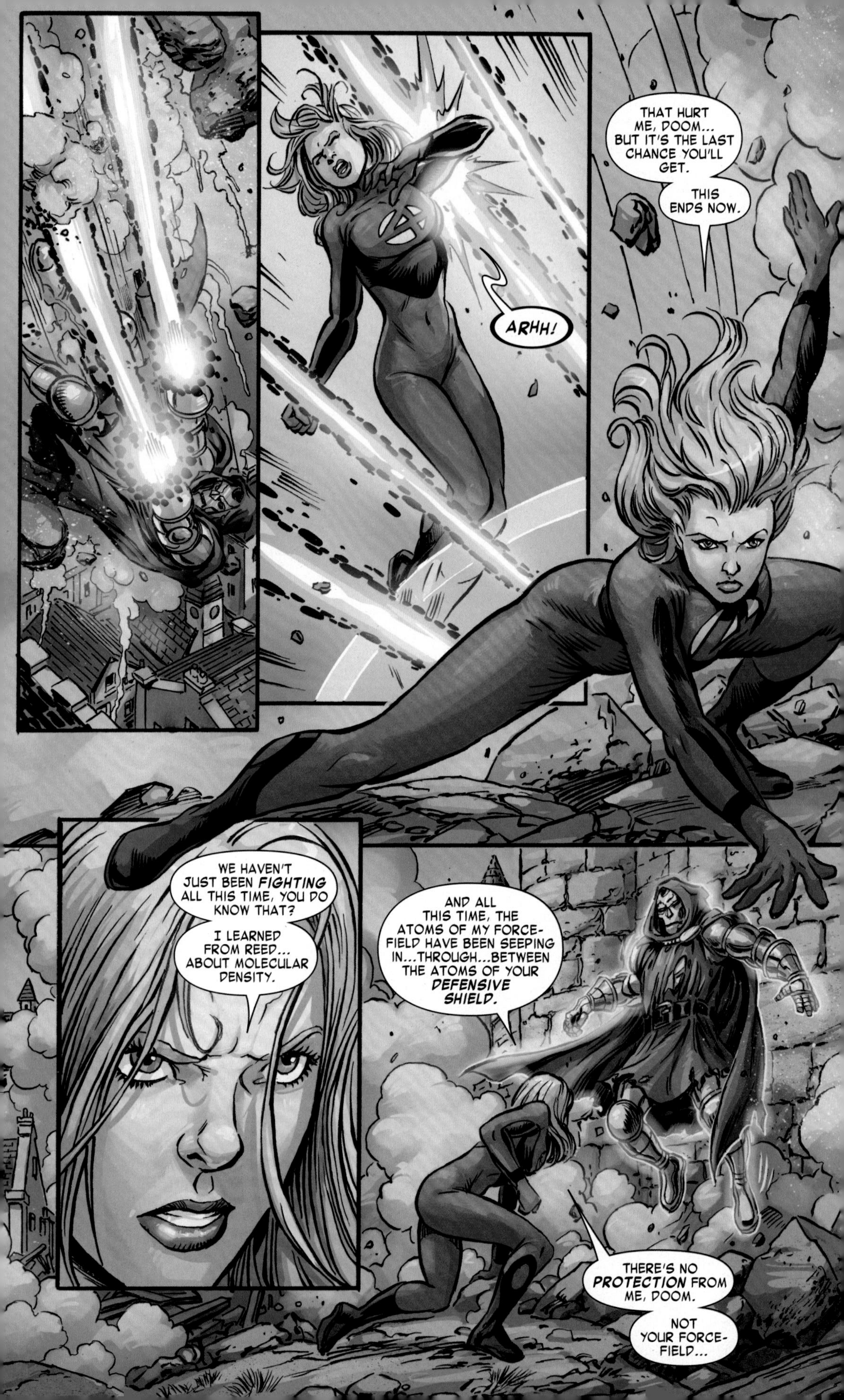
ARHH!
THAT HURT ME, DOOM... BUT IT'S THE LAST CHANCE YOU'LL GET.
THIS ENDS NOW.
WE HAVEN'T JUST BEEN FIGHTING ALL THIS TIME, YOU DO KNOW THAT?
I LEARNED FROM REED... ABOUT MOLECULAR DENSITY.
AND ALL THIS TIME, THE ATOMS OF MY FORCE-FIELD HAVE BEEN SEEPING IN...THROUGH...BETWEEN THE ATOMS OF YOUR DEFENSIVE SHIELD.
THERE'S NO PROTECTION FROM ME, DOOM.
NOT YOUR FORCE-FIELD...

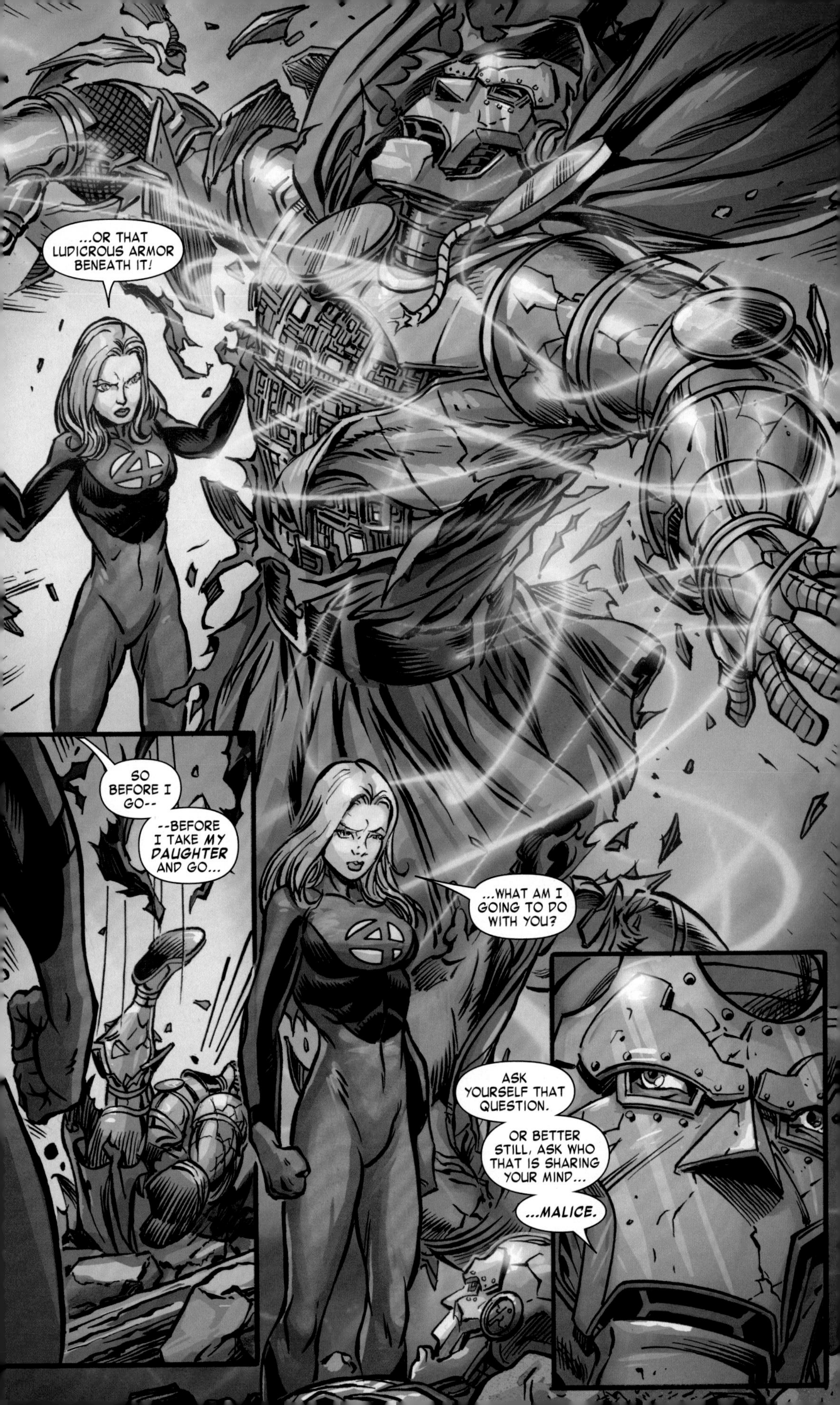

...OR THAT LUDICROUS ARMOR BENEATH IT!
SO BEFORE I GO--
--BEFORE I TAKE *MY DAUGHTER* AND GO...
...WHAT AM I GOING TO DO WITH YOU?
ASK YOURSELF THAT QUESTION.
OR BETTER STILL, ASK WHO THAT IS SHARING YOUR MIND...
...MALICE.

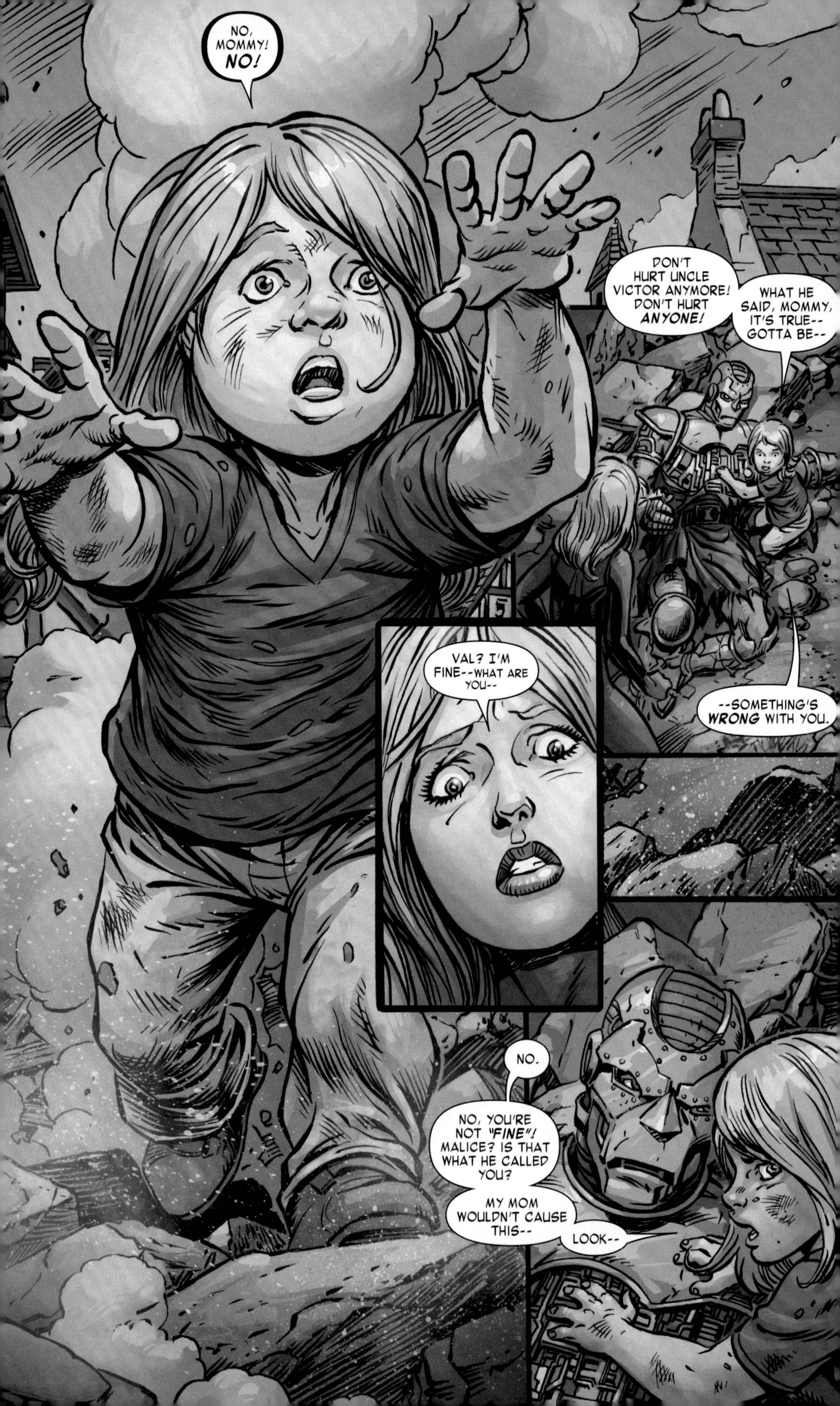
NO, MOMMY! NO!
DON'T HURT UNCLE VICTOR ANYMORE! DON'T HURT ANYONE!
WHAT HE SAID, MOMMY, IT'S TRUE-- GOTTA BE--
--SOMETHING'S WRONG WITH YOU.
VAL? I'M FINE--WHAT ARE YOU--
NO.
NO, YOU'RE NOT "FINE"! MALICE? IS THAT WHAT HE CALLED YOU?
MY MOM WOULDN'T CAUSE THIS--
LOOK--

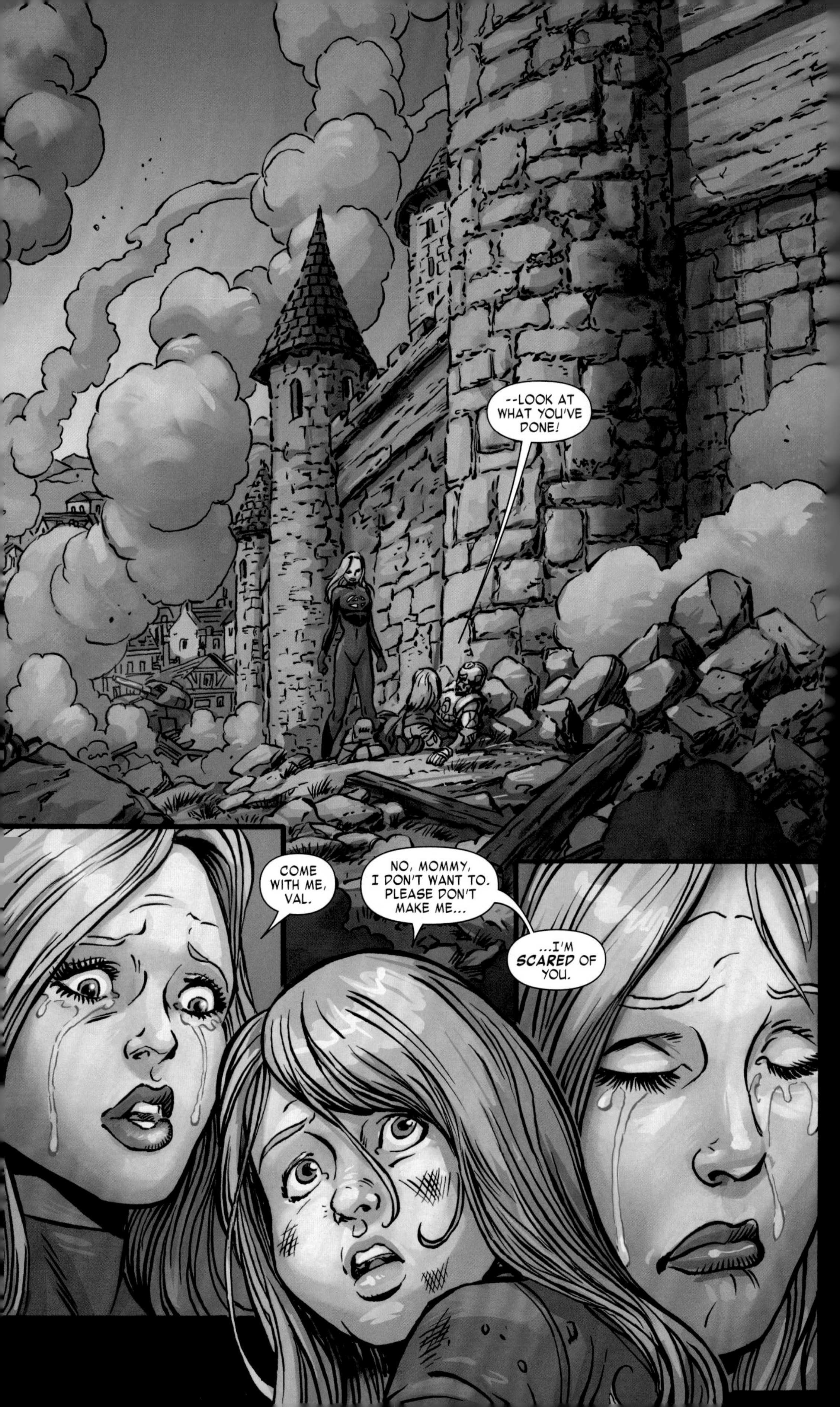
--LOOK AT WHAT YOU'VE DONE!
COME WITH ME, VAL.
NO, MOMMY, I DON'T WANT TO. PLEASE DON'T MAKE ME...
...I'M SCARED OF YOU.

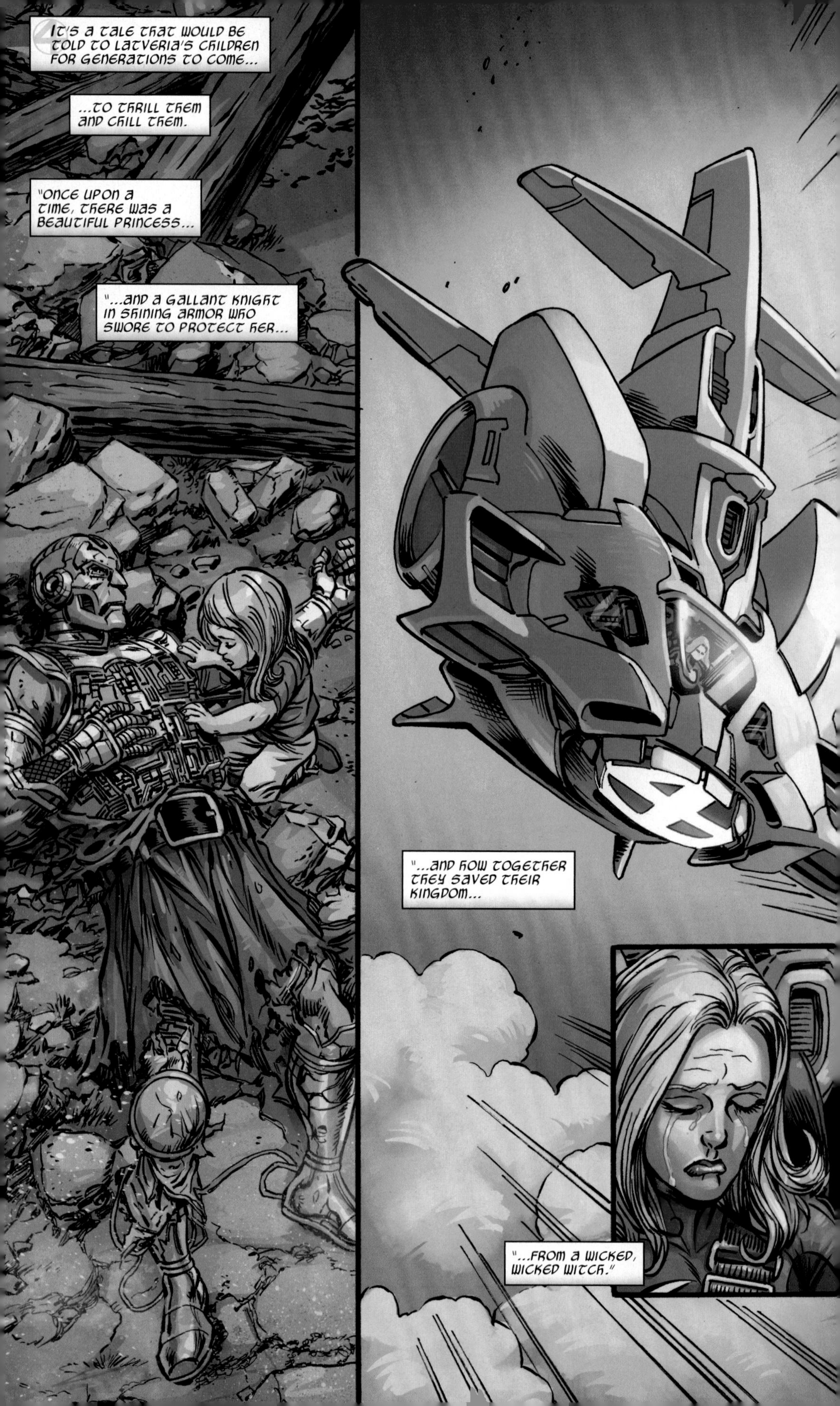
IT'S A TALE THAT WOULD BE TOLD TO LATVERIA'S CHILDREN FOR GENERATIONS TO COME...
...TO THRILL THEM AND CHILL THEM.
"ONCE UPON A TIME, THERE WAS A BEAUTIFUL PRINCESS...
"...AND A GALLANT KNIGHT IN SHINING ARMOR WHO SWORE TO PROTECT HER...
"...AND HOW TOGETHER THEY SAVED THEIR KINGDOM...
"...FROM A WICKED, WICKED WITCH."

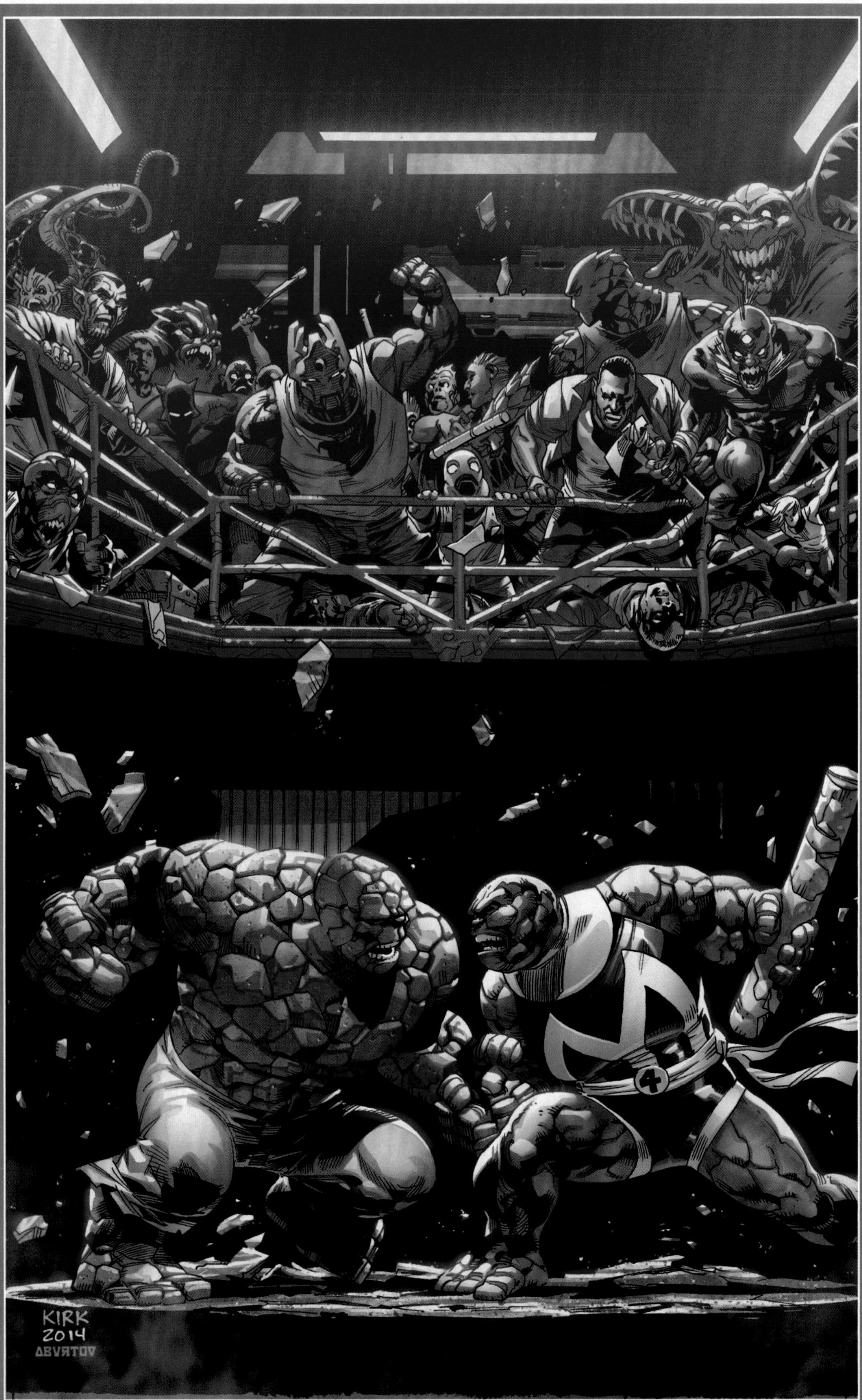
KIRK
2014
ABYRTOV

ELEVEN

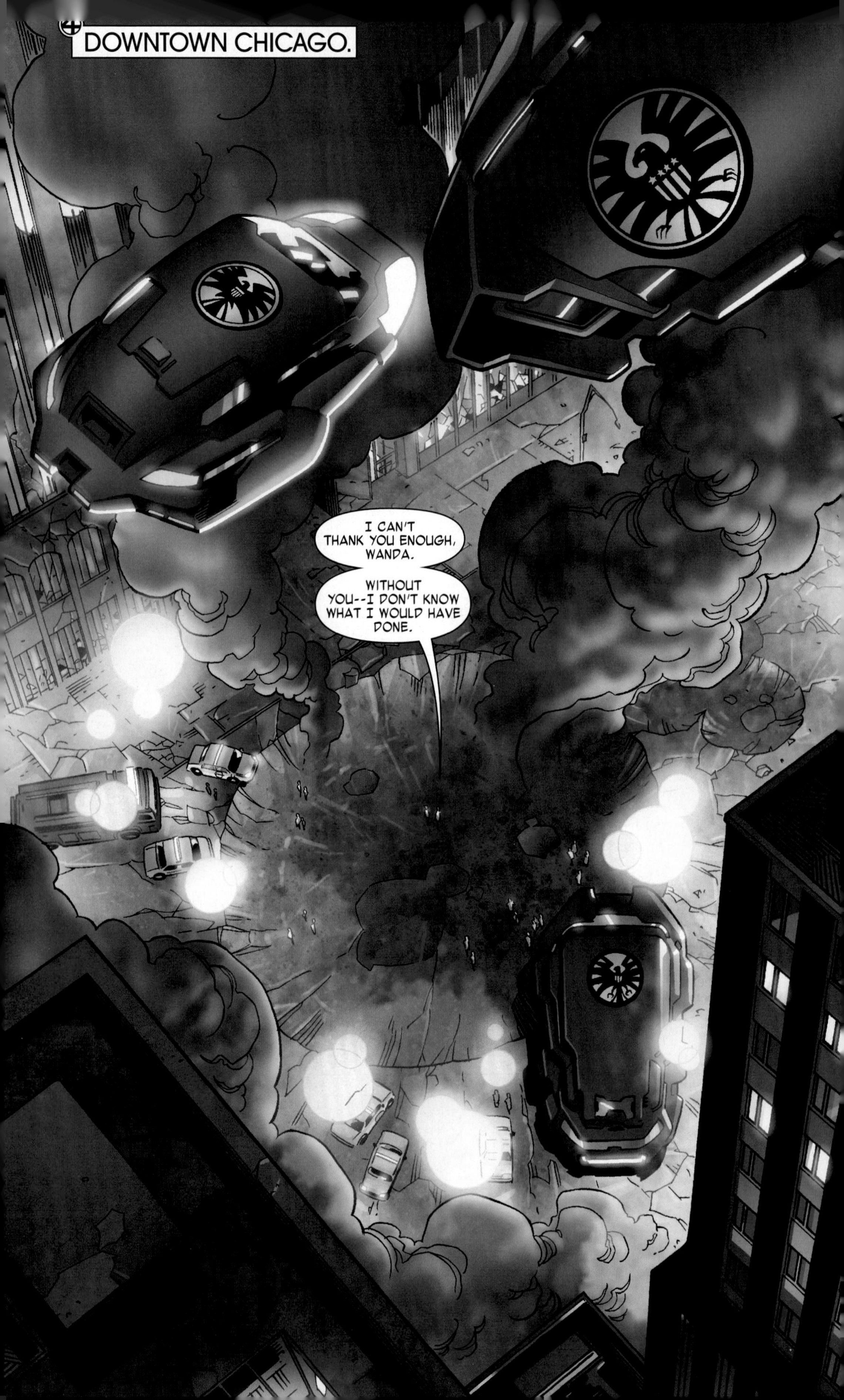
DOWNTOWN CHICAGO.
I CAN'T THANK YOU ENOUGH, WANDA.
WITHOUT YOU--I DON'T KNOW WHAT I WOULD HAVE DONE.

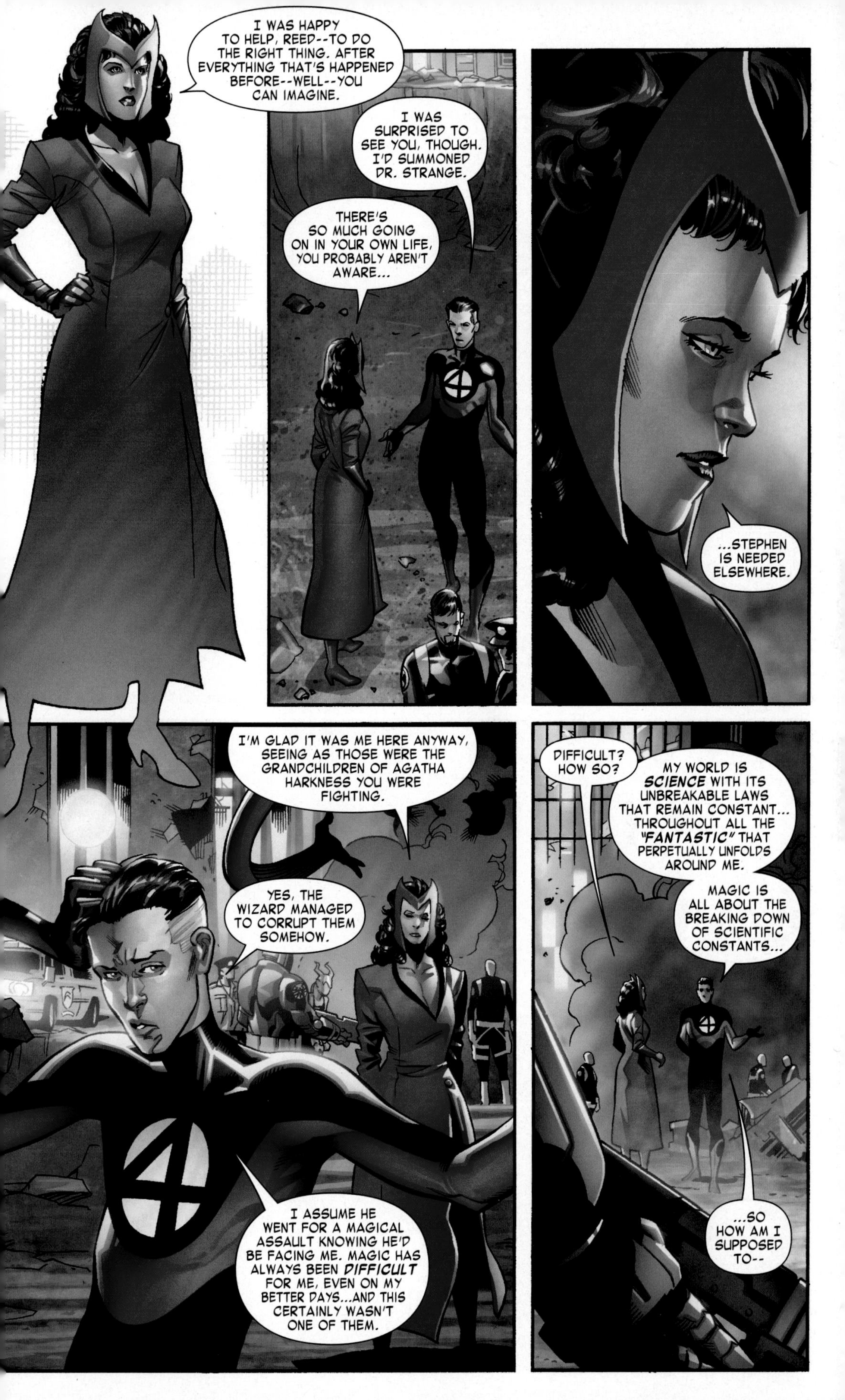
I WAS HAPPY TO HELP, REED--TO DO THE RIGHT THING. AFTER EVERYTHING THAT'S HAPPENED BEFORE--WELL--YOU CAN IMAGINE.
I WAS SURPRISED TO SEE YOU, THOUGH. I'D SUMMONED DR. STRANGE.
THERE'S SO MUCH GOING ON IN YOUR OWN LIFE, YOU PROBABLY AREN'T AWARE...
...STEPHEN IS NEEDED ELSEWHERE.
I'M GLAD IT WAS ME HERE ANYWAY, SEEING AS THOSE WERE THE GRANDCHILDREN OF AGATHA HARKNESS YOU WERE FIGHTING.
YES, THE WIZARD MANAGED TO CORRUPT THEM SOMEHOW.
I ASSUME HE WENT FOR A MAGICAL ASSAULT KNOWING HE'D BE FACING ME. MAGIC HAS ALWAYS BEEN *DIFFICULT* FOR ME, EVEN ON MY BETTER DAYS...AND THIS CERTAINLY WASN'T ONE OF THEM.
DIFFICULT? HOW SO?
MY WORLD IS *SCIENCE* WITH ITS UNBREAKABLE LAWS THAT REMAIN CONSTANT... THROUGHOUT ALL THE *"FANTASTIC"* THAT PERPETUALLY UNFOLDS AROUND ME.
MAGIC IS ALL ABOUT THE BREAKING DOWN OF SCIENTIFIC CONSTANTS...
...SO HOW AM I SUPPOSED TO--

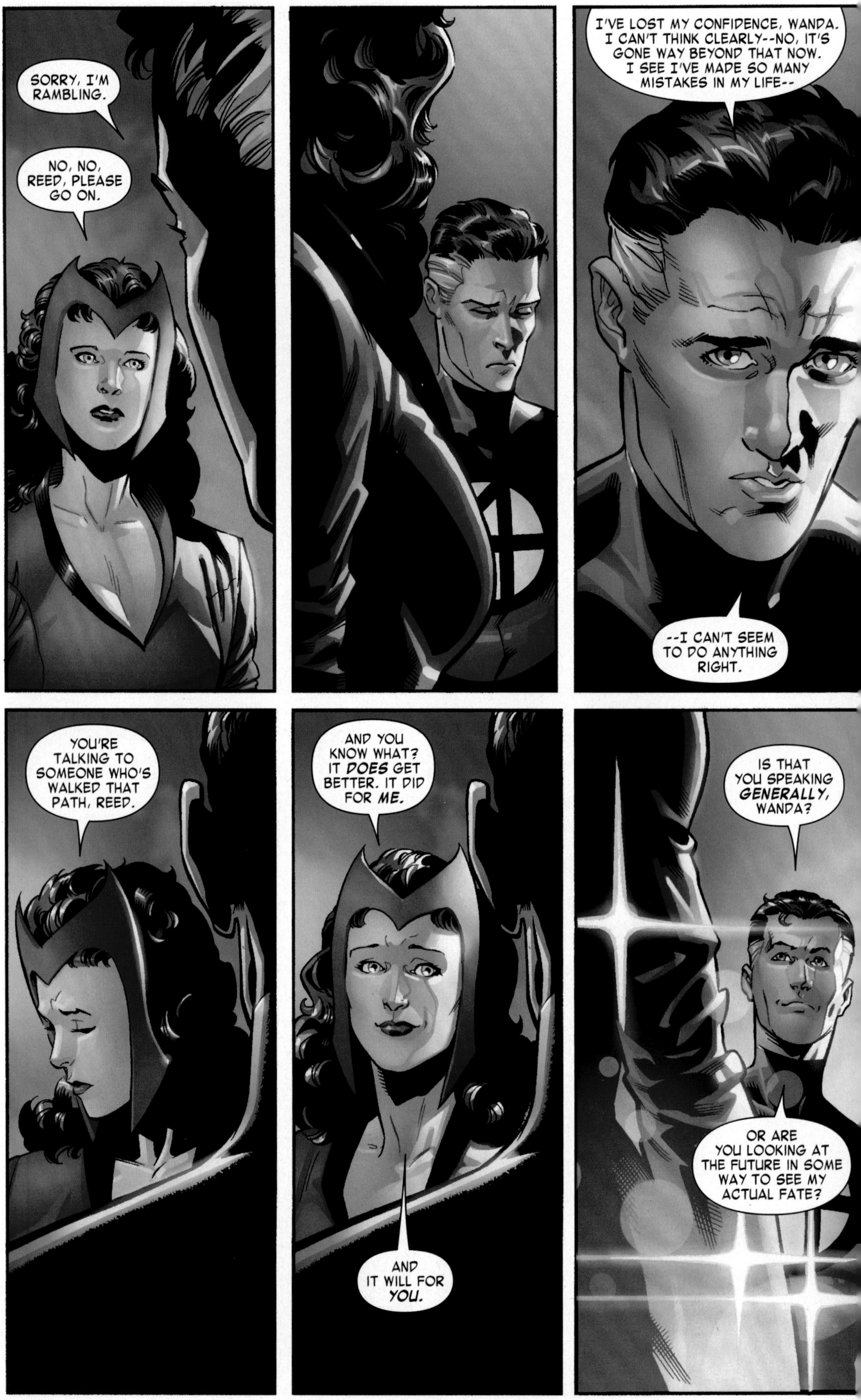
SORRY, I'M RAMBLING.
NO, NO, REED, PLEASE GO ON.
I'VE LOST MY CONFIDENCE, WANDA. I CAN'T THINK CLEARLY--NO, IT'S GONE WAY BEYOND THAT NOW. I SEE I'VE MADE SO MANY MISTAKES IN MY LIFE--
--I CAN'T SEEM TO DO ANYTHING RIGHT.
YOU'RE TALKING TO SOMEONE WHO'S WALKED THAT PATH, REED.
AND YOU KNOW WHAT? IT *DOES* GET BETTER. IT DID FOR *ME.*
AND IT WILL FOR *YOU.*
IS THAT YOU SPEAKING *GENERALLY,* WANDA?
OR ARE YOU LOOKING AT THE FUTURE IN SOME WAY TO SEE MY ACTUAL FATE?

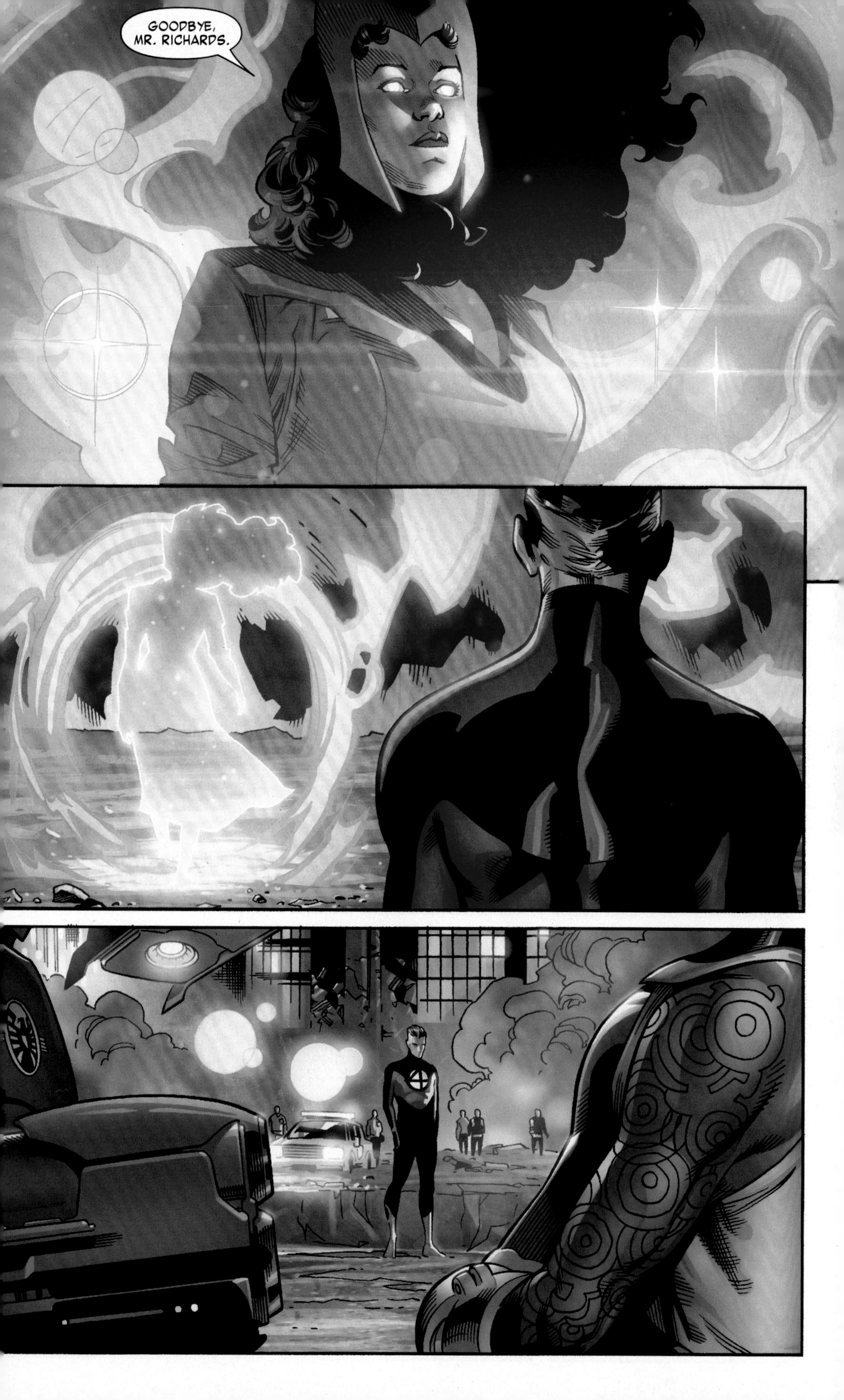
GOODBYE, MR. RICHARDS.

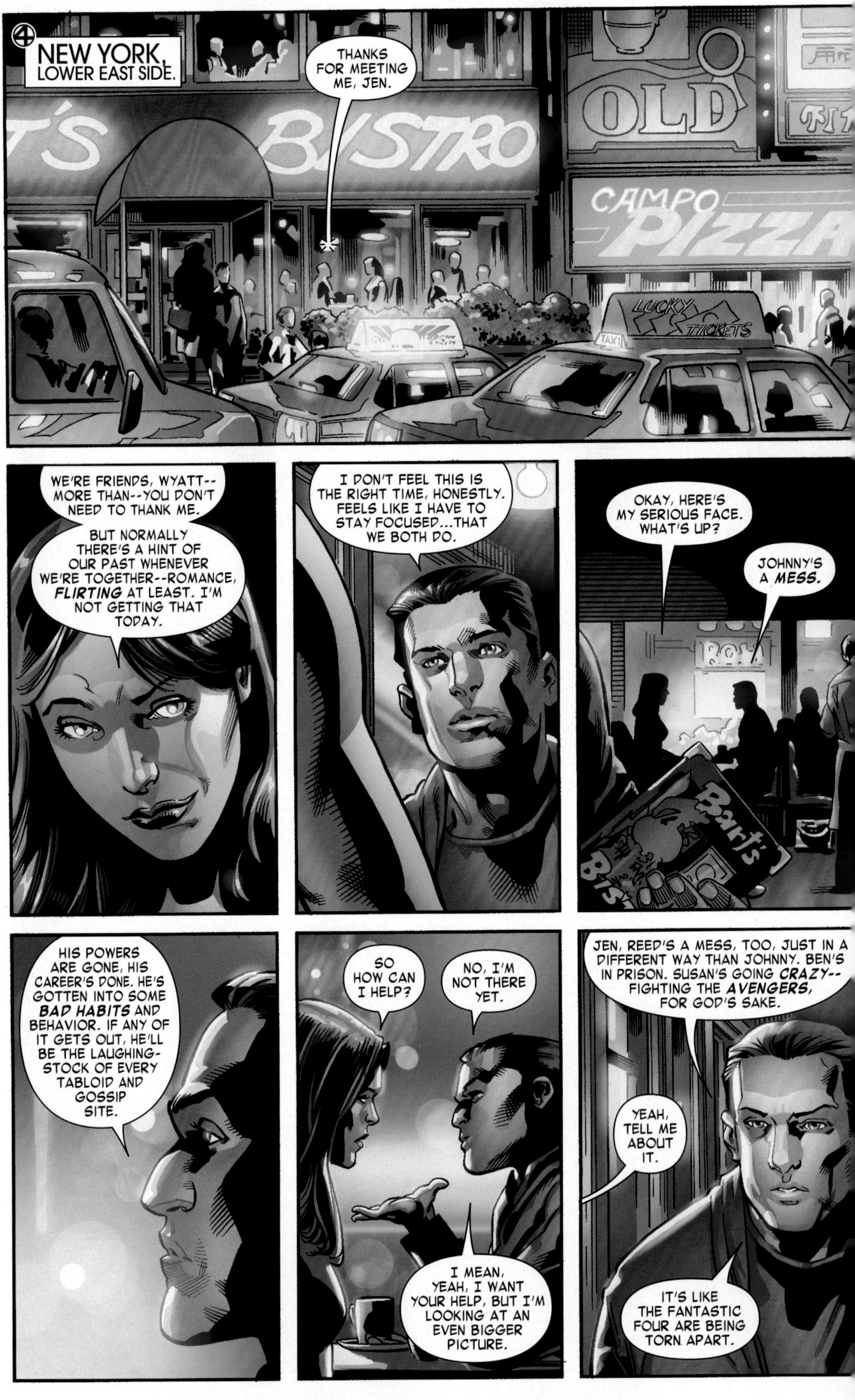
4
NEW YORK, LOWER EAST SIDE.
THANKS FOR MEETING ME, JEN.
BISTRO
OLD
CAMPO PIZZA
LUCKY TICKETS
TAXI
WE'RE FRIENDS, WYATT--MORE THAN--YOU DON'T NEED TO THANK ME.
BUT NORMALLY THERE'S A HINT OF OUR PAST WHENEVER WE'RE TOGETHER--ROMANCE, FLIRTING AT LEAST. I'M NOT GETTING THAT TODAY.
I DON'T FEEL THIS IS THE RIGHT TIME, HONESTLY. FEELS LIKE I HAVE TO STAY FOCUSED...THAT WE BOTH DO.
OKAY, HERE'S MY SERIOUS FACE. WHAT'S UP?
JOHNNY'S A MESS.
Bart's
HIS POWERS ARE GONE, HIS CAREER'S DONE. HE'S GOTTEN INTO SOME BAD HABITS AND BEHAVIOR. IF ANY OF IT GETS OUT, HE'LL BE THE LAUGHING-STOCK OF EVERY TABLOID AND GOSSIP SITE.
SO HOW CAN I HELP?
NO, I'M NOT THERE YET.
I MEAN, YEAH, I WANT YOUR HELP, BUT I'M LOOKING AT AN EVEN BIGGER PICTURE.
JEN, REED'S A MESS, TOO, JUST IN A DIFFERENT WAY THAN JOHNNY. BEN'S IN PRISON. SUSAN'S GOING CRAZY--FIGHTING THE AVENGERS, FOR GOD'S SAKE.
YEAH, TELL ME ABOUT IT.
IT'S LIKE THE FANTASTIC FOUR ARE BEING TORN APART.

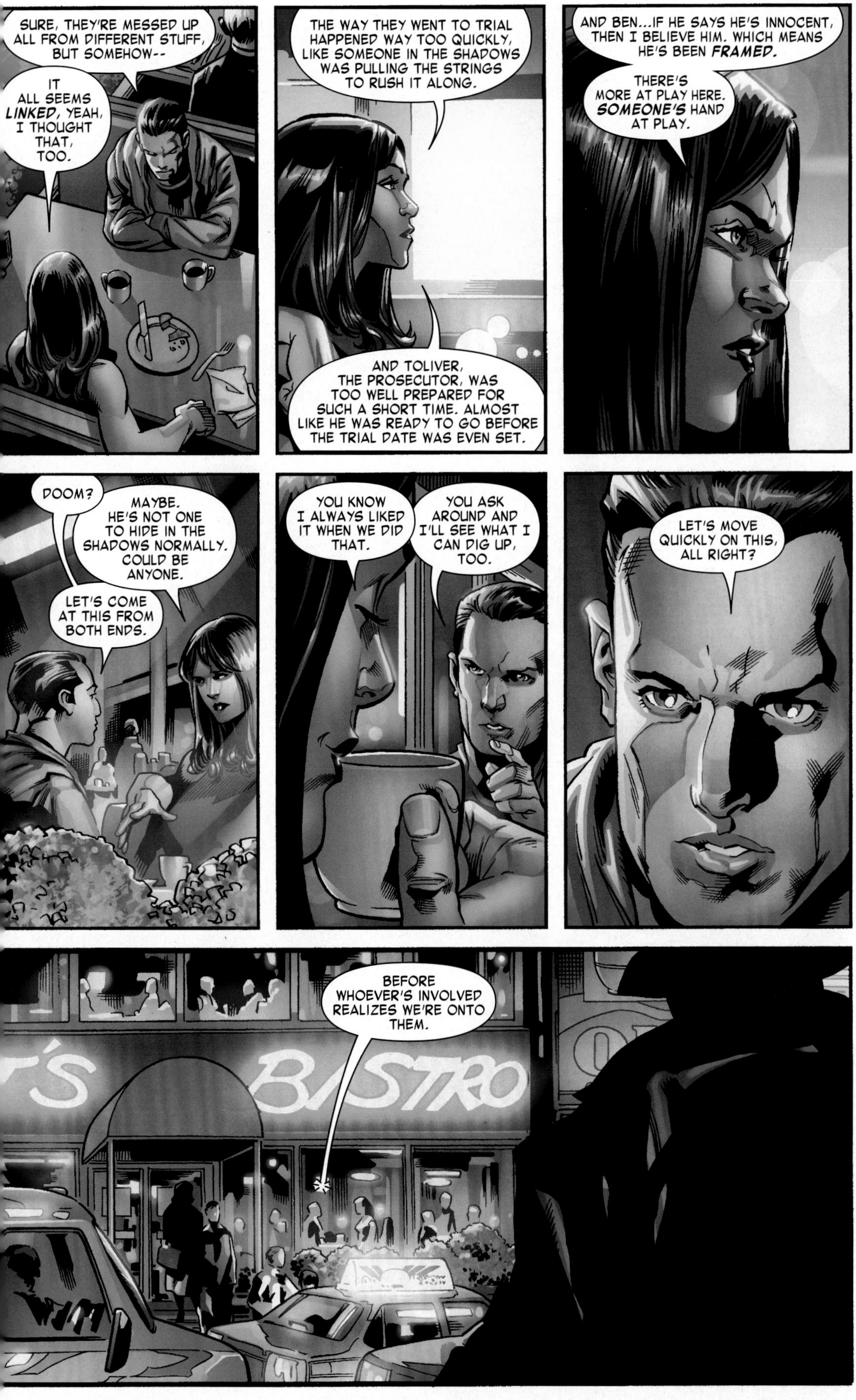
SURE, THEY'RE MESSED UP ALL FROM DIFFERENT STUFF, BUT SOMEHOW--
IT ALL SEEMS LINKED, YEAH, I THOUGHT THAT, TOO.
THE WAY THEY WENT TO TRIAL HAPPENED WAY TOO QUICKLY, LIKE SOMEONE IN THE SHADOWS WAS PULLING THE STRINGS TO RUSH IT ALONG.
AND TOLIVER, THE PROSECUTOR, WAS TOO WELL PREPARED FOR SUCH A SHORT TIME. ALMOST LIKE HE WAS READY TO GO BEFORE THE TRIAL DATE WAS EVEN SET.
AND BEN...IF HE SAYS HE'S INNOCENT, THEN I BELIEVE HIM. WHICH MEANS HE'S BEEN FRAMED.
THERE'S MORE AT PLAY HERE. SOMEONE'S HAND AT PLAY.
DOOM?
MAYBE. HE'S NOT ONE TO HIDE IN THE SHADOWS NORMALLY. COULD BE ANYONE.
LET'S COME AT THIS FROM BOTH ENDS.
YOU KNOW I ALWAYS LIKED IT WHEN WE DID THAT.
YOU ASK AROUND AND I'LL SEE WHAT I CAN DIG UP, TOO.
LET'S MOVE QUICKLY ON THIS, ALL RIGHT?
BEFORE WHOEVER'S INVOLVED REALIZES WE'RE ONTO THEM.
'S BISTRO

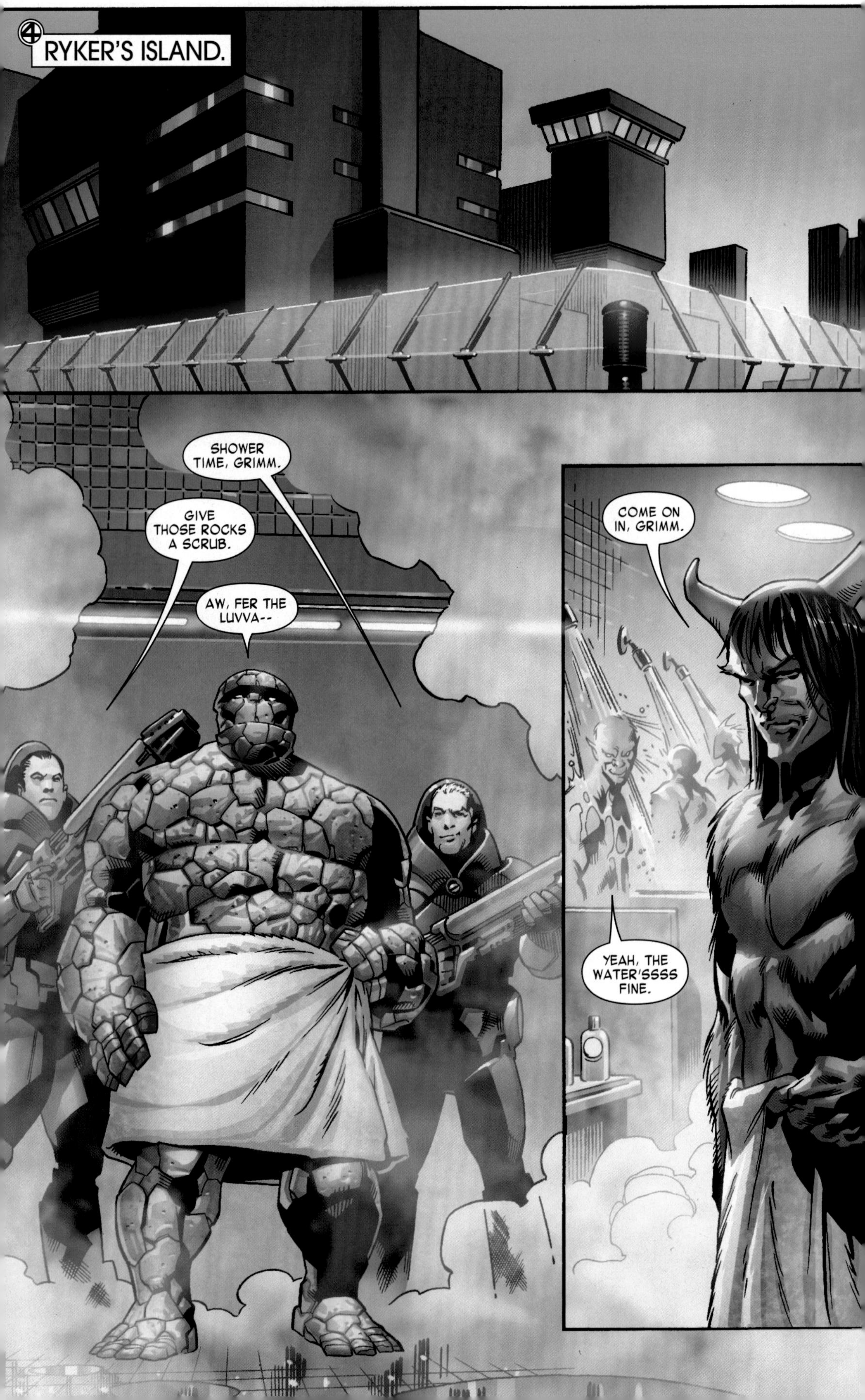
RYKER'S ISLAND.
SHOWER TIME, GRIMM.
GIVE THOSE ROCKS A SCRUB.
AW, FER THE LUVVA--
COME ON IN, GRIMM.
YEAH, THE WATER'SSSS FINE.

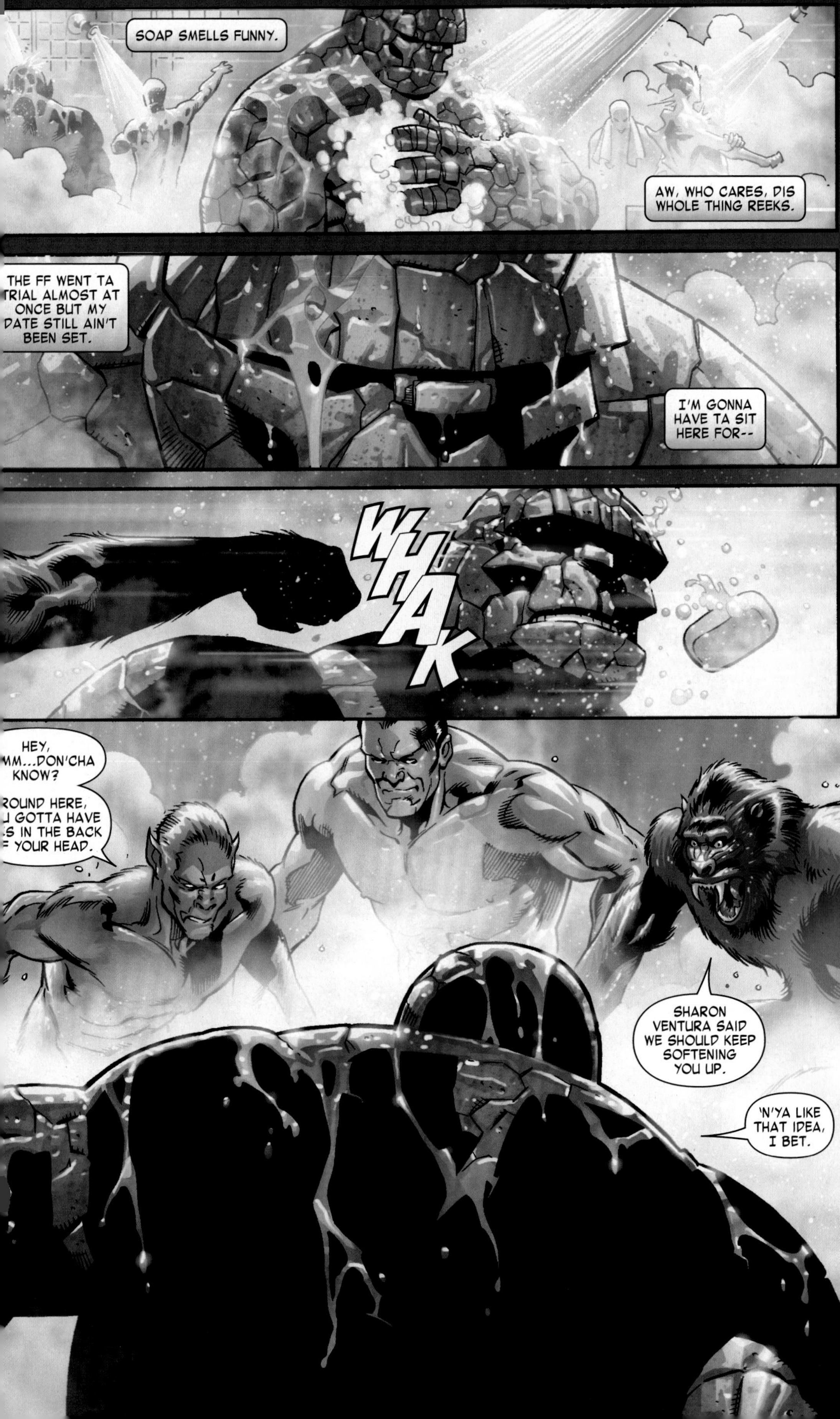
SOAP SMELLS FUNNY.
AW, WHO CARES, DIS WHOLE THING REEKS.
THE FF WENT TA TRIAL ALMOST AT ONCE BUT MY DATE STILL AIN'T BEEN SET.
I'M GONNA HAVE TA SIT HERE FOR--
WHAK
HEY, MM...DON'CHA KNOW?
ROUND HERE, GOTTA HAVE S IN THE BACK F YOUR HEAD.
SHARON VENTURA SAID WE SHOULD KEEP SOFTENING YOU UP.
'N'YA LIKE THAT IDEA, I BET.

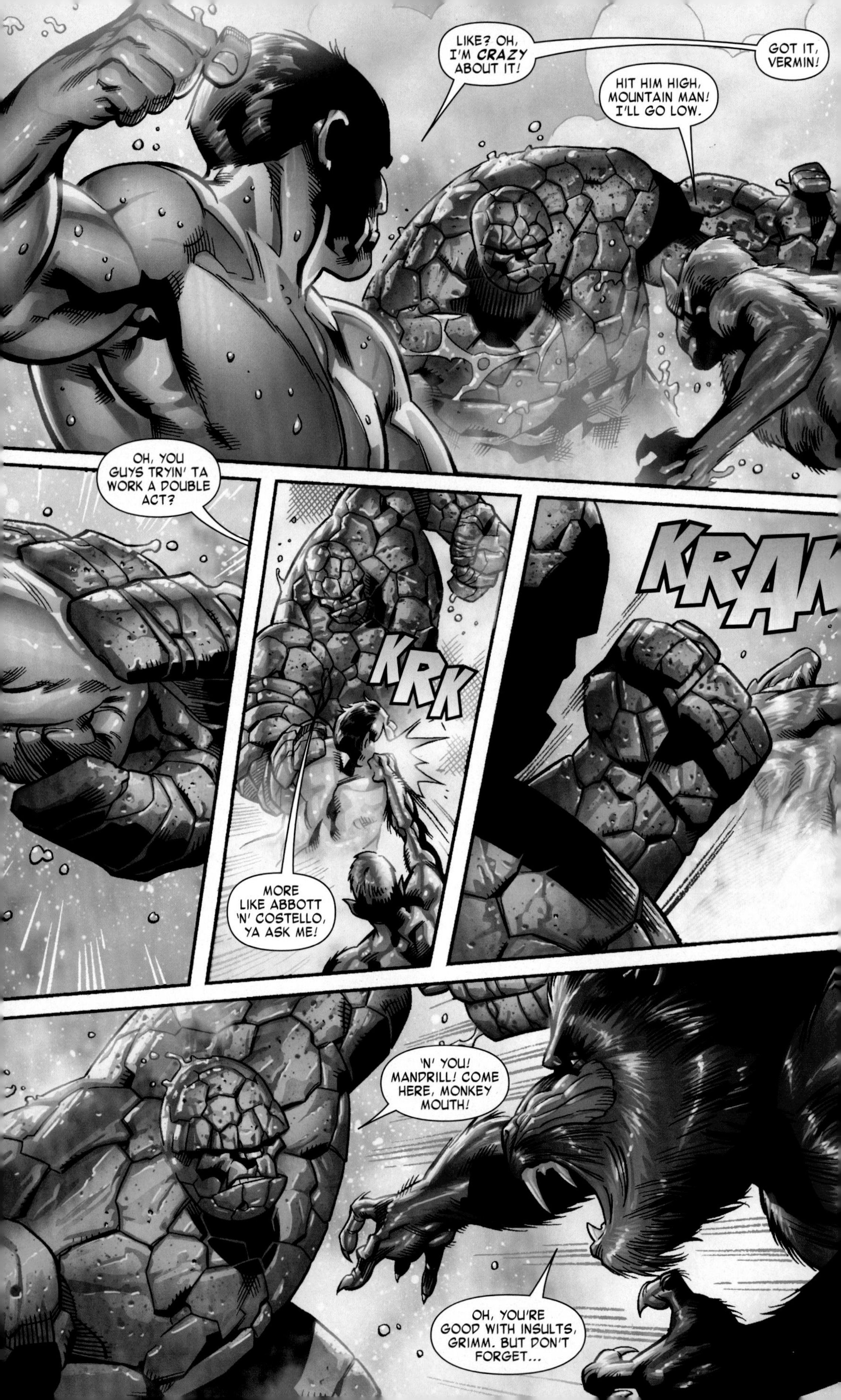
LIKE? OH, I'M CRAZY ABOUT IT!
GOT IT, VERMIN!
HIT HIM HIGH, MOUNTAIN MAN! I'LL GO LOW.
OH, YOU GUYS TRYIN' TA WORK A DOUBLE ACT?
KRK
MORE LIKE ABBOTT 'N' COSTELLO, YA ASK ME!
KRAK
'N' YOU! MANDRILL! COME HERE, MONKEY MOUTH!
OH, YOU'RE GOOD WITH INSULTS, GRIMM. BUT DON'T FORGET...

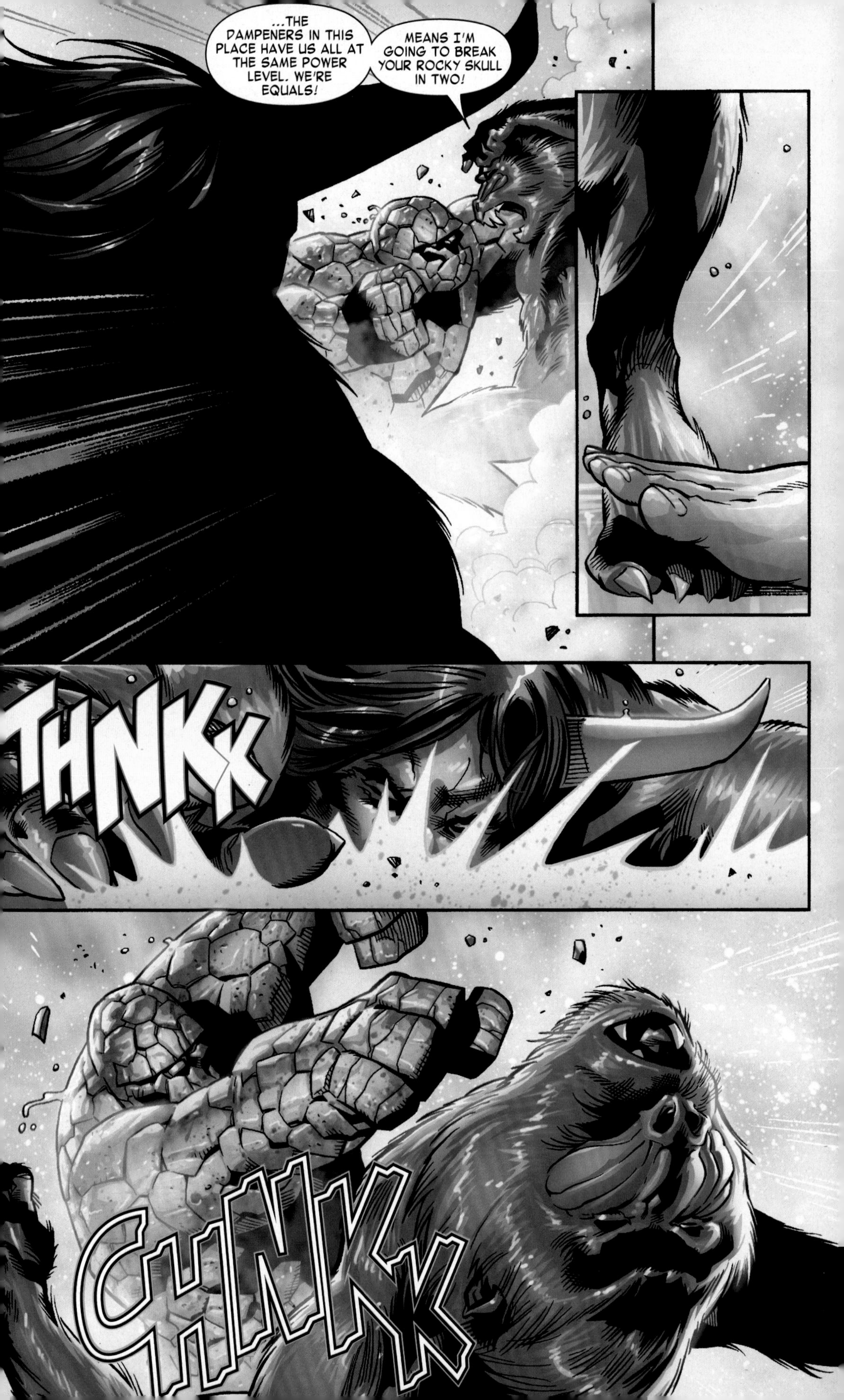
...THE DAMPENERS IN THIS PLACE HAVE US ALL AT THE SAME POWER LEVEL. WE'RE EQUALS!
MEANS I'M GOING TO BREAK YOUR ROCKY SKULL IN TWO!
THNKK
CHNKK

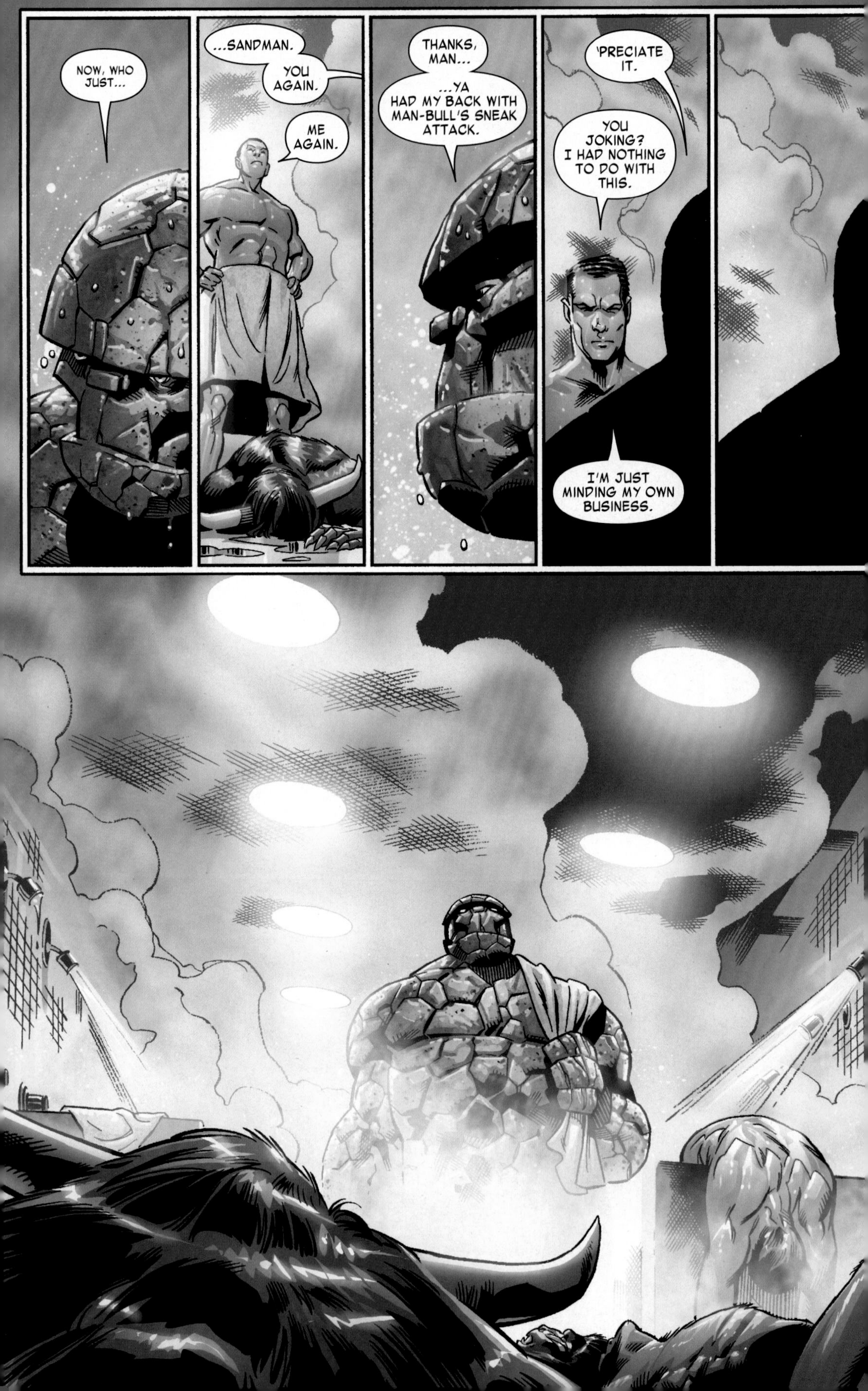
NOW, WHO JUST...
...SANDMAN.
YOU AGAIN.
ME AGAIN.
THANKS, MAN...
...YA HAD MY BACK WITH MAN-BULL'S SNEAK ATTACK.
'PRECIATE IT.
YOU JOKING? I HAD NOTHING TO DO WITH THIS.
I'M JUST MINDING MY OWN BUSINESS.

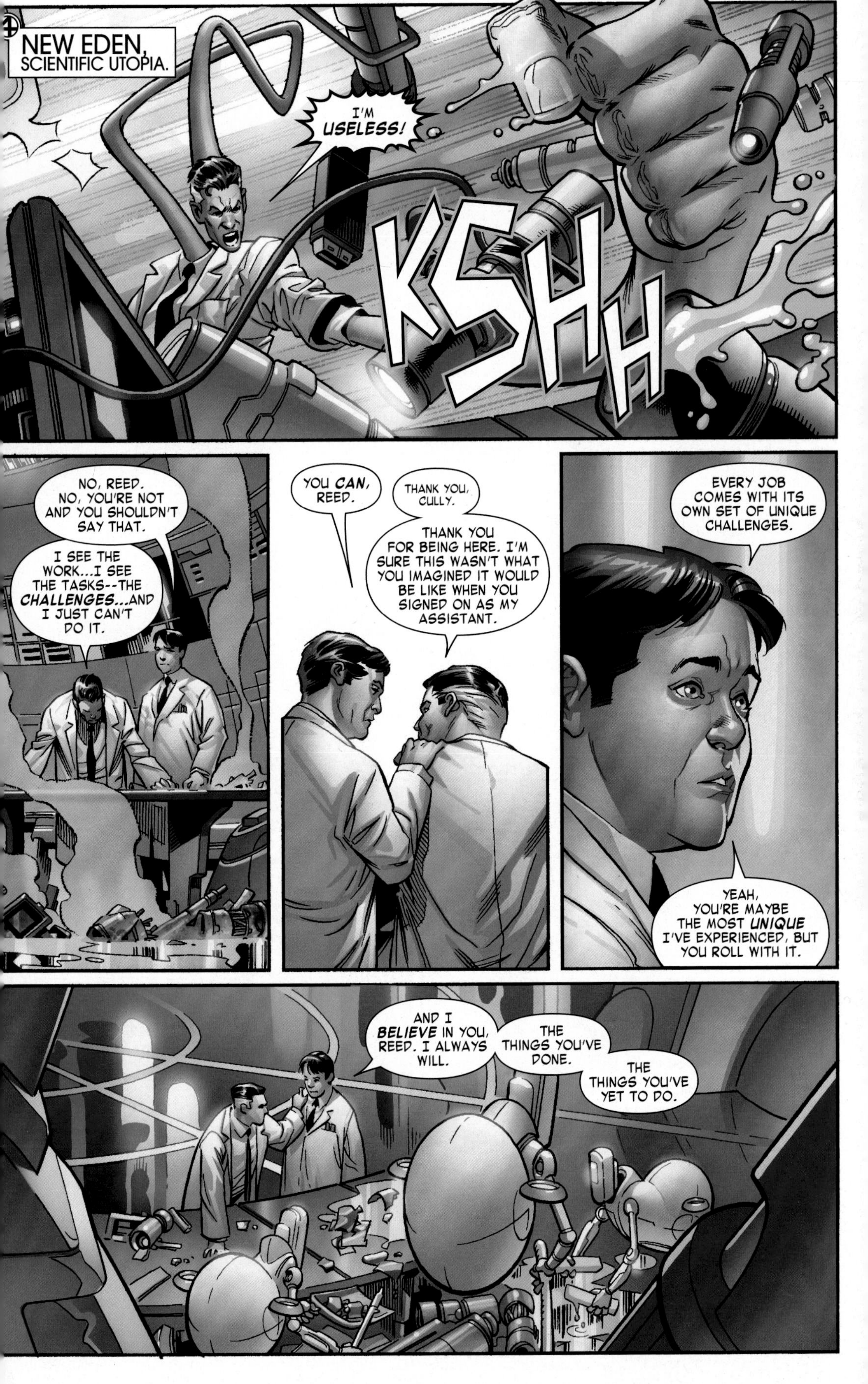
NEW EDEN, SCIENTIFIC UTOPIA.
I'M USELESS!
KSHH
NO, REED. NO, YOU'RE NOT AND YOU SHOULDN'T SAY THAT.
I SEE THE WORK...I SEE THE TASKS--THE CHALLENGES...AND I JUST CAN'T DO IT.
YOU CAN, REED.
THANK YOU, CULLY.
THANK YOU FOR BEING HERE. I'M SURE THIS WASN'T WHAT YOU IMAGINED IT WOULD BE LIKE WHEN YOU SIGNED ON AS MY ASSISTANT.
EVERY JOB COMES WITH ITS OWN SET OF UNIQUE CHALLENGES.
YEAH, YOU'RE MAYBE THE MOST UNIQUE I'VE EXPERIENCED, BUT YOU ROLL WITH IT.
AND I BELIEVE IN YOU, REED. I ALWAYS WILL.
THE THINGS YOU'VE DONE.
THE THINGS YOU'VE YET TO DO.

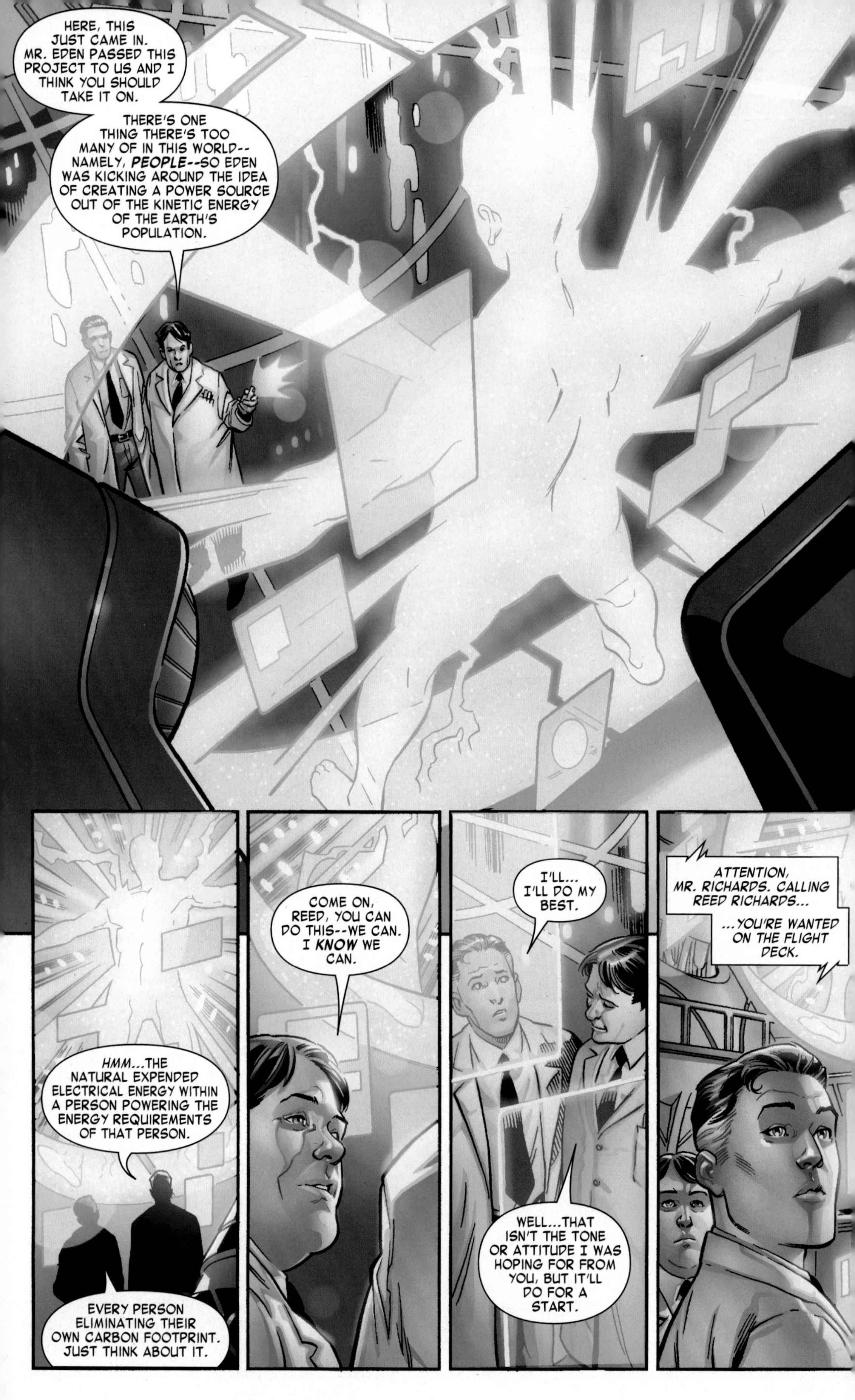
HERE, THIS JUST CAME IN. MR. EDEN PASSED THIS PROJECT TO US AND I THINK YOU SHOULD TAKE IT ON.
THERE'S ONE THING THERE'S TOO MANY OF IN THIS WORLD--NAMELY, PEOPLE--SO EDEN WAS KICKING AROUND THE IDEA OF CREATING A POWER SOURCE OUT OF THE KINETIC ENERGY OF THE EARTH'S POPULATION.
HMM...THE NATURAL EXPENDED ELECTRICAL ENERGY WITHIN A PERSON POWERING THE ENERGY REQUIREMENTS OF THAT PERSON.
EVERY PERSON ELIMINATING THEIR OWN CARBON FOOTPRINT. JUST THINK ABOUT IT.
COME ON, REED, YOU CAN DO THIS--WE CAN. I KNOW WE CAN.
I'LL... I'LL DO MY BEST.
WELL...THAT ISN'T THE TONE OR ATTITUDE I WAS HOPING FOR FROM YOU, BUT IT'LL DO FOR A START.
ATTENTION, MR. RICHARDS. CALLING REED RICHARDS...
...YOU'RE WANTED ON THE FLIGHT DECK.

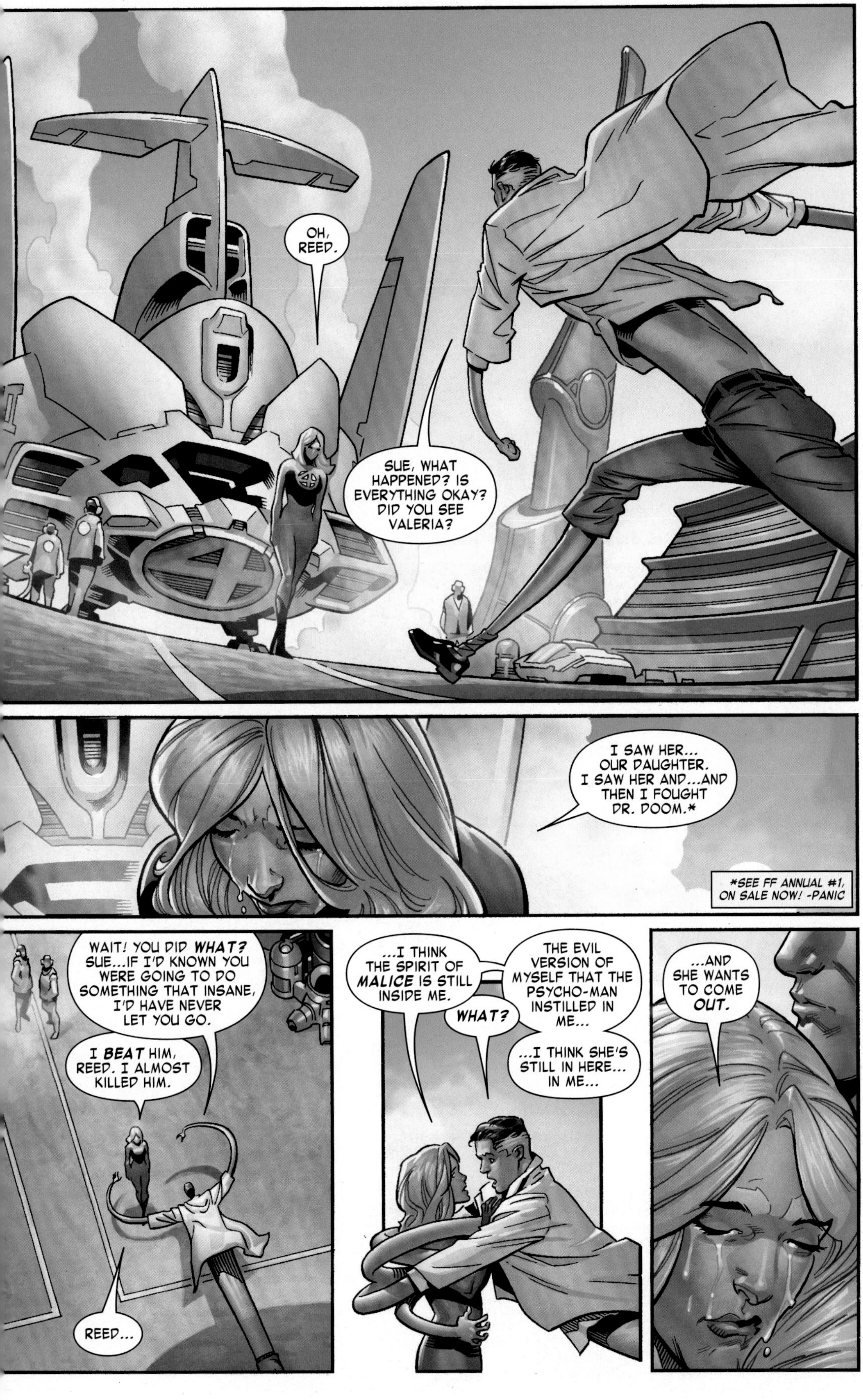

OH, REED.
SUE, WHAT HAPPENED? IS EVERYTHING OKAY? DID YOU SEE VALERIA?
I SAW HER... OUR DAUGHTER. I SAW HER AND...AND THEN I FOUGHT DR. DOOM.*
*SEE FF ANNUAL #1, ON SALE NOW! -PANIC
WAIT! YOU DID WHAT? SUE...IF I'D KNOWN YOU WERE GOING TO DO SOMETHING THAT INSANE, I'D HAVE NEVER LET YOU GO.
I BEAT HIM, REED. I ALMOST KILLED HIM.
REED...
...I THINK THE SPIRIT OF MALICE IS STILL INSIDE ME.
WHAT?
THE EVIL VERSION OF MYSELF THAT THE PSYCHO-MAN INSTILLED IN ME...
...I THINK SHE'S STILL IN HERE... IN ME...
...AND SHE WANTS TO COME OUT.

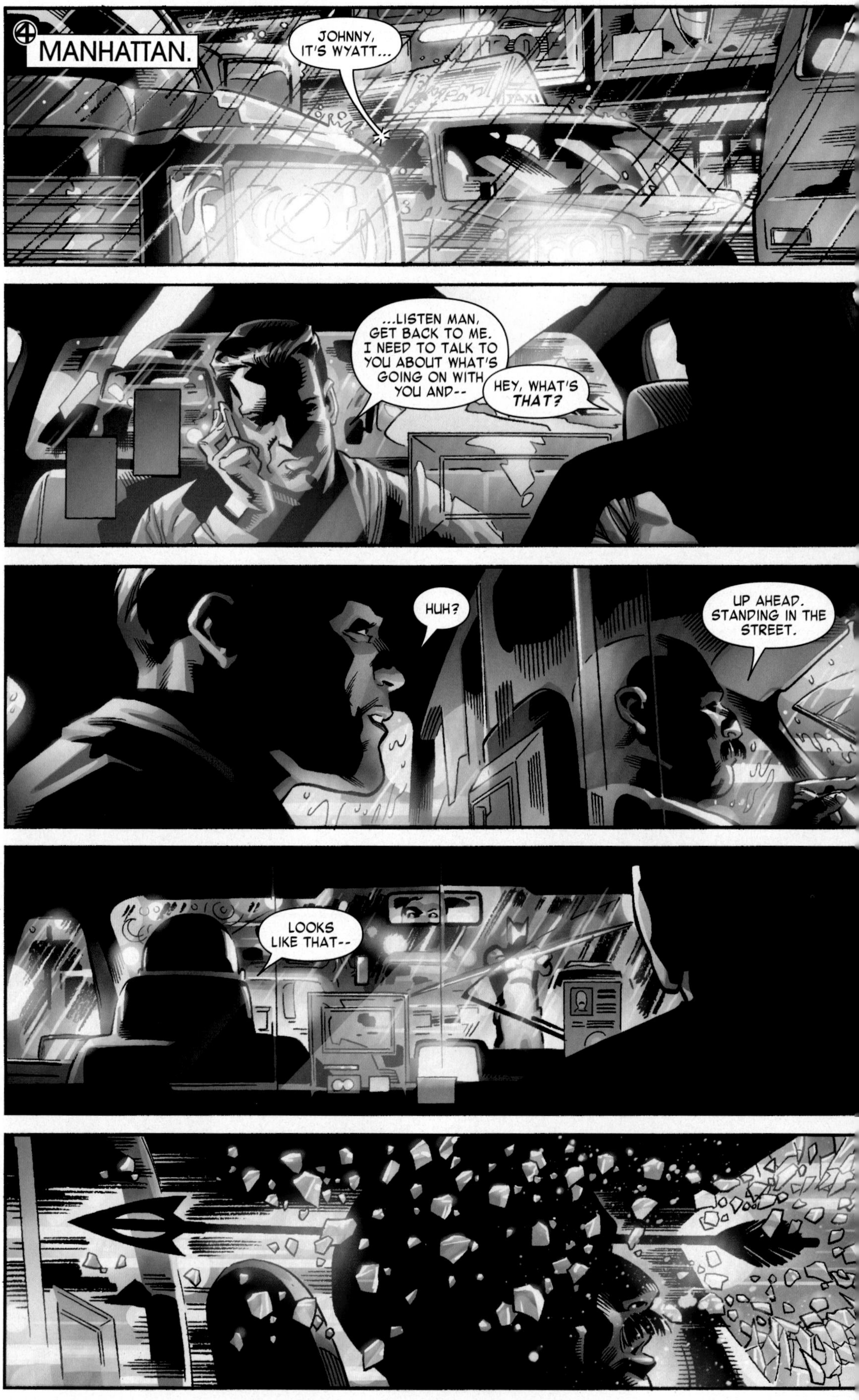
4
MANHATTAN.
JOHNNY, IT'S WYATT...
...LISTEN MAN, GET BACK TO ME. I NEED TO TALK TO YOU ABOUT WHAT'S GOING ON WITH YOU AND--
HEY, WHAT'S THAT?
HUH?
UP AHEAD. STANDING IN THE STREET.
LOOKS LIKE THAT--

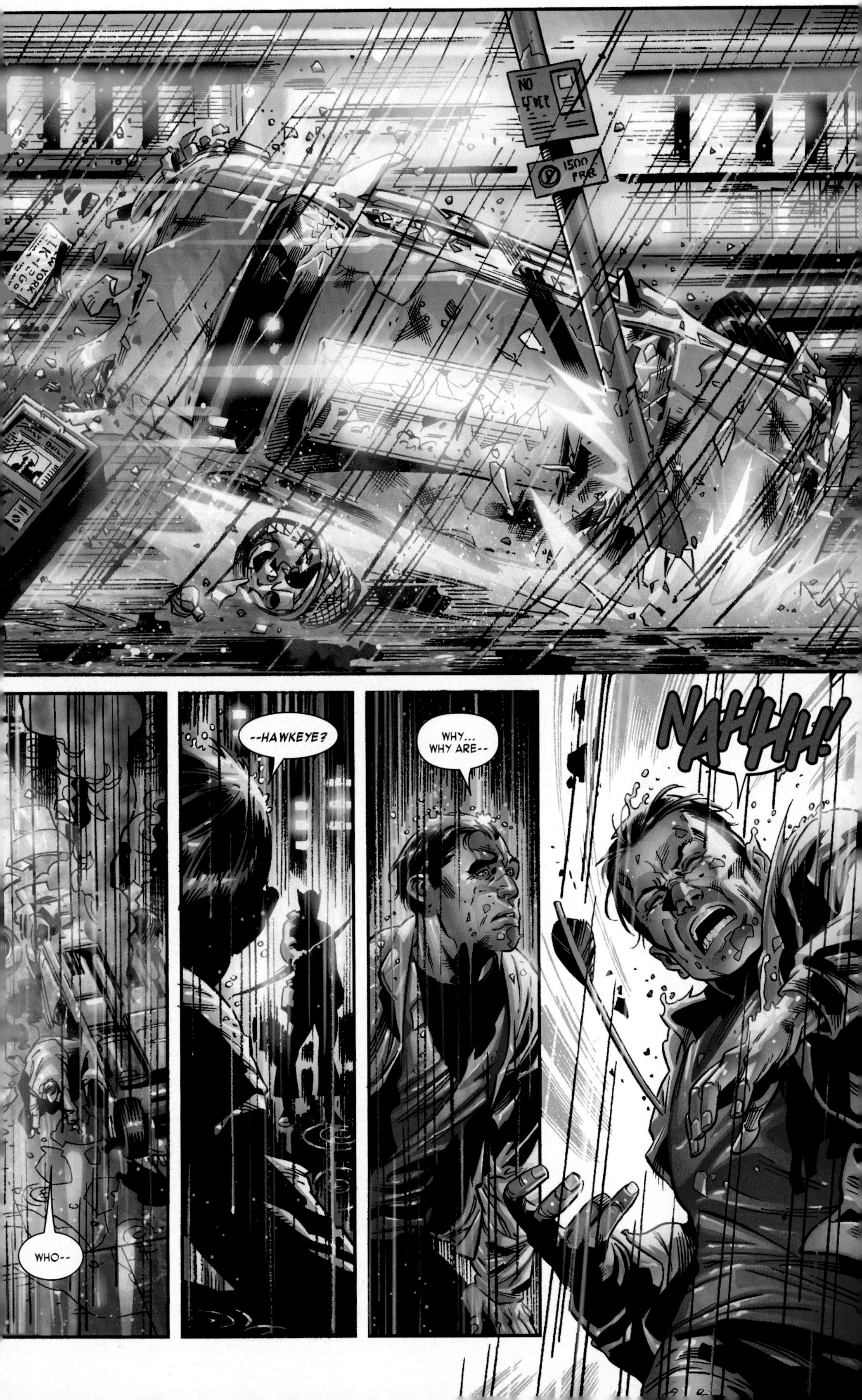
NO
1500 FREE
WHO--
--HAWKEYE?
WHY... WHY ARE--
NAHHH!

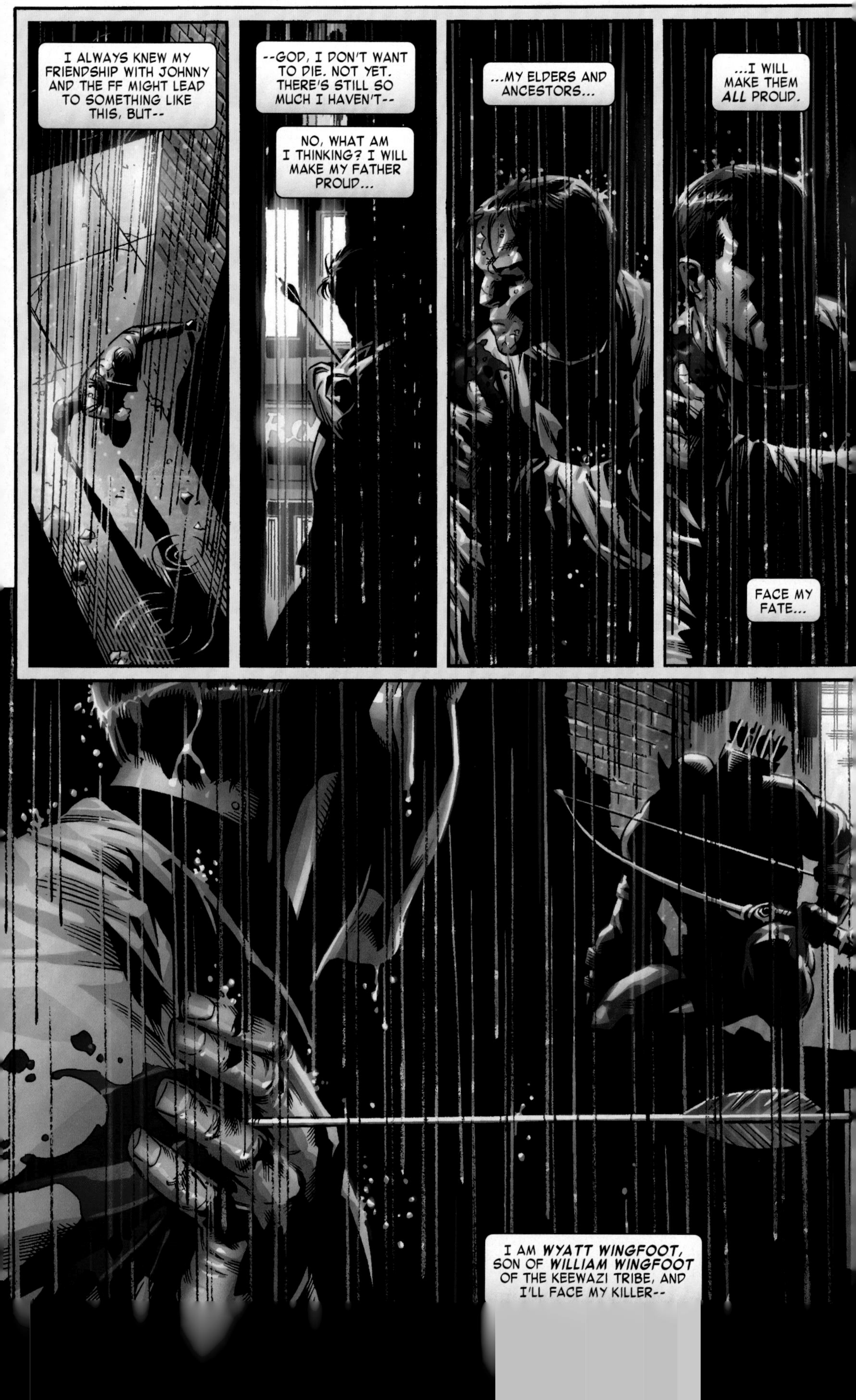
I ALWAYS KNEW MY FRIENDSHIP WITH JOHNNY AND THE FF MIGHT LEAD TO SOMETHING LIKE THIS, BUT--
--GOD, I DON'T WANT TO DIE. NOT YET. THERE'S STILL SO MUCH I HAVEN'T--
NO, WHAT AM I THINKING? I WILL MAKE MY FATHER PROUD...
...MY ELDERS AND ANCESTORS...
...I WILL MAKE THEM ALL PROUD.
FACE MY FATE...
I AM WYATT WINGFOOT, SON OF WILLIAM WINGFOOT OF THE KEEWAZI TRIBE, AND I'LL FACE MY KILLER--

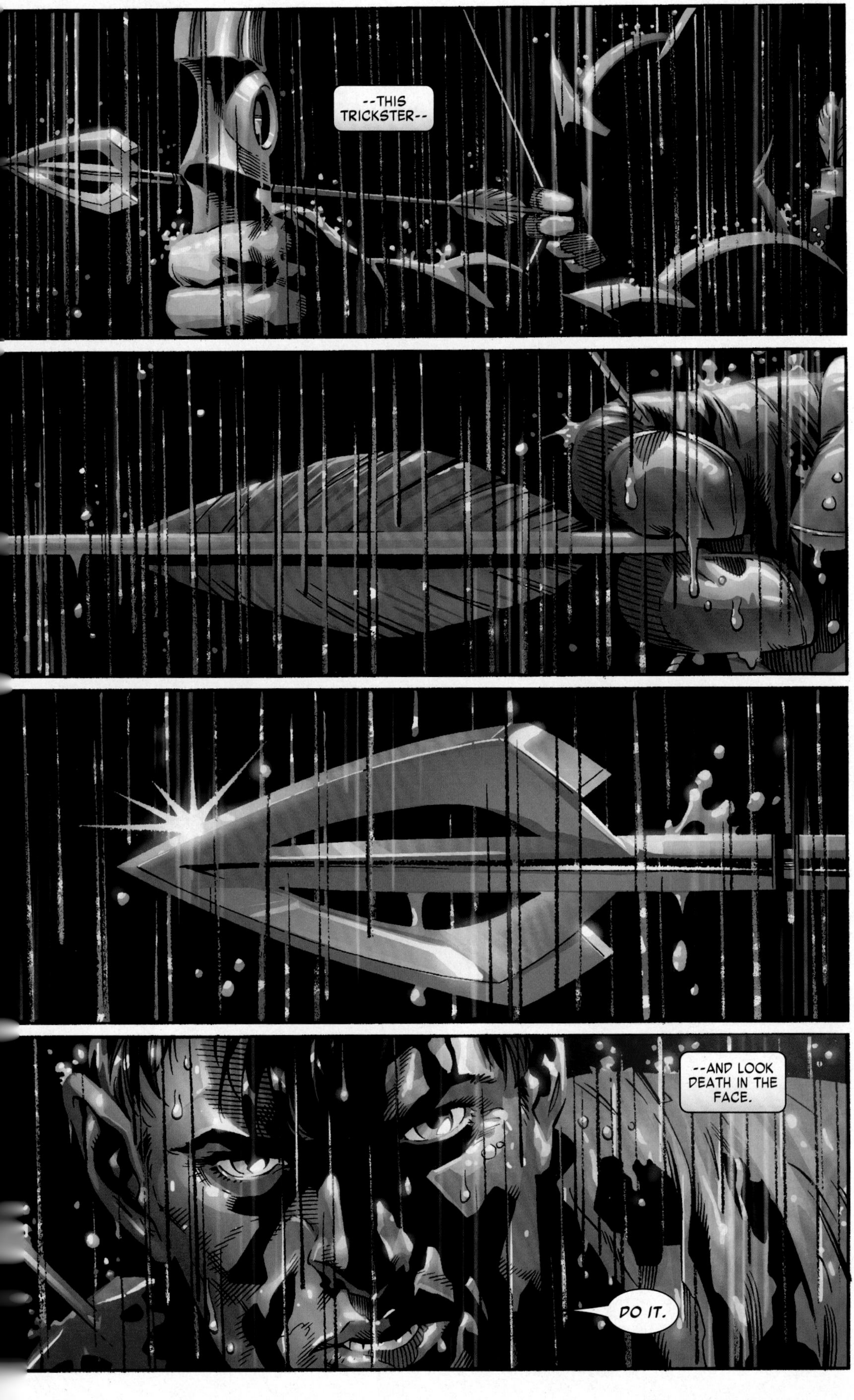
--THIS TRICKSTER--
--AND LOOK DEATH IN THE FACE.
DO IT.

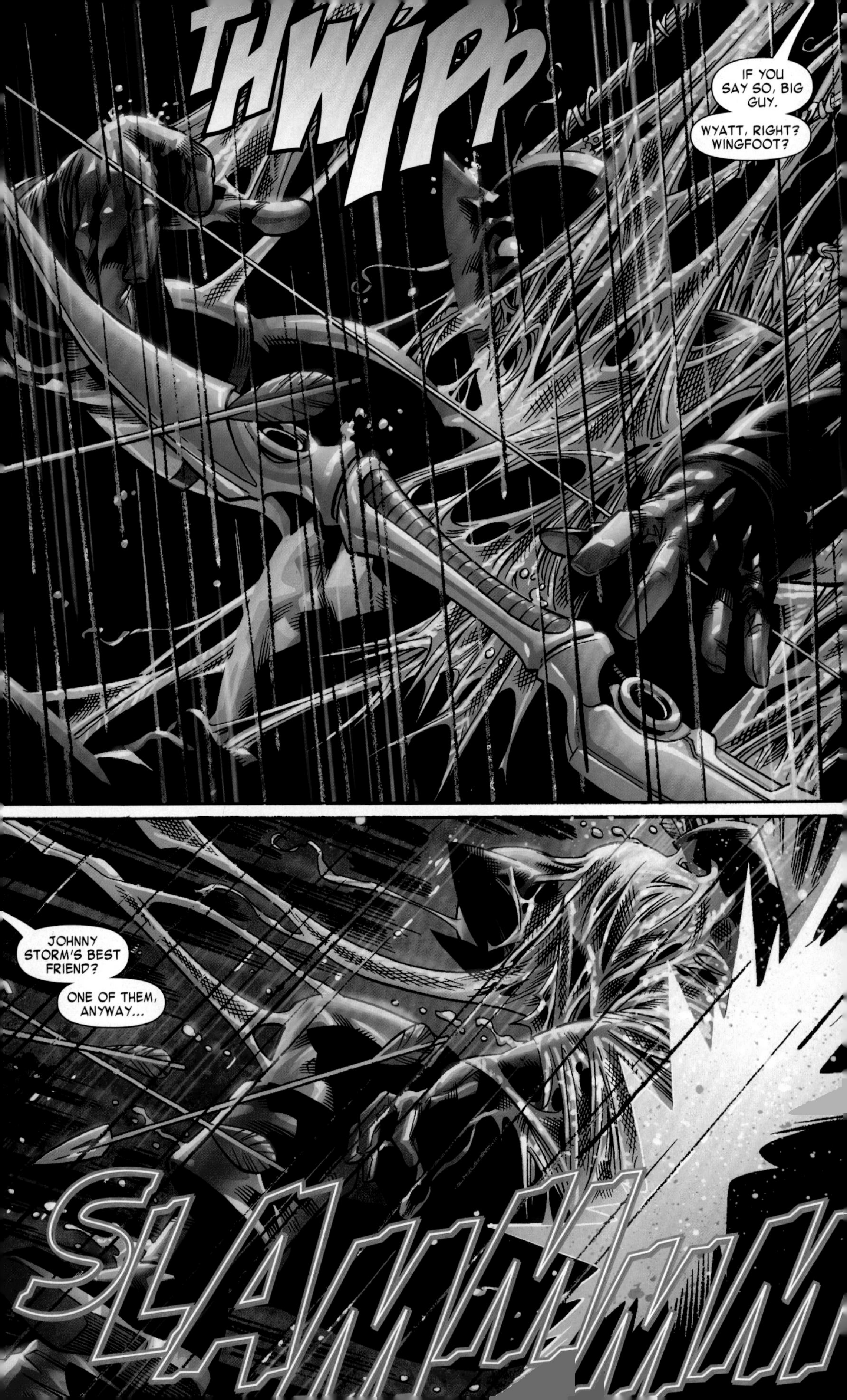
THWIPP
IF YOU SAY SO, BIG GUY.
WYATT, RIGHT? WINGFOOT?
JOHNNY STORM'S BEST FRIEND?
ONE OF THEM, ANYWAY...
SLAMMMMM

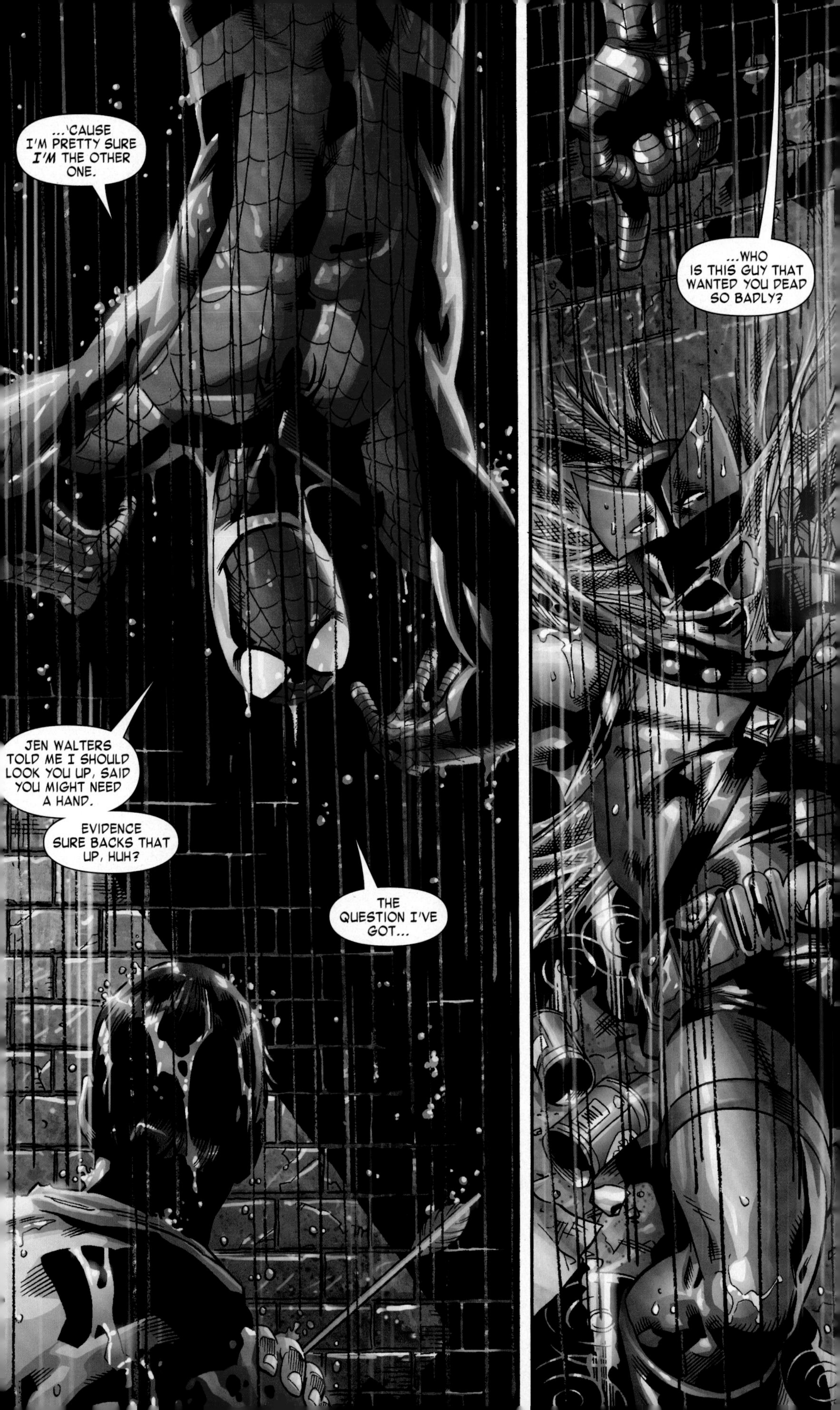
...'CAUSE I'M PRETTY SURE I'M THE OTHER ONE.
JEN WALTERS TOLD ME I SHOULD LOOK YOU UP, SAID YOU MIGHT NEED A HAND.
EVIDENCE SURE BACKS THAT UP, HUH?
THE QUESTION I'VE GOT...
...WHO IS THIS GUY THAT WANTED YOU DEAD SO BADLY?

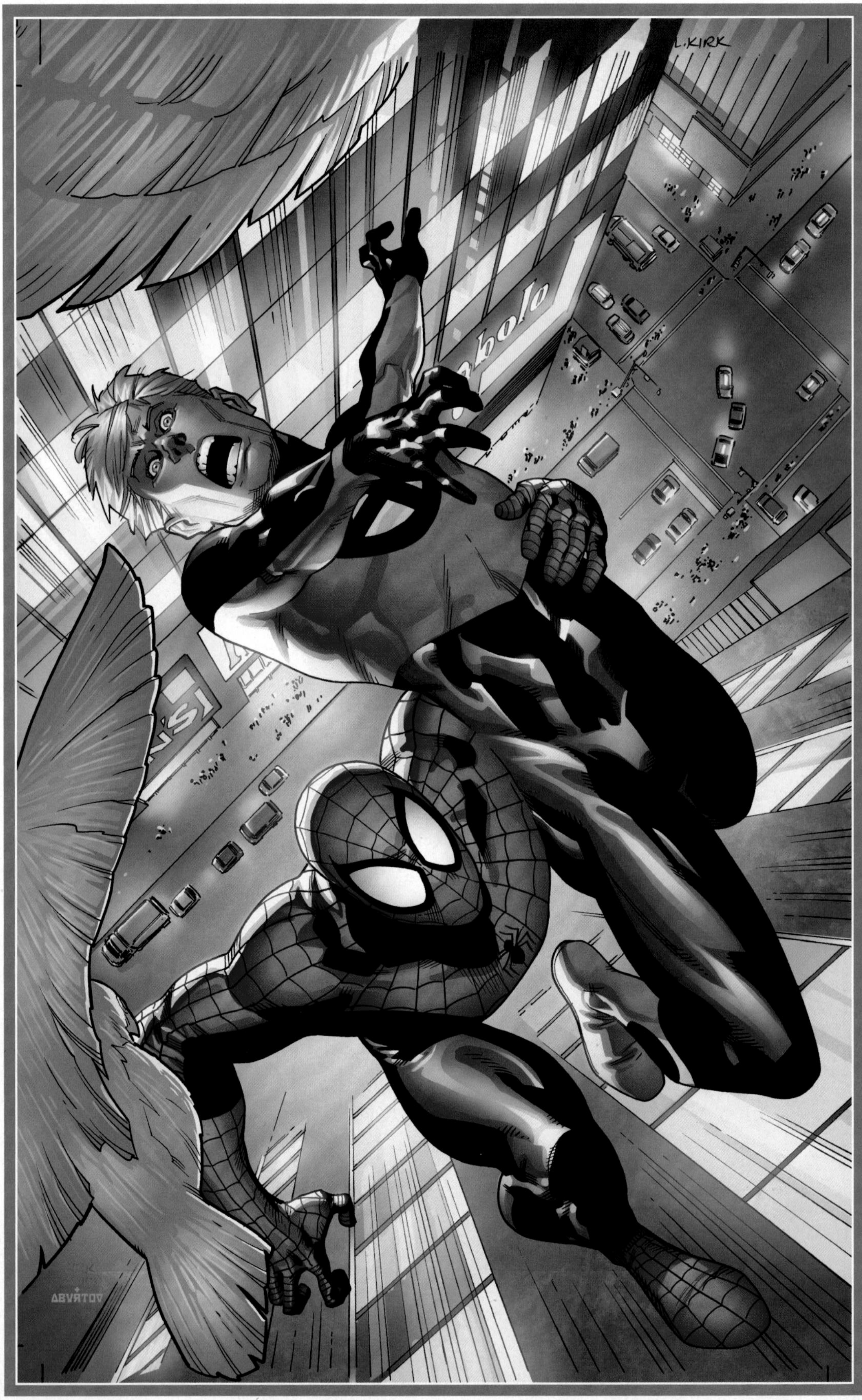
L.KIRK

TWELVE

MY NAME IS *JOHNNY STORM* AND I'M AN *IDIOT.*

I NEVER SHOULD HAVE LIED ABOUT GALACTUS' UNDERPANTS.

I DIDN'T ACT LIKE I SAID I DID. NO, TRUTH IS, BACK THEN I WAS SIMPLY FREAKING OUT LIKE THE REST OF MANHATTAN.

AND NOW--RIGHT NOW IN THE PRESENT, IT'S JUST *ME* WHO'S FREAKING OUT ALL BY MY LONESOME.

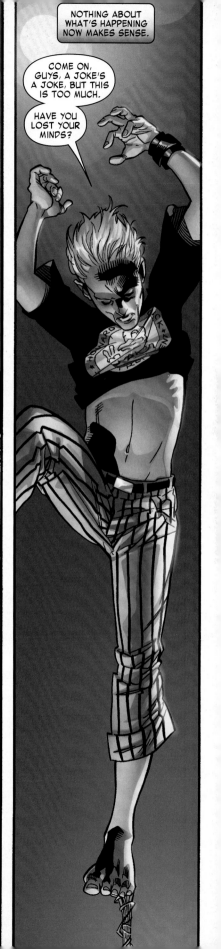

NOTHING ABOUT WHAT'S HAPPENING NOW MAKES SENSE.

COME ON, GUYS, A JOKE'S A JOKE, BUT THIS IS TOO MUCH.

HAVE YOU LOST YOUR MINDS?

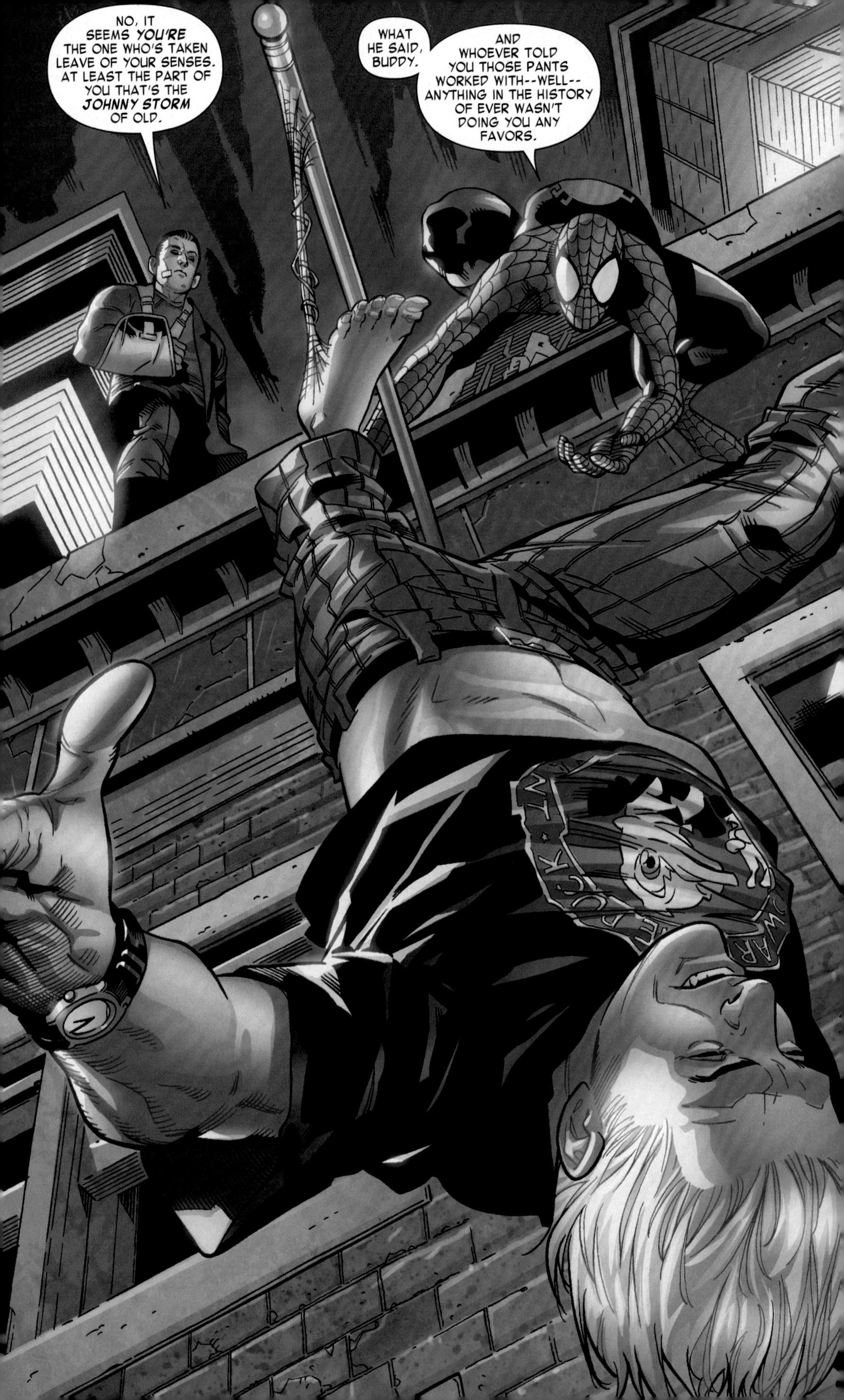
NO, IT SEEMS YOU'RE THE ONE WHO'S TAKEN LEAVE OF YOUR SENSES. AT LEAST THE PART OF YOU THAT'S THE JOHNNY STORM OF OLD.
WHAT HE SAID, BUDDY.
AND WHOEVER TOLD YOU THOSE PANTS WORKED WITH--WELL--ANYTHING IN THE HISTORY OF EVER WASN'T DOING YOU ANY FAVORS.

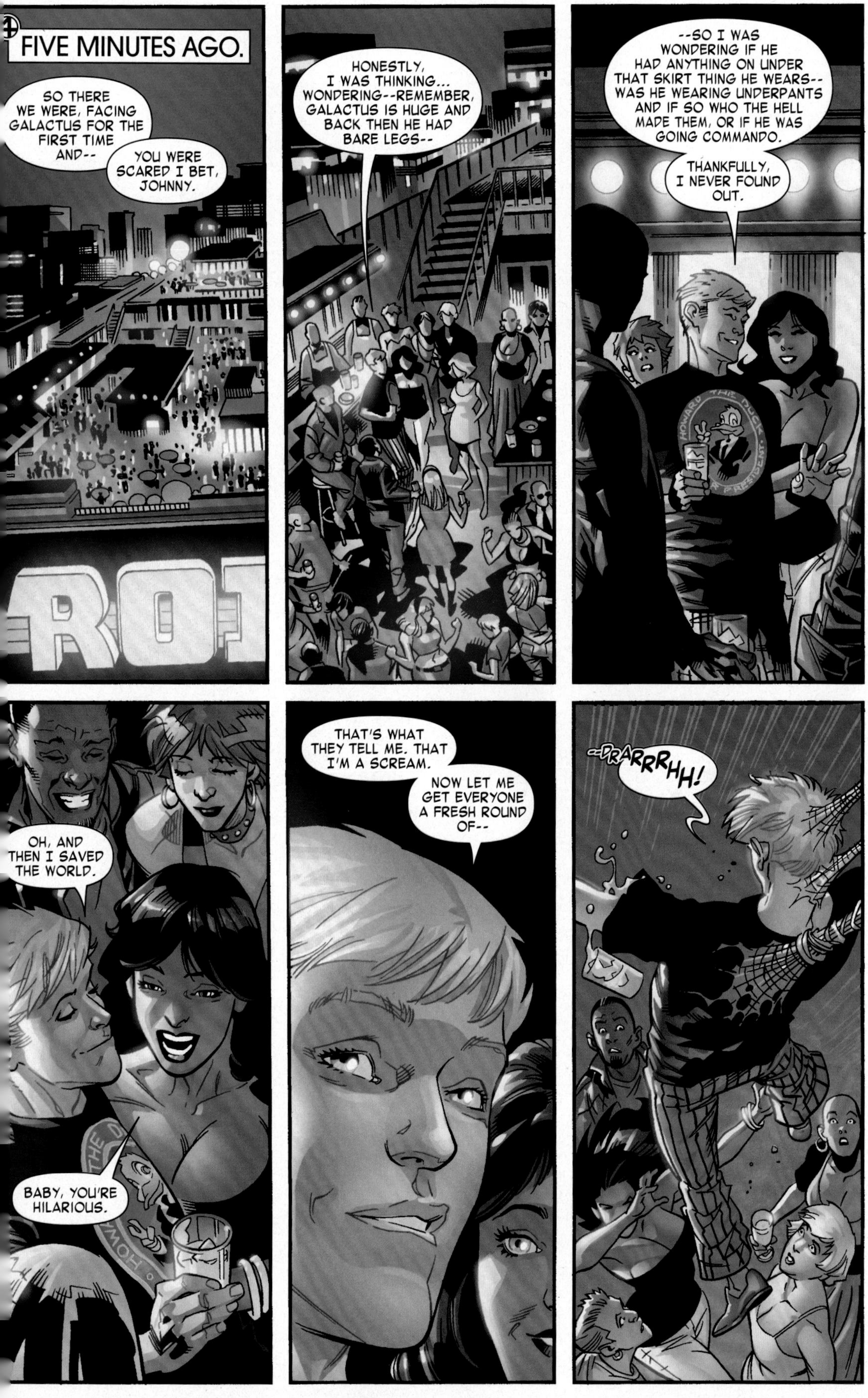
FIVE MINUTES AGO.
SO THERE WE WERE, FACING GALACTUS FOR THE FIRST TIME AND--
YOU WERE SCARED I BET, JOHNNY.
HONESTLY, I WAS THINKING... WONDERING--REMEMBER, GALACTUS IS HUGE AND BACK THEN HE HAD BARE LEGS--
--SO I WAS WONDERING IF HE HAD ANYTHING ON UNDER THAT SKIRT THING HE WEARS--WAS HE WEARING UNDERPANTS AND IF SO WHO THE HELL MADE THEM, OR IF HE WAS GOING COMMANDO.
THANKFULLY, I NEVER FOUND OUT.
HOWARD THE DUCK FOR PRESIDENT
OH, AND THEN I SAVED THE WORLD.
BABY, YOU'RE HILARIOUS.
THAT'S WHAT THEY TELL ME. THAT I'M A SCREAM.
NOW LET ME GET EVERYONE A FRESH ROUND OF--
--DRARRRHH!

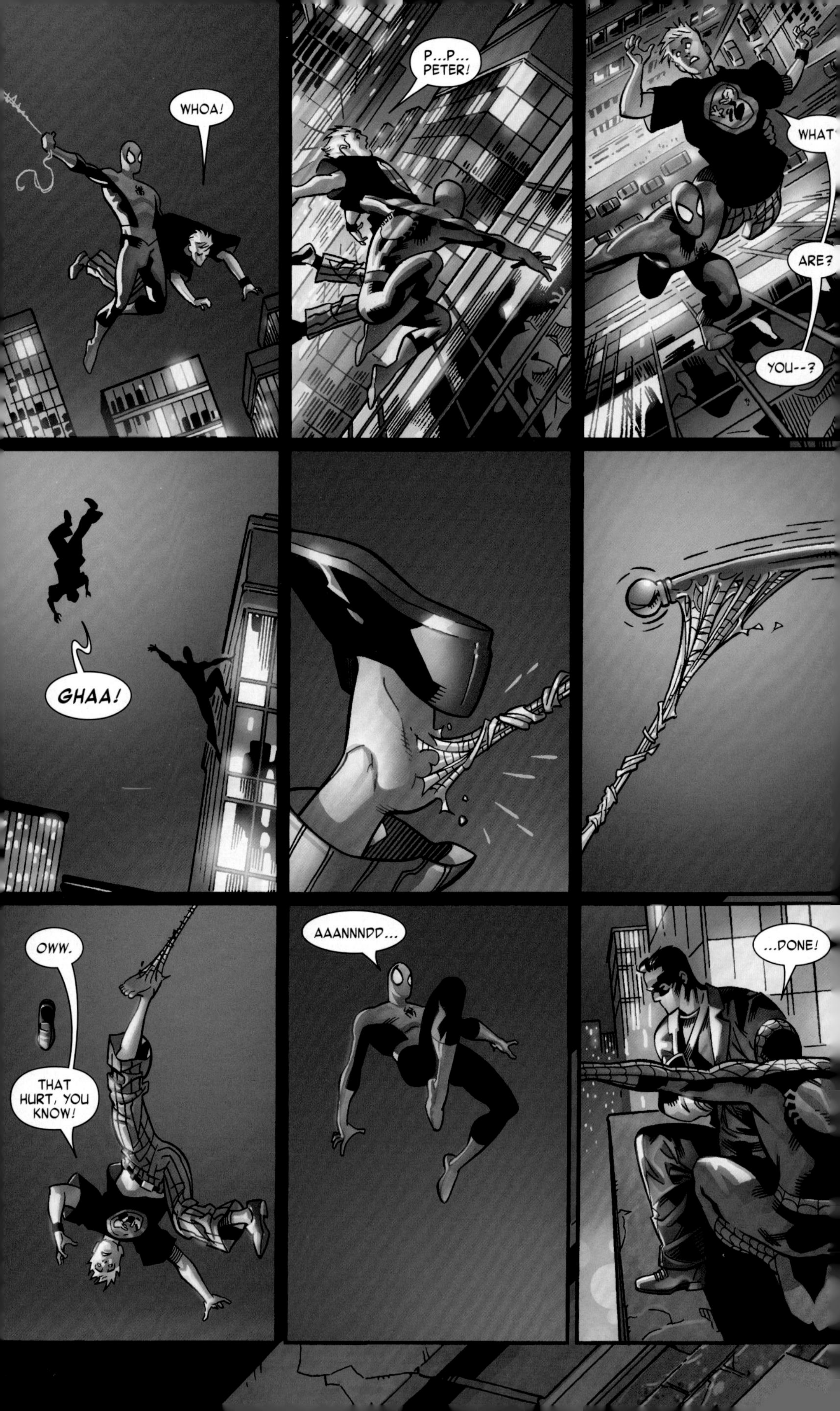

WHOA!
P...P... PETER!
WHAT
ARE?
YOU--?
GHAA!
OWW.
THAT HURT, YOU KNOW!
AAANNNDD...
...DONE!

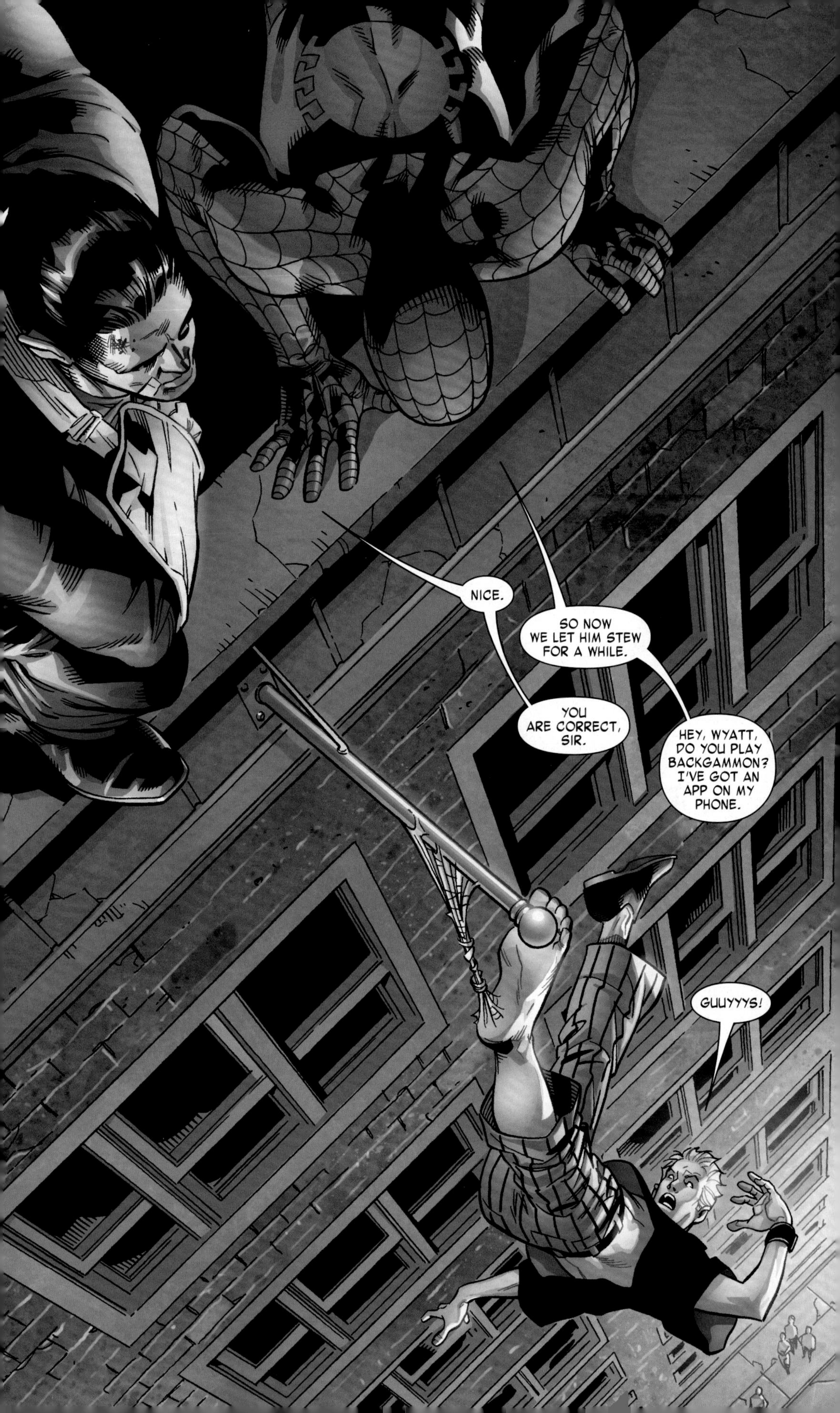
NICE.
SO NOW WE LET HIM STEW FOR A WHILE.
YOU ARE CORRECT, SIR.
HEY, WYATT, DO YOU PLAY BACKGAMMON? I'VE GOT AN APP ON MY PHONE.
GUUYYYS!

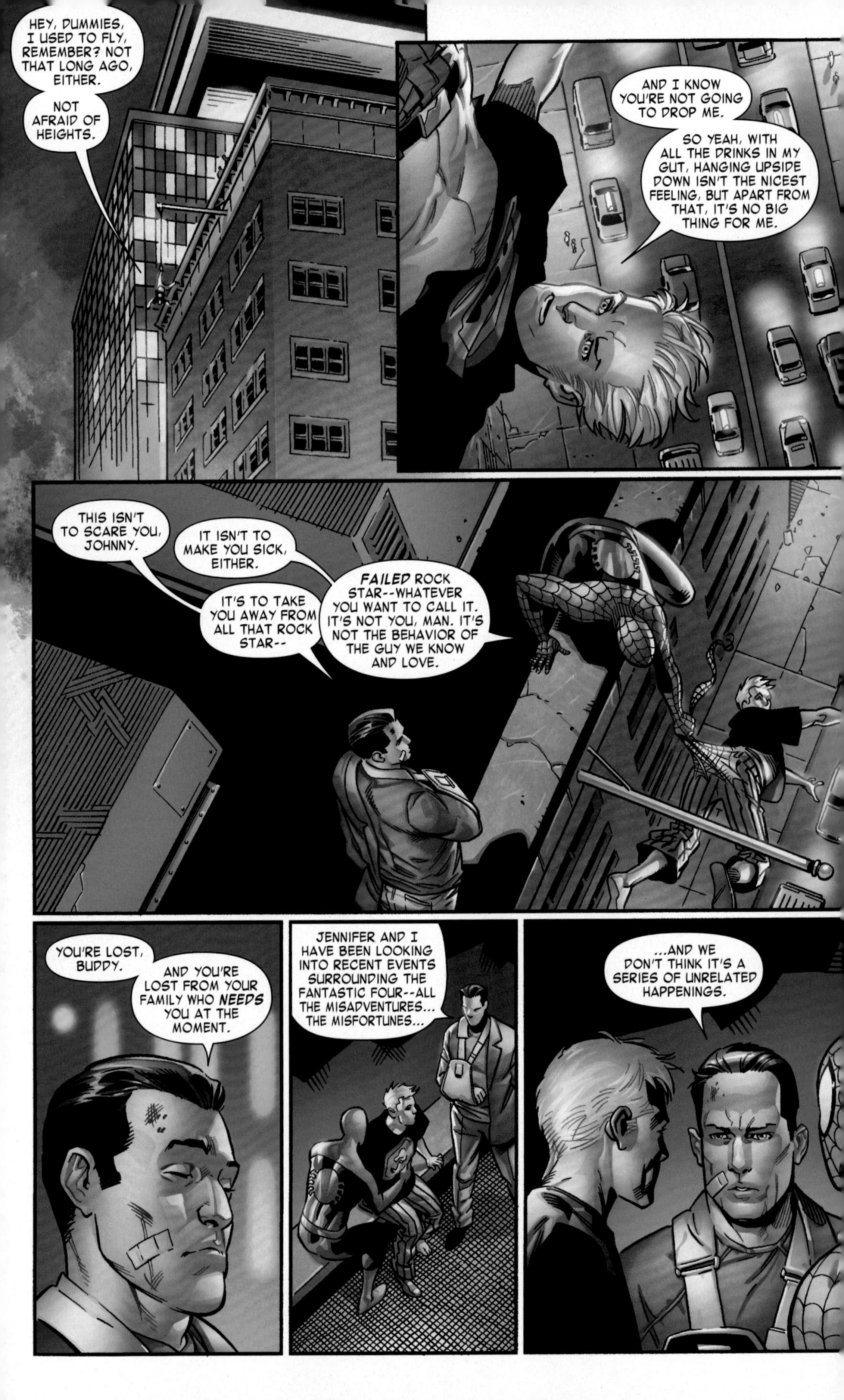
HEY, DUMMIES, I USED TO FLY, REMEMBER? NOT THAT LONG AGO, EITHER.
NOT AFRAID OF HEIGHTS.
AND I KNOW YOU'RE NOT GOING TO DROP ME.
SO YEAH, WITH ALL THE DRINKS IN MY GUT, HANGING UPSIDE DOWN ISN'T THE NICEST FEELING, BUT APART FROM THAT, IT'S NO BIG THING FOR ME.
THIS ISN'T TO SCARE YOU, JOHNNY.
IT ISN'T TO MAKE YOU SICK, EITHER.
IT'S TO TAKE YOU AWAY FROM ALL THAT ROCK STAR--
FAILED ROCK STAR--WHATEVER YOU WANT TO CALL IT. IT'S NOT YOU, MAN. IT'S NOT THE BEHAVIOR OF THE GUY WE KNOW AND LOVE.
YOU'RE LOST, BUDDY.
AND YOU'RE LOST FROM YOUR FAMILY WHO *NEEDS* YOU AT THE MOMENT.
JENNIFER AND I HAVE BEEN LOOKING INTO RECENT EVENTS SURROUNDING THE FANTASTIC FOUR--ALL THE MISADVENTURES... THE MISFORTUNES...
...AND WE DON'T THINK IT'S A SERIES OF UNRELATED HAPPENINGS.

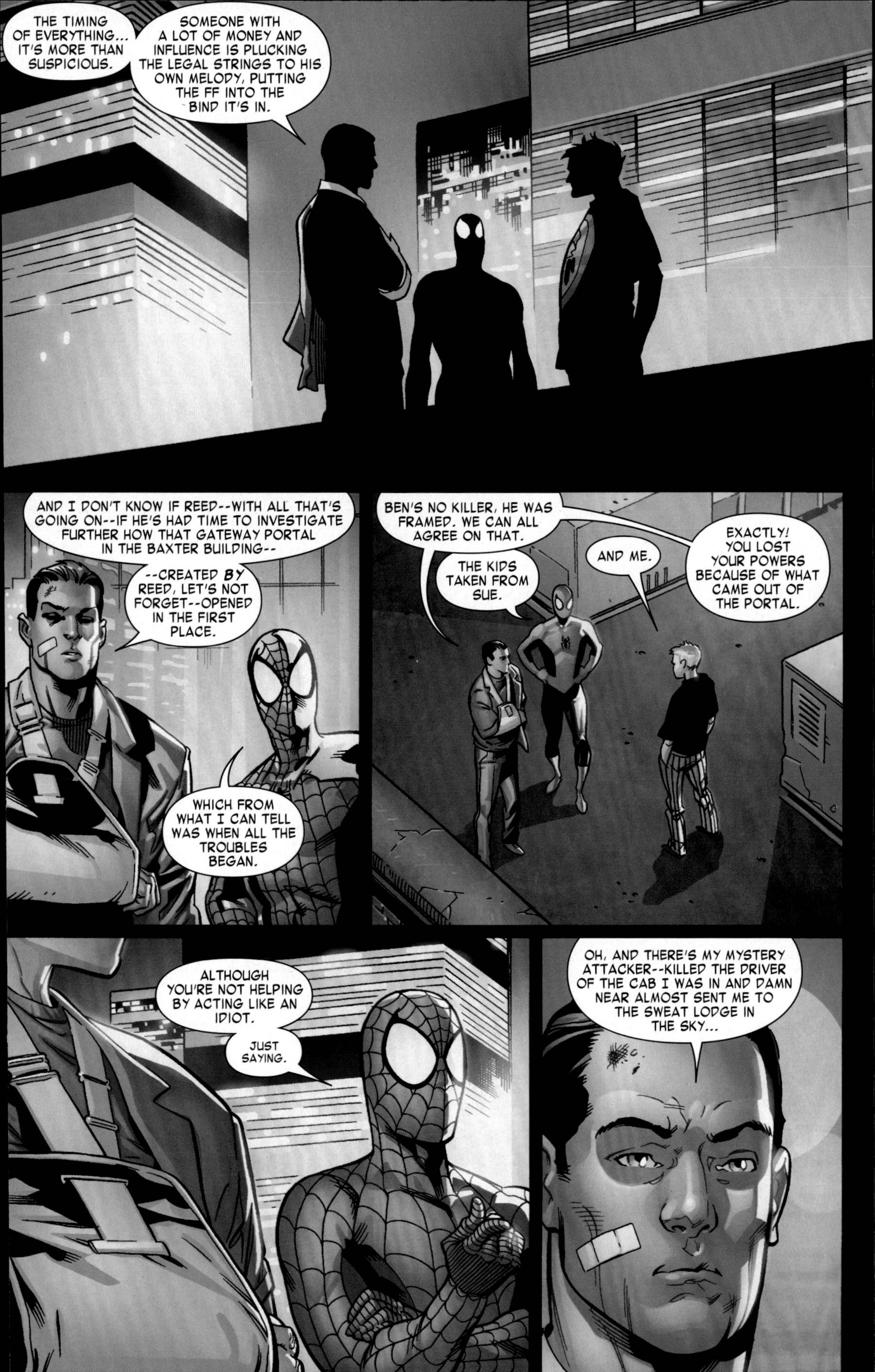

THE TIMING OF EVERYTHING... IT'S MORE THAN SUSPICIOUS.
SOMEONE WITH A LOT OF MONEY AND INFLUENCE IS PLUCKING THE LEGAL STRINGS TO HIS OWN MELODY, PUTTING THE FF INTO THE BIND IT'S IN.
AND I DON'T KNOW IF REED--WITH ALL THAT'S GOING ON--IF HE'S HAD TIME TO INVESTIGATE FURTHER HOW THAT GATEWAY PORTAL IN THE BAXTER BUILDING--
--CREATED BY REED, LET'S NOT FORGET--OPENED IN THE FIRST PLACE.
WHICH FROM WHAT I CAN TELL WAS WHEN ALL THE TROUBLES BEGAN.
BEN'S NO KILLER, HE WAS FRAMED. WE CAN ALL AGREE ON THAT.
THE KIDS TAKEN FROM SUE.
AND ME.
EXACTLY! YOU LOST YOUR POWERS BECAUSE OF WHAT CAME OUT OF THE PORTAL.
ALTHOUGH YOU'RE NOT HELPING BY ACTING LIKE AN IDIOT.
JUST SAYING.
OH, AND THERE'S MY MYSTERY ATTACKER--KILLED THE DRIVER OF THE CAB I WAS IN AND DAMN NEAR ALMOST SENT ME TO THE SWEAT LODGE IN THE SKY...

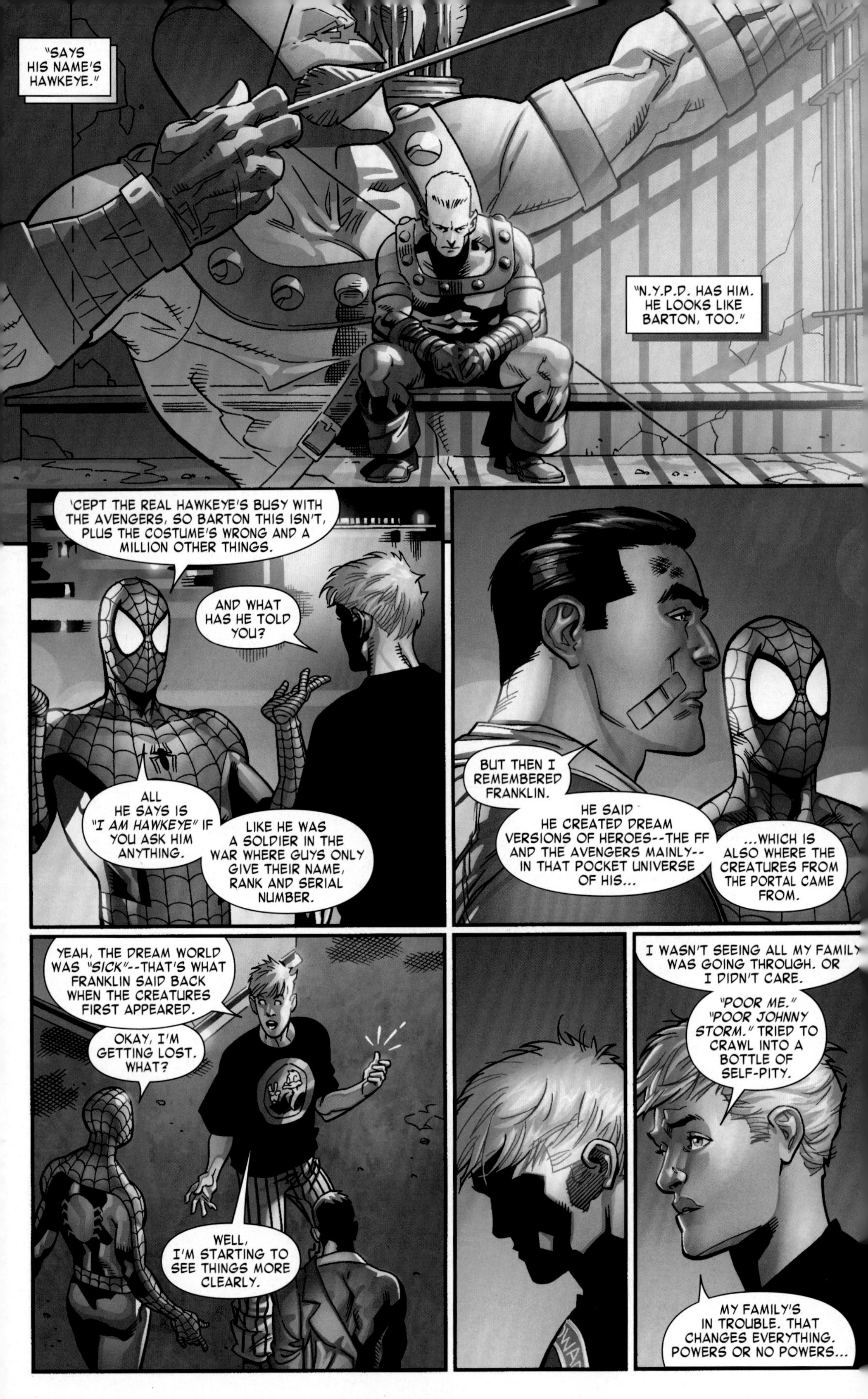
"SAYS HIS NAME'S HAWKEYE."
"N.Y.P.D. HAS HIM. HE LOOKS LIKE BARTON, TOO."
'CEPT THE REAL HAWKEYE'S BUSY WITH THE AVENGERS, SO BARTON THIS ISN'T, PLUS THE COSTUME'S WRONG AND A MILLION OTHER THINGS.
AND WHAT HAS HE TOLD YOU?
ALL HE SAYS IS "I AM HAWKEYE" IF YOU ASK HIM ANYTHING.
LIKE HE WAS A SOLDIER IN THE WAR WHERE GUYS ONLY GIVE THEIR NAME, RANK AND SERIAL NUMBER.
BUT THEN I REMEMBERED FRANKLIN.
HE SAID HE CREATED DREAM VERSIONS OF HEROES--THE FF AND THE AVENGERS MAINLY--IN THAT POCKET UNIVERSE OF HIS...
...WHICH IS ALSO WHERE THE CREATURES FROM THE PORTAL CAME FROM.
YEAH, THE DREAM WORLD WAS "SICK"--THAT'S WHAT FRANKLIN SAID BACK WHEN THE CREATURES FIRST APPEARED.
OKAY, I'M GETTING LOST. WHAT?
WELL, I'M STARTING TO SEE THINGS MORE CLEARLY.
I WASN'T SEEING ALL MY FAMILY WAS GOING THROUGH. OR I DIDN'T CARE.
"POOR ME." "POOR JOHNNY STORM." TRIED TO CRAWL INTO A BOTTLE OF SELF-PITY.
MY FAMILY'S IN TROUBLE. THAT CHANGES EVERYTHING. POWERS OR NO POWERS...

RYKER'S ISLAND.

"...I'M COMING BACK."

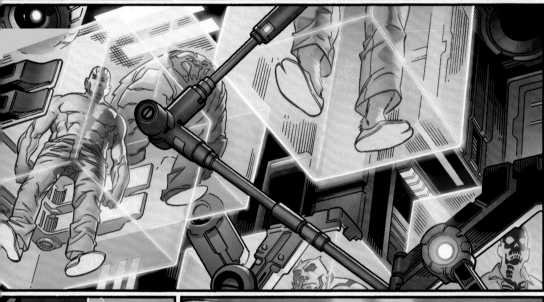

BEN.

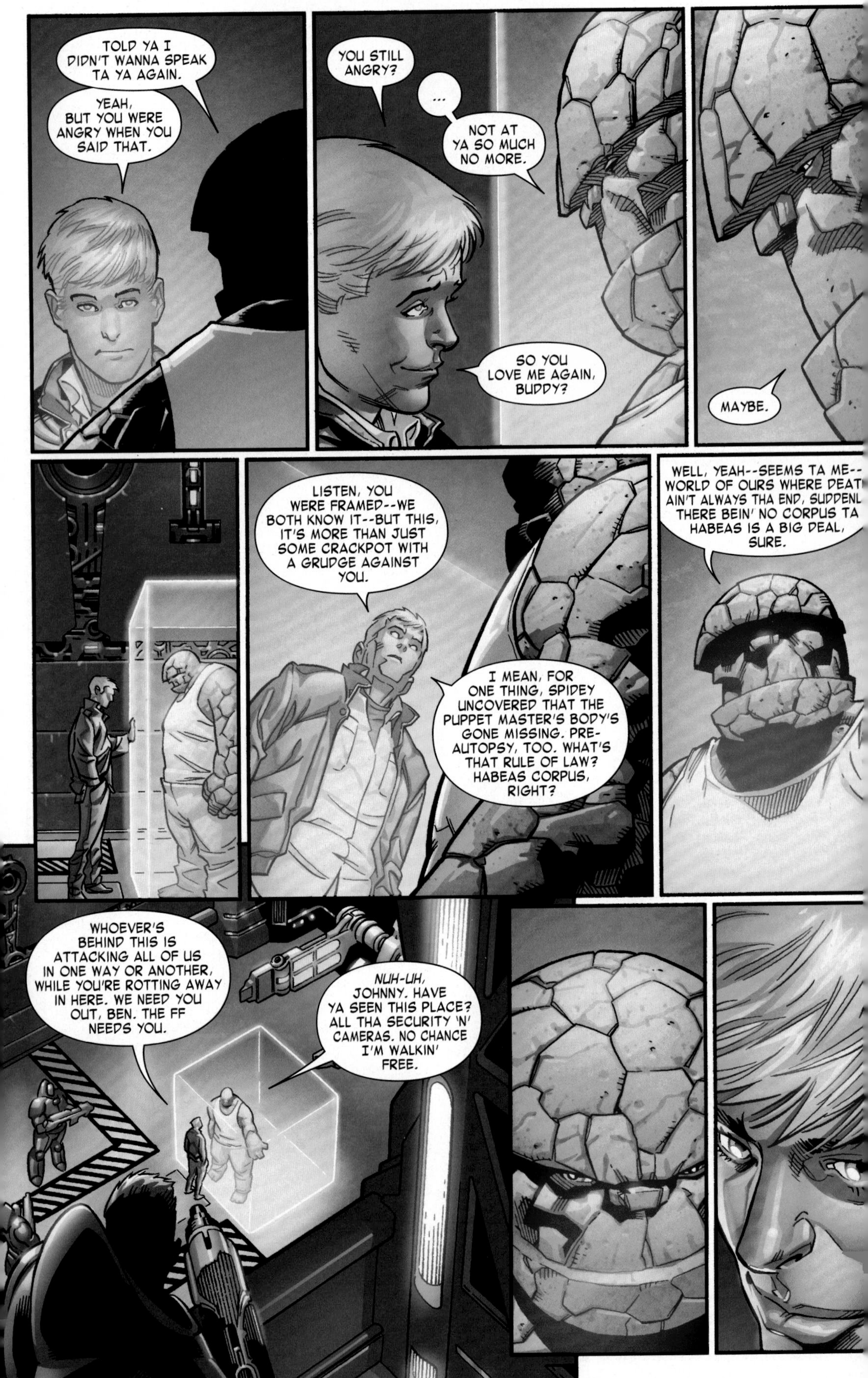
TOLD YA I DIDN'T WANNA SPEAK TA YA AGAIN.
YEAH, BUT YOU WERE ANGRY WHEN YOU SAID THAT.
YOU STILL ANGRY?
...
NOT AT YA SO MUCH NO MORE.
SO YOU LOVE ME AGAIN, BUDDY?
MAYBE.
LISTEN, YOU WERE FRAMED--WE BOTH KNOW IT--BUT THIS, IT'S MORE THAN JUST SOME CRACKPOT WITH A GRUDGE AGAINST YOU.
I MEAN, FOR ONE THING, SPIDEY UNCOVERED THAT THE PUPPET MASTER'S BODY'S GONE MISSING. PRE-AUTOPSY, TOO. WHAT'S THAT RULE OF LAW? HABEAS CORPUS, RIGHT?
WELL, YEAH--SEEMS TA ME-- WORLD OF OURS WHERE DEAT AIN'T ALWAYS THA END, SUDDENL THERE BEIN' NO CORPUS TA HABEAS IS A BIG DEAL, SURE.
WHOEVER'S BEHIND THIS IS ATTACKING ALL OF US IN ONE WAY OR ANOTHER, WHILE YOU'RE ROTTING AWAY IN HERE. WE NEED YOU OUT, BEN. THE FF NEEDS YOU.
NUH-UH, JOHNNY. HAVE YA SEEN THIS PLACE? ALL THA SECURITY 'N' CAMERAS. NO CHANCE I'M WALKIN' FREE.

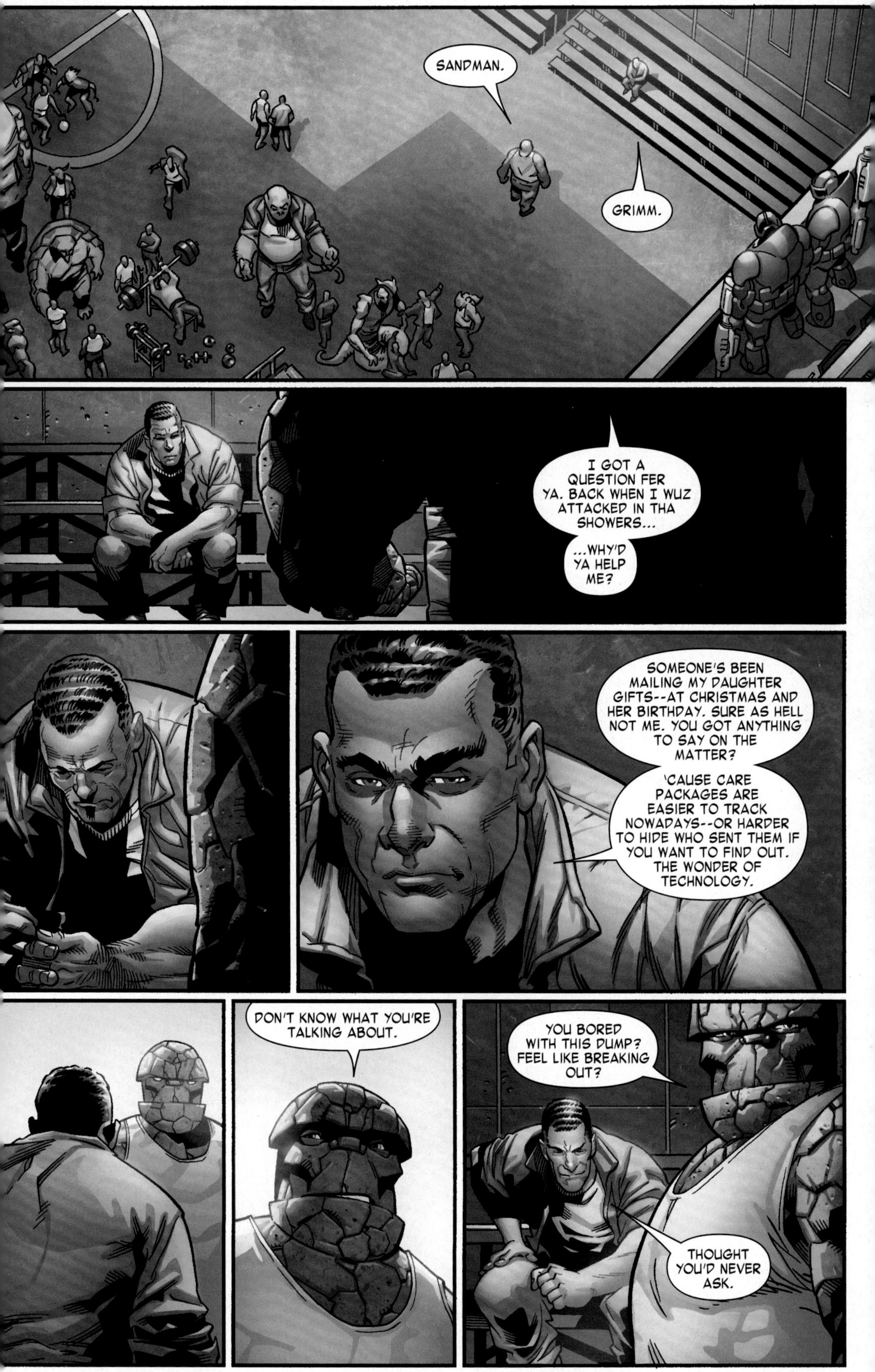

SANDMAN.
GRIMM.
I GOT A QUESTION FER YA. BACK WHEN I WUZ ATTACKED IN THA SHOWERS...
...WHY'D YA HELP ME?
SOMEONE'S BEEN MAILING MY DAUGHTER GIFTS--AT CHRISTMAS AND HER BIRTHDAY. SURE AS HELL NOT ME. YOU GOT ANYTHING TO SAY ON THE MATTER?
'CAUSE CARE PACKAGES ARE EASIER TO TRACK NOWADAYS--OR HARDER TO HIDE WHO SENT THEM IF YOU WANT TO FIND OUT. THE WONDER OF TECHNOLOGY.
DON'T KNOW WHAT YOU'RE TALKING ABOUT.
YOU BORED WITH THIS DUMP? FEEL LIKE BREAKING OUT?
THOUGHT YOU'D NEVER ASK.

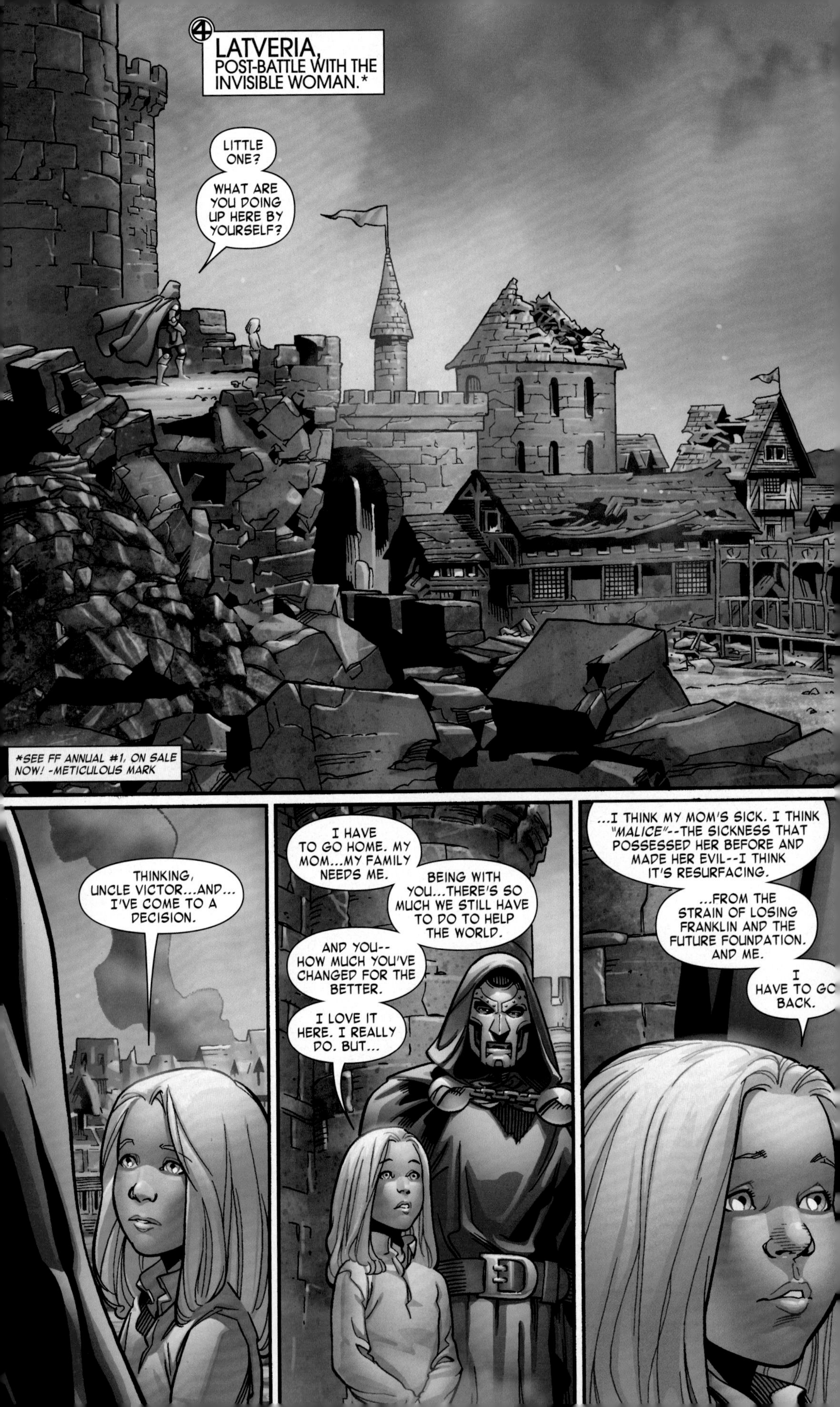
LATVERIA, POST-BATTLE WITH THE INVISIBLE WOMAN.*
LITTLE ONE?
WHAT ARE YOU DOING UP HERE BY YOURSELF?
*SEE FF ANNUAL #1, ON SALE NOW! -METICULOUS MARK
THINKING, UNCLE VICTOR...AND... I'VE COME TO A DECISION.
I HAVE TO GO HOME. MY MOM...MY FAMILY NEEDS ME.
BEING WITH YOU...THERE'S SO MUCH WE STILL HAVE TO DO TO HELP THE WORLD.
AND YOU--HOW MUCH YOU'VE CHANGED FOR THE BETTER.
I LOVE IT HERE. I REALLY DO. BUT...
...I THINK MY MOM'S SICK. I THINK "MALICE"--THE SICKNESS THAT POSSESSED HER BEFORE AND MADE HER EVIL--I THINK IT'S RESURFACING.
...FROM THE STRAIN OF LOSING FRANKLIN AND THE FUTURE FOUNDATION. AND ME.
I HAVE TO GO BACK.

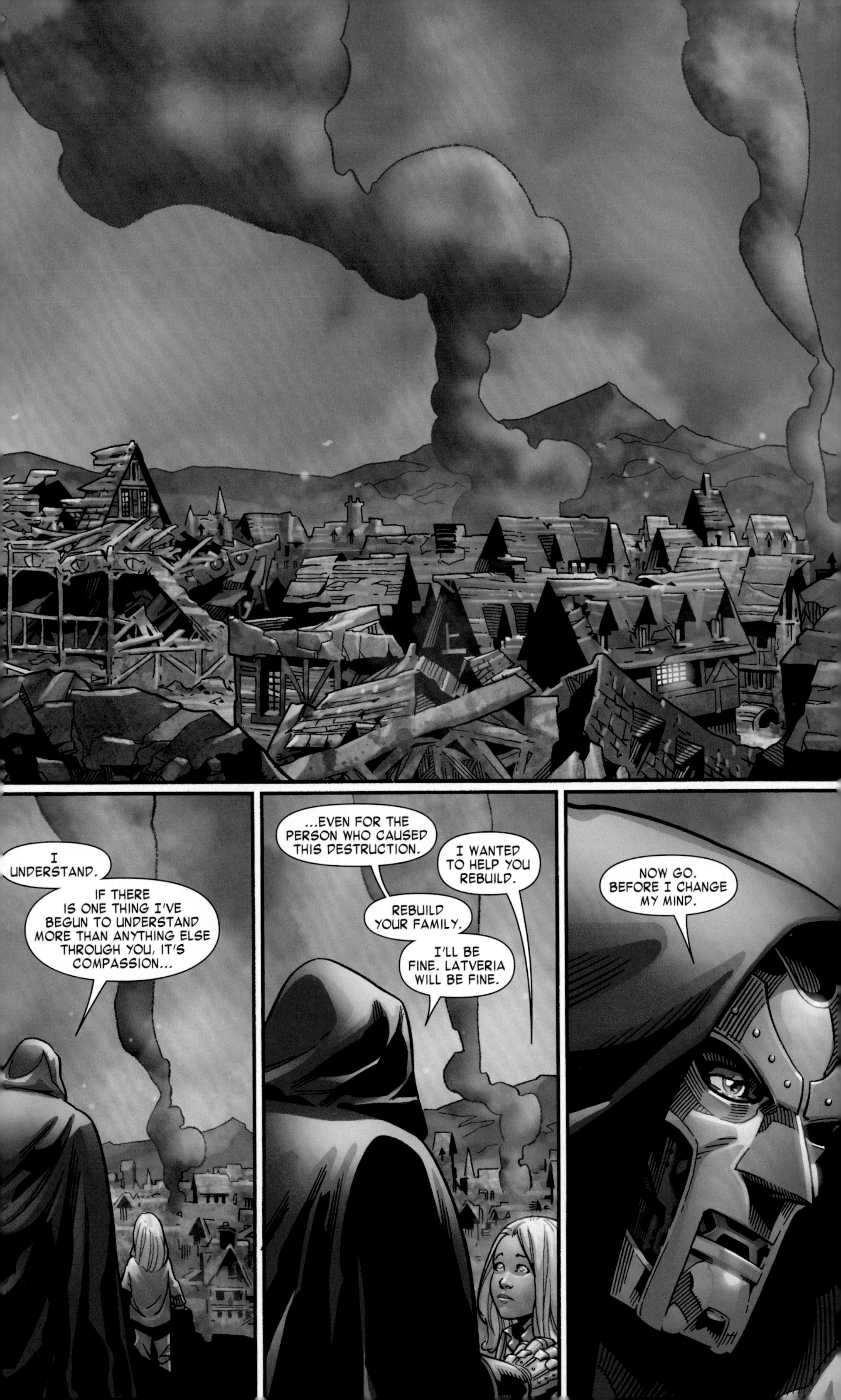
I UNDERSTAND.
IF THERE IS ONE THING I'VE BEGUN TO UNDERSTAND MORE THAN ANYTHING ELSE THROUGH YOU, IT'S COMPASSION...
...EVEN FOR THE PERSON WHO CAUSED THIS DESTRUCTION.
I WANTED TO HELP YOU REBUILD.
REBUILD YOUR FAMILY.
I'LL BE FINE. LATVERIA WILL BE FINE.
NOW GO. BEFORE I CHANGE MY MIND.

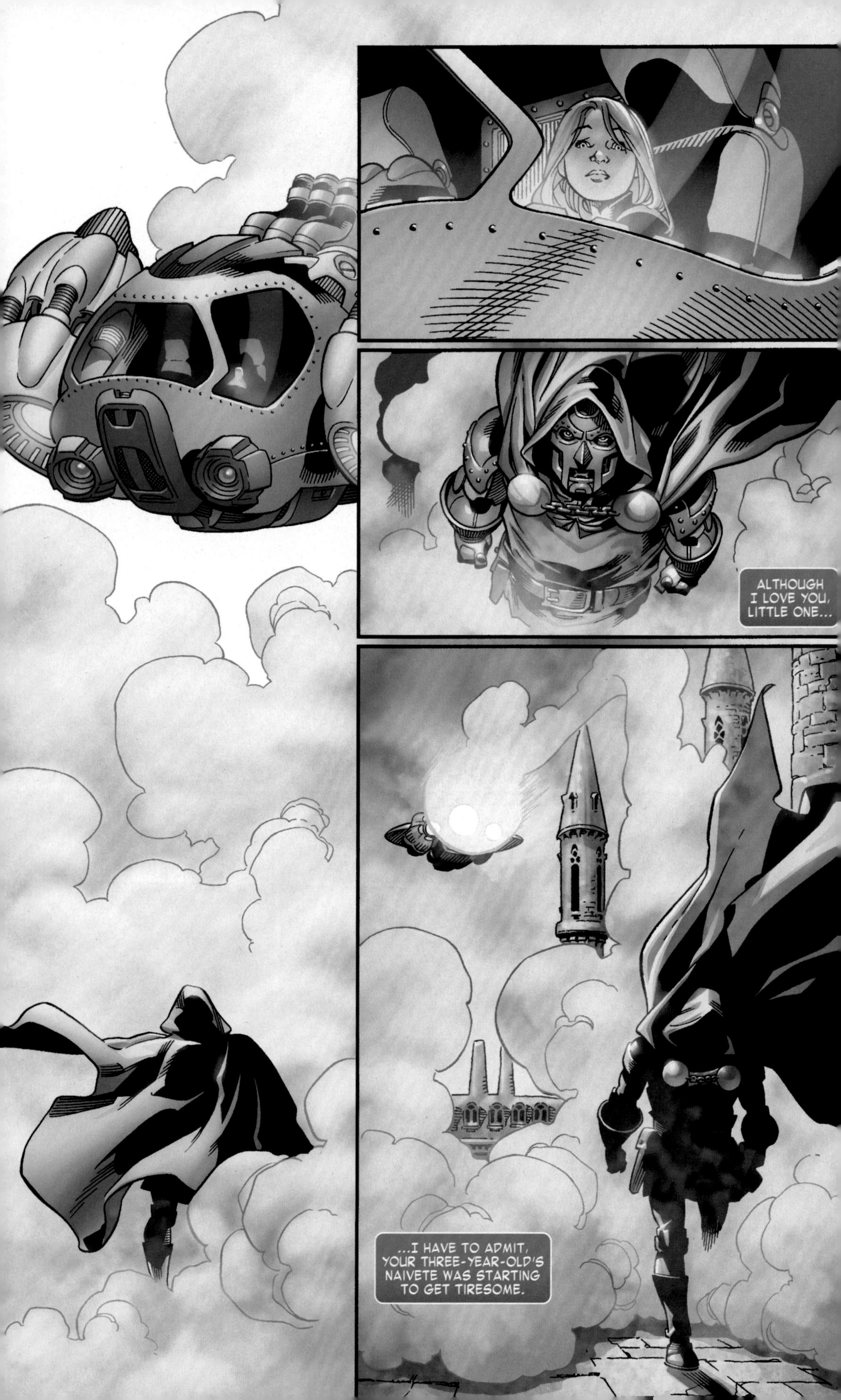

ALTHOUGH I LOVE YOU, LITTLE ONE...
...I HAVE TO ADMIT, YOUR THREE-YEAR-OLD'S NAIVETE WAS STARTING TO GET TIRESOME.

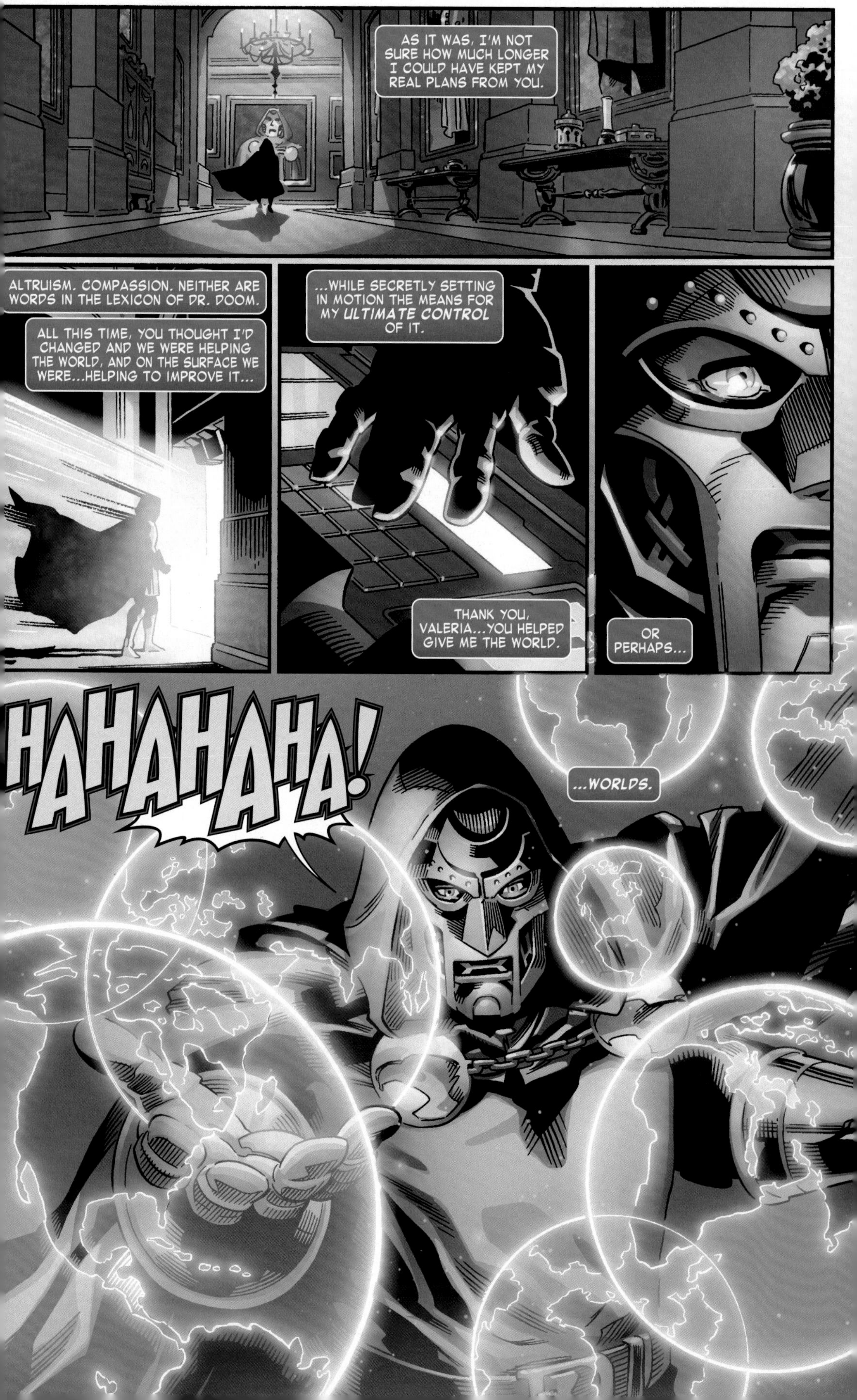

AS IT WAS, I'M NOT SURE HOW MUCH LONGER I COULD HAVE KEPT MY REAL PLANS FROM YOU.
ALTRUISM. COMPASSION. NEITHER ARE WORDS IN THE LEXICON OF DR. DOOM.
ALL THIS TIME, YOU THOUGHT I'D CHANGED AND WE WERE HELPING THE WORLD, AND ON THE SURFACE WE WERE...HELPING TO IMPROVE IT...
...WHILE SECRETLY SETTING IN MOTION THE MEANS FOR MY *ULTIMATE CONTROL* OF IT.
THANK YOU, VALERIA...YOU HELPED GIVE ME THE WORLD.
OR PERHAPS...
HAHAHAHA!
...WORLDS.

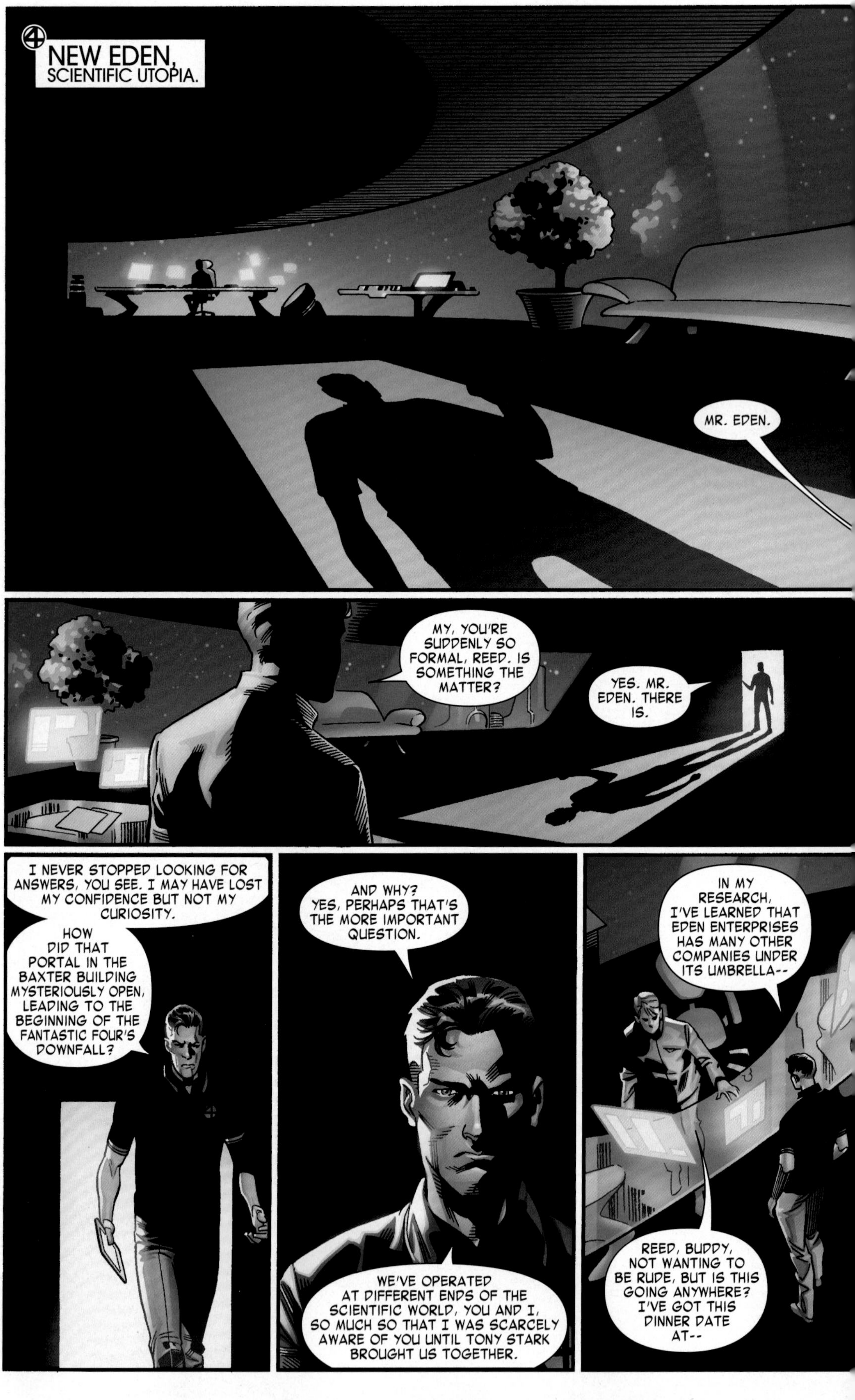
NEW EDEN, SCIENTIFIC UTOPIA.
MR. EDEN.
MY, YOU'RE SUDDENLY SO FORMAL, REED. IS SOMETHING THE MATTER?
YES. MR. EDEN. THERE IS.
I NEVER STOPPED LOOKING FOR ANSWERS, YOU SEE. I MAY HAVE LOST MY CONFIDENCE BUT NOT MY CURIOSITY.
HOW DID THAT PORTAL IN THE BAXTER BUILDING MYSTERIOUSLY OPEN, LEADING TO THE BEGINNING OF THE FANTASTIC FOUR'S DOWNFALL?
AND WHY? YES, PERHAPS THAT'S THE MORE IMPORTANT QUESTION.
WE'VE OPERATED AT DIFFERENT ENDS OF THE SCIENTIFIC WORLD, YOU AND I, SO MUCH SO THAT I WAS SCARCELY AWARE OF YOU UNTIL TONY STARK BROUGHT US TOGETHER.
IN MY RESEARCH, I'VE LEARNED THAT EDEN ENTERPRISES HAS MANY OTHER COMPANIES UNDER ITS UMBRELLA--
REED, BUDDY, NOT WANTING TO BE RUDE, BUT IS THIS GOING ANYWHERE? I'VE GOT THIS DINNER DATE AT--

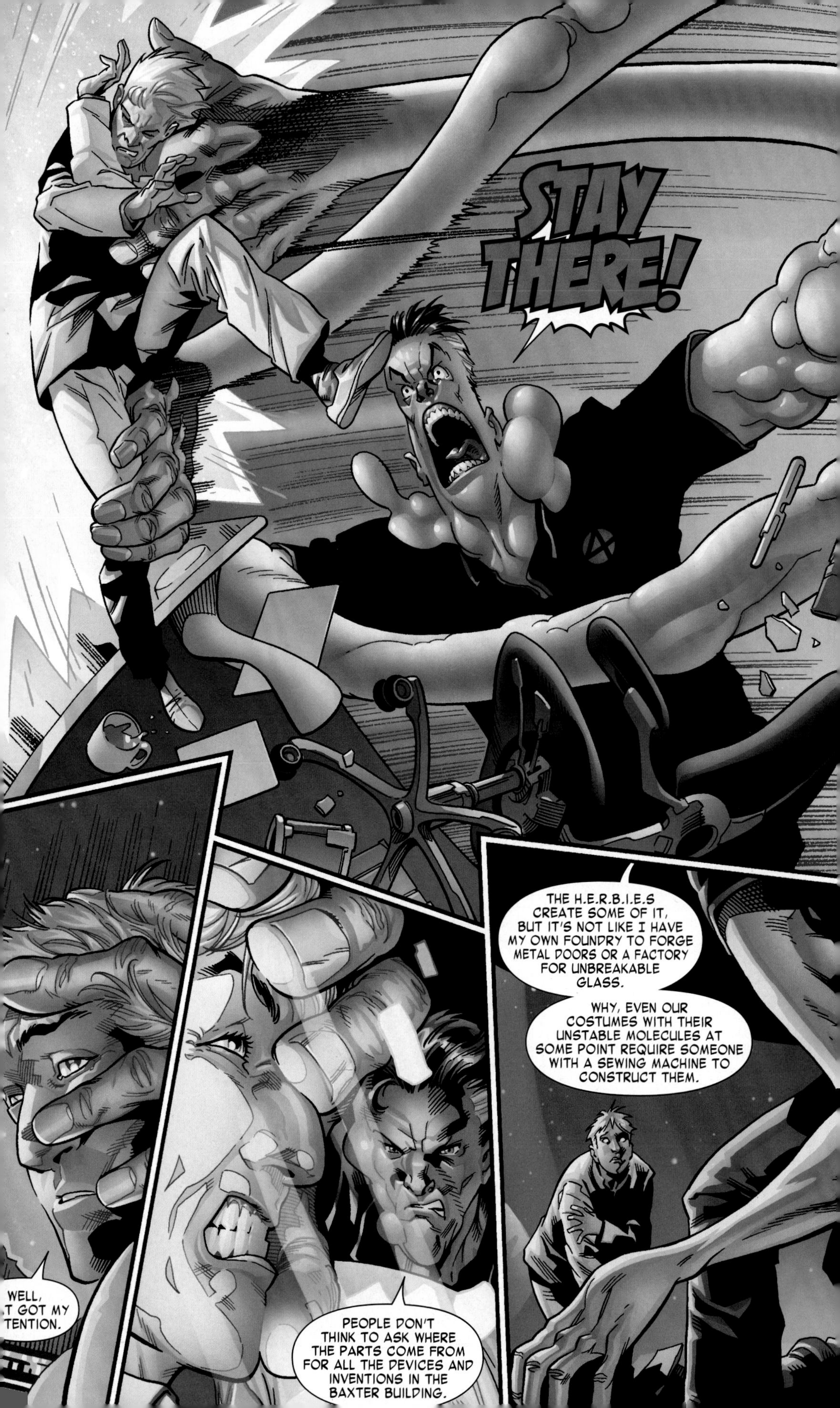
STAY THERE!
WELL, ...T GOT MY ...TENTION.
PEOPLE DON'T THINK TO ASK WHERE THE PARTS COME FROM FOR ALL THE DEVICES AND INVENTIONS IN THE BAXTER BUILDING.
THE H.E.R.B.I.E.S CREATE SOME OF IT, BUT IT'S NOT LIKE I HAVE MY OWN FOUNDRY TO FORGE METAL DOORS OR A FACTORY FOR UNBREAKABLE GLASS.
WHY, EVEN OUR COSTUMES WITH THEIR UNSTABLE MOLECULES AT SOME POINT REQUIRE SOMEONE WITH A SEWING MACHINE TO CONSTRUCT THEM.

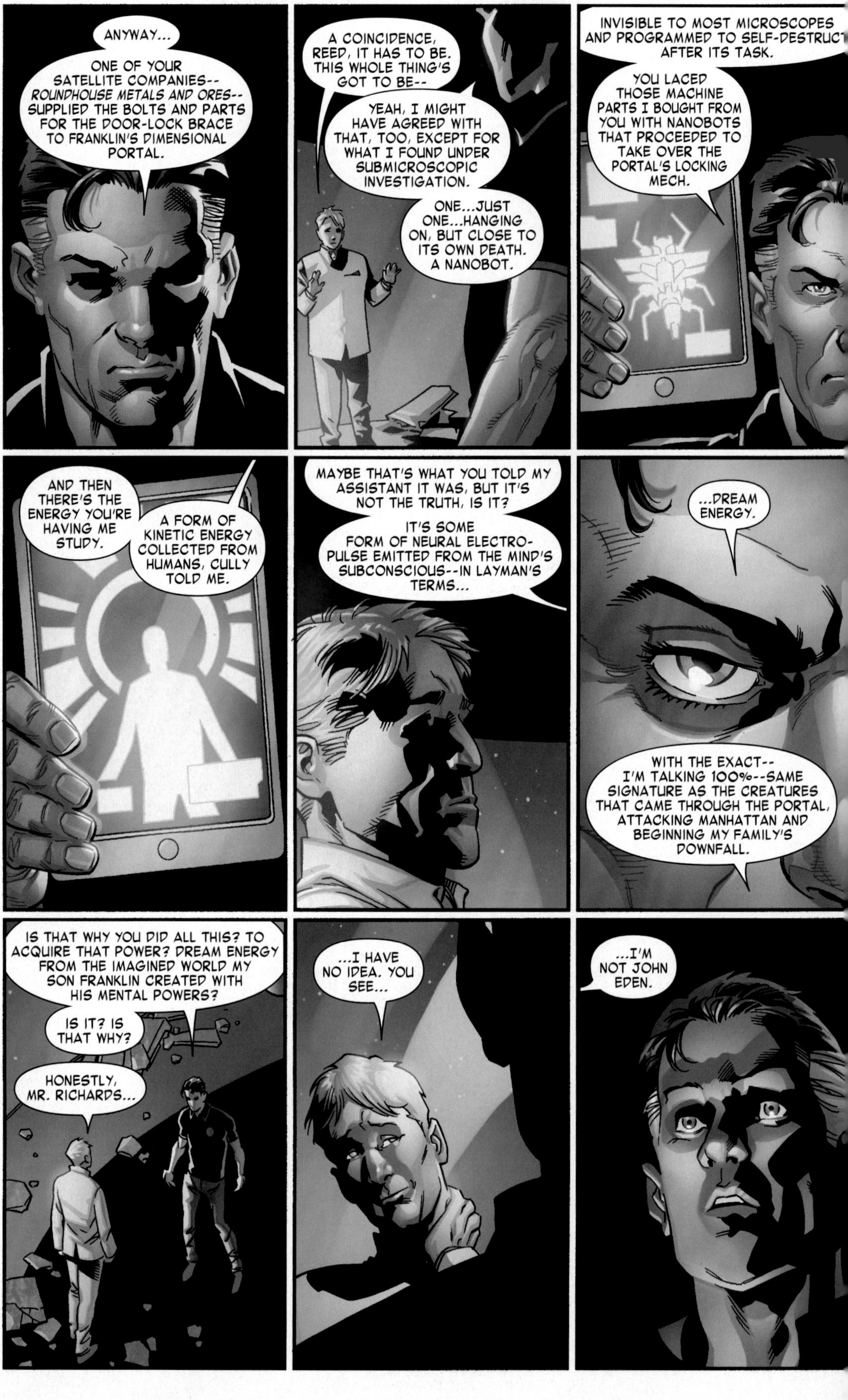
ANYWAY...
ONE OF YOUR SATELLITE COMPANIES-- *ROUNDHOUSE METALS AND ORES*-- SUPPLIED THE BOLTS AND PARTS FOR THE DOOR-LOCK BRACE TO FRANKLIN'S DIMENSIONAL PORTAL.
A COINCIDENCE, REED, IT HAS TO BE. THIS WHOLE THING'S GOT TO BE--
YEAH, I MIGHT HAVE AGREED WITH THAT, TOO, EXCEPT FOR WHAT I FOUND UNDER SUBMICROSCOPIC INVESTIGATION.
ONE...JUST ONE...HANGING ON, BUT CLOSE TO ITS OWN DEATH. A NANOBOT.
INVISIBLE TO MOST MICROSCOPES AND PROGRAMMED TO SELF-DESTRUCT AFTER ITS TASK.
YOU LACED THOSE MACHINE PARTS I BOUGHT FROM YOU WITH NANOBOTS THAT PROCEEDED TO TAKE OVER THE PORTAL'S LOCKING MECH.
AND THEN THERE'S THE ENERGY YOU'RE HAVING ME STUDY.
A FORM OF KINETIC ENERGY COLLECTED FROM HUMANS, CULLY TOLD ME.
MAYBE THAT'S WHAT YOU TOLD MY ASSISTANT IT WAS, BUT IT'S NOT THE TRUTH, IS IT?
IT'S SOME FORM OF NEURAL ELECTRO-PULSE EMITTED FROM THE MIND'S SUBCONSCIOUS--IN LAYMAN'S TERMS...
...DREAM ENERGY.
WITH THE EXACT-- I'M TALKING 100%--SAME SIGNATURE AS THE CREATURES THAT CAME THROUGH THE PORTAL, ATTACKING MANHATTAN AND BEGINNING MY FAMILY'S DOWNFALL.
IS THAT WHY YOU DID ALL THIS? TO ACQUIRE THAT POWER? DREAM ENERGY FROM THE IMAGINED WORLD MY SON FRANKLIN CREATED WITH HIS MENTAL POWERS?
IS IT? IS THAT WHY?
HONESTLY, MR. RICHARDS...
...I HAVE NO IDEA. YOU SEE...
...I'M NOT JOHN EDEN.

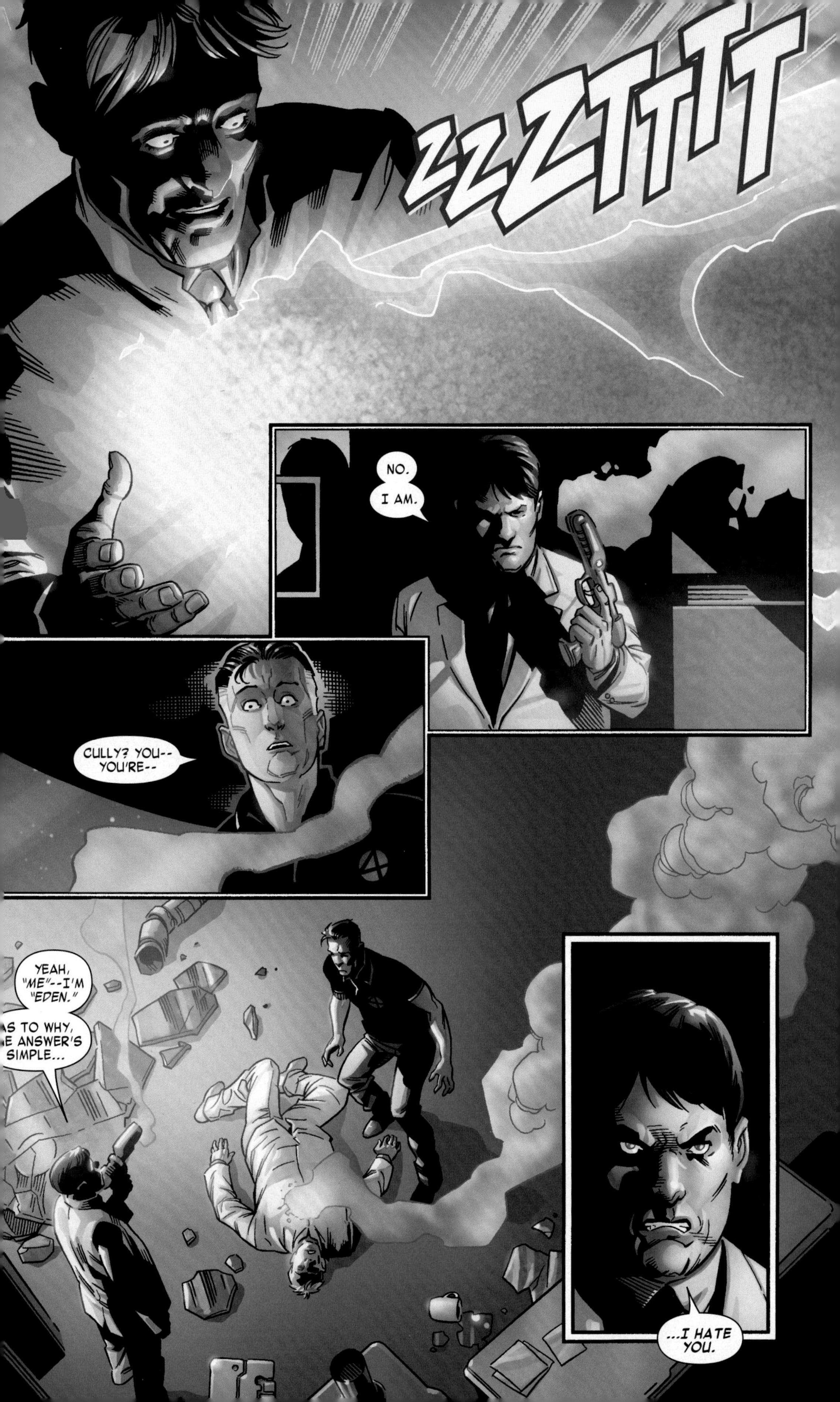
ZZZTTTT
NO.
I AM.
CULLY? YOU-- YOU'RE--
YEAH, "ME"--I'M "EDEN."
AS TO WHY, THE ANSWER'S SIMPLE...
...I HATE YOU.

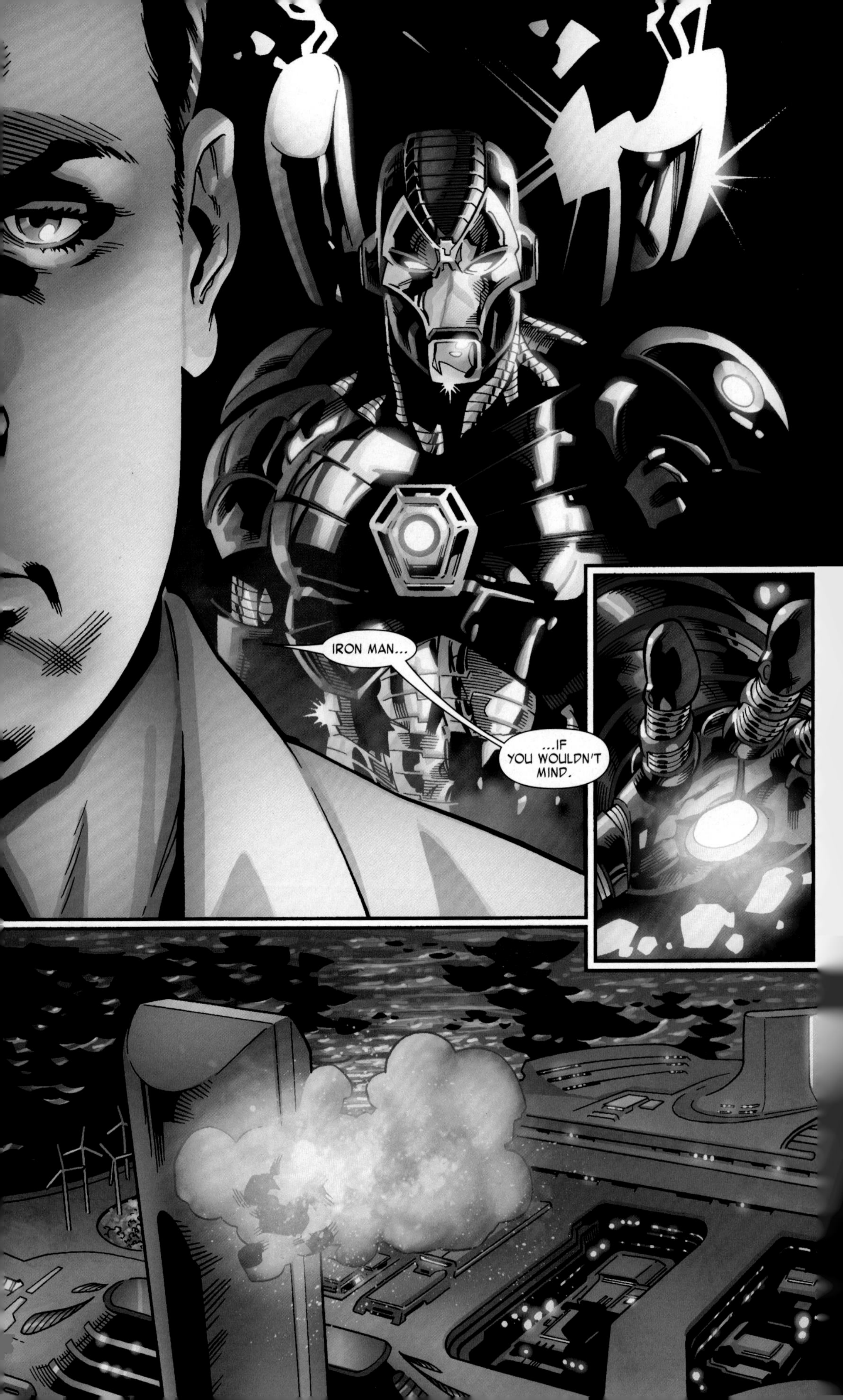
IRON MAN...
...IF YOU WOULDN'T MIND.

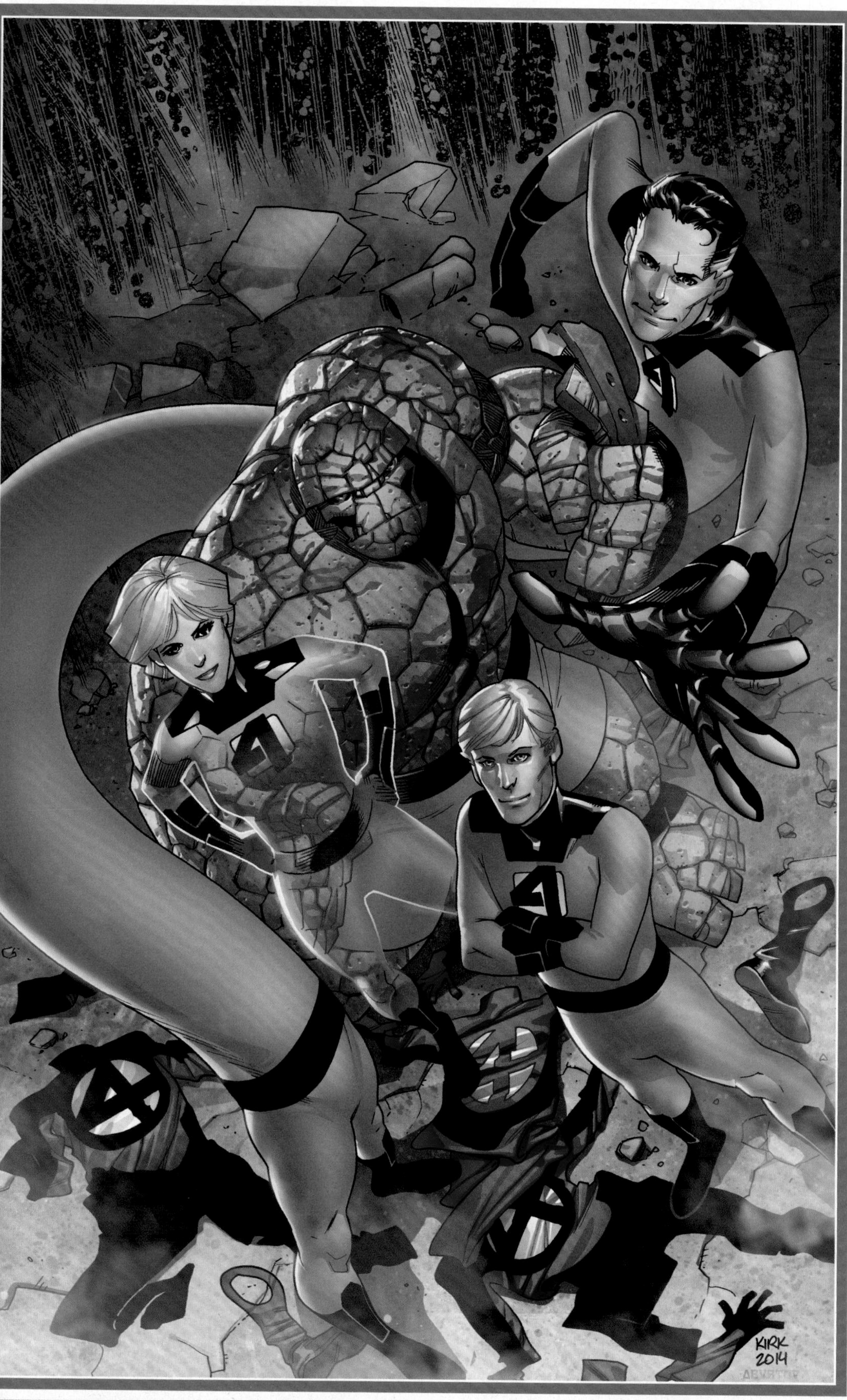
KIRK
2014

THIRTEEN

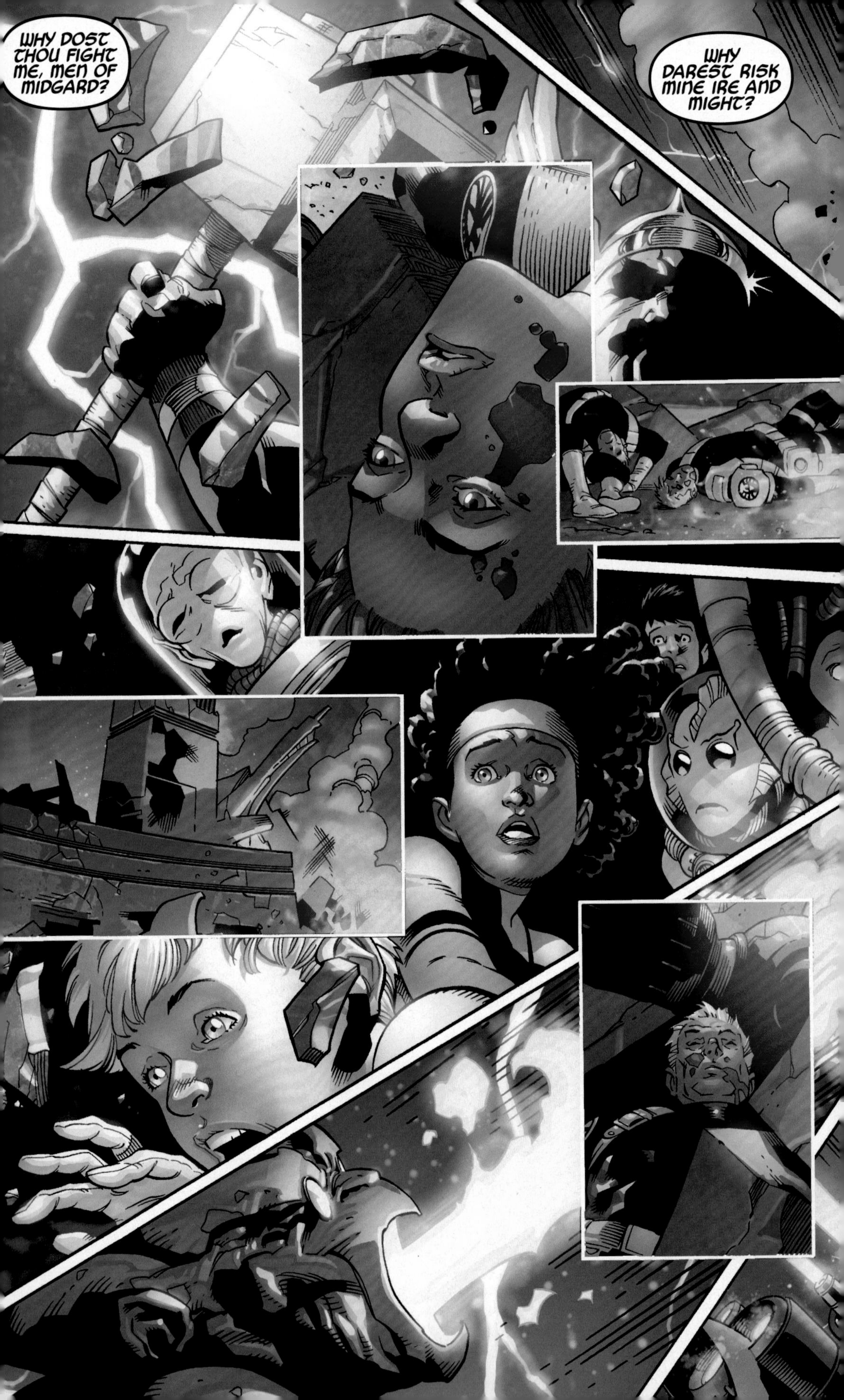
WHY DOST THOU FIGHT ME, MEN OF MIDGARD?
WHY DAREST RISK MINE IRE AND MIGHT?

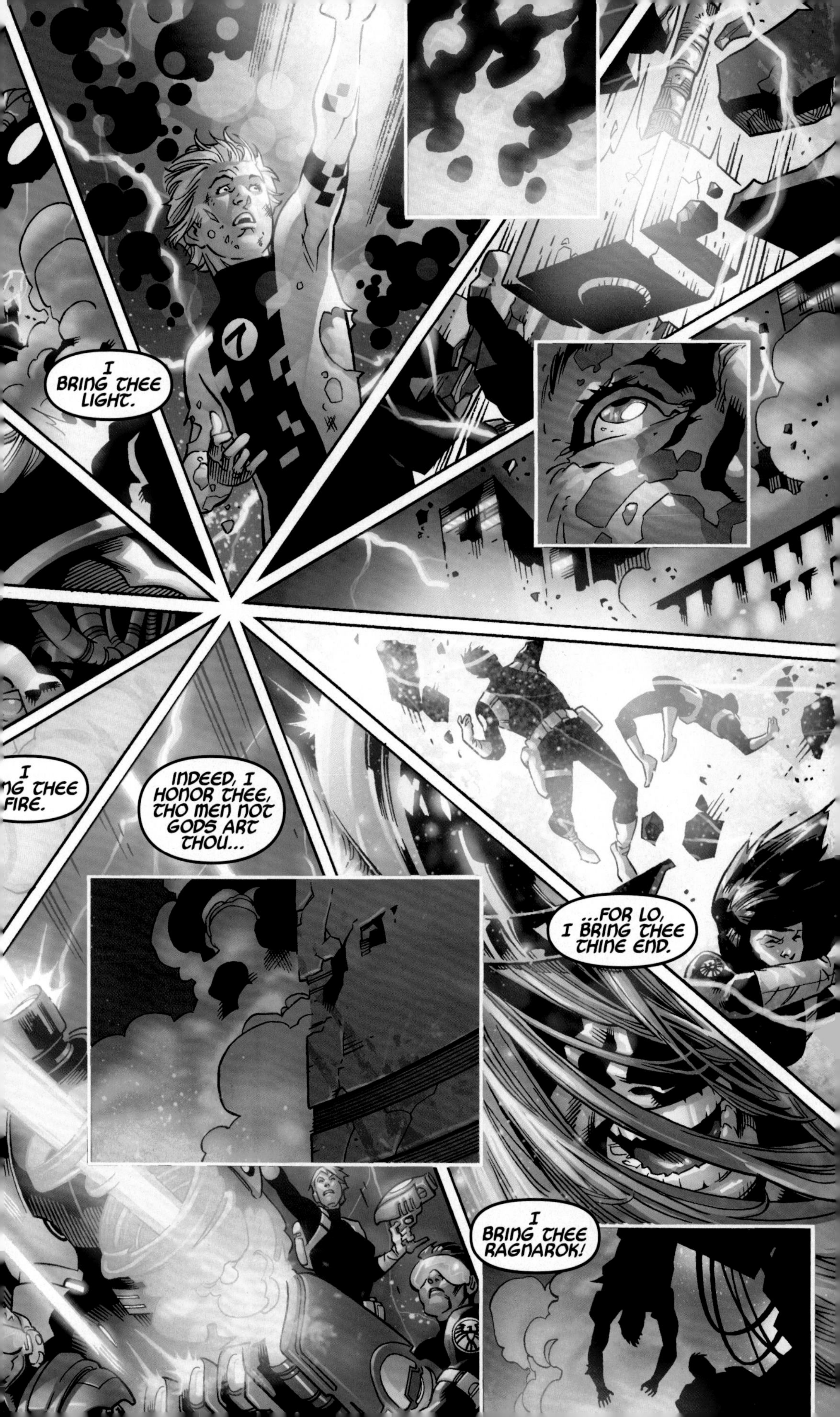
I BRING THEE LIGHT.
I ...NG THEE FIRE.
INDEED, I HONOR THEE, THO MEN NOT GODS ART THOU...
...FOR LO, I BRING THEE THINE END.
I BRING THEE RAGNAROK!

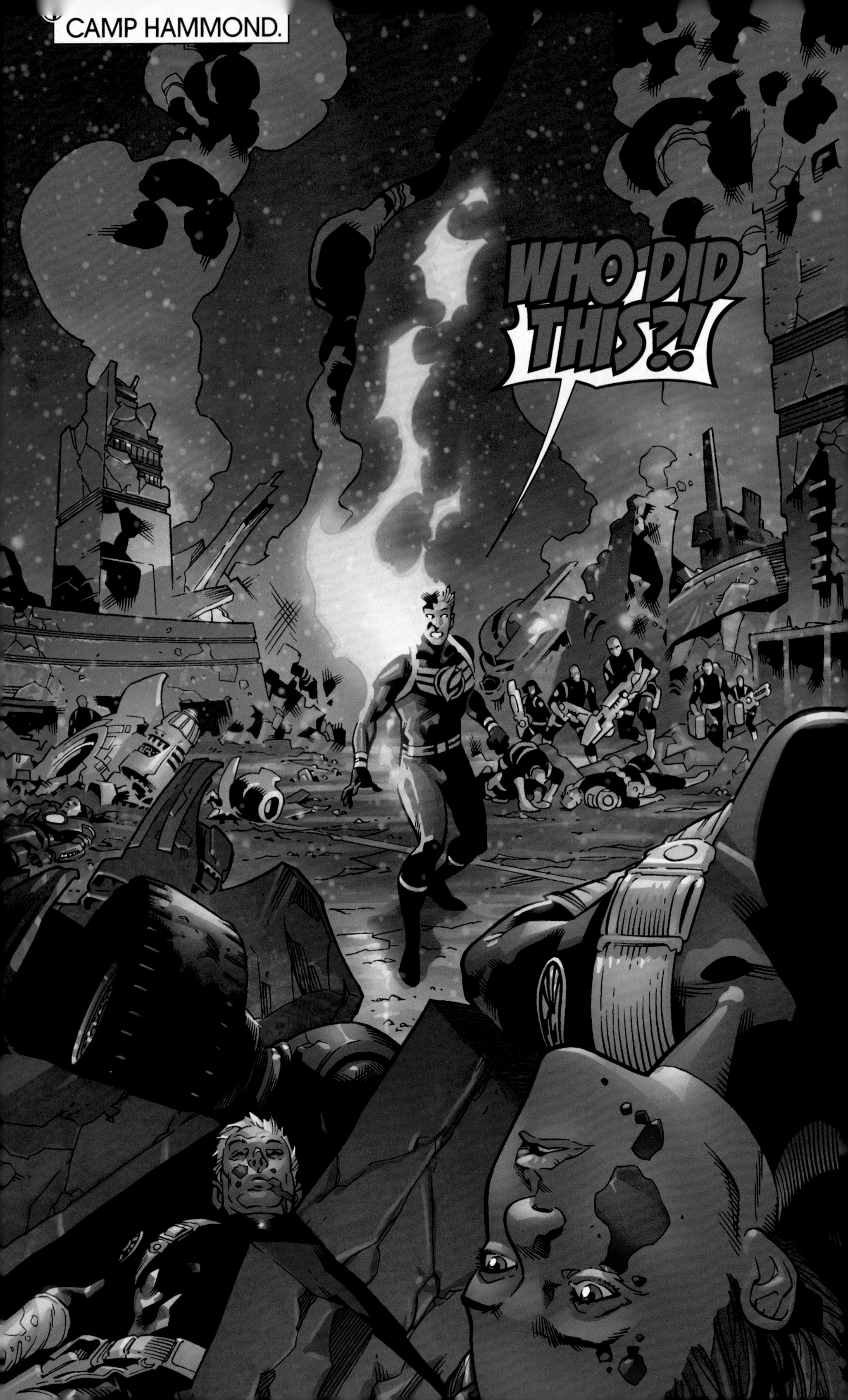
CAMP HAMMOND.
WHO DID THIS?!

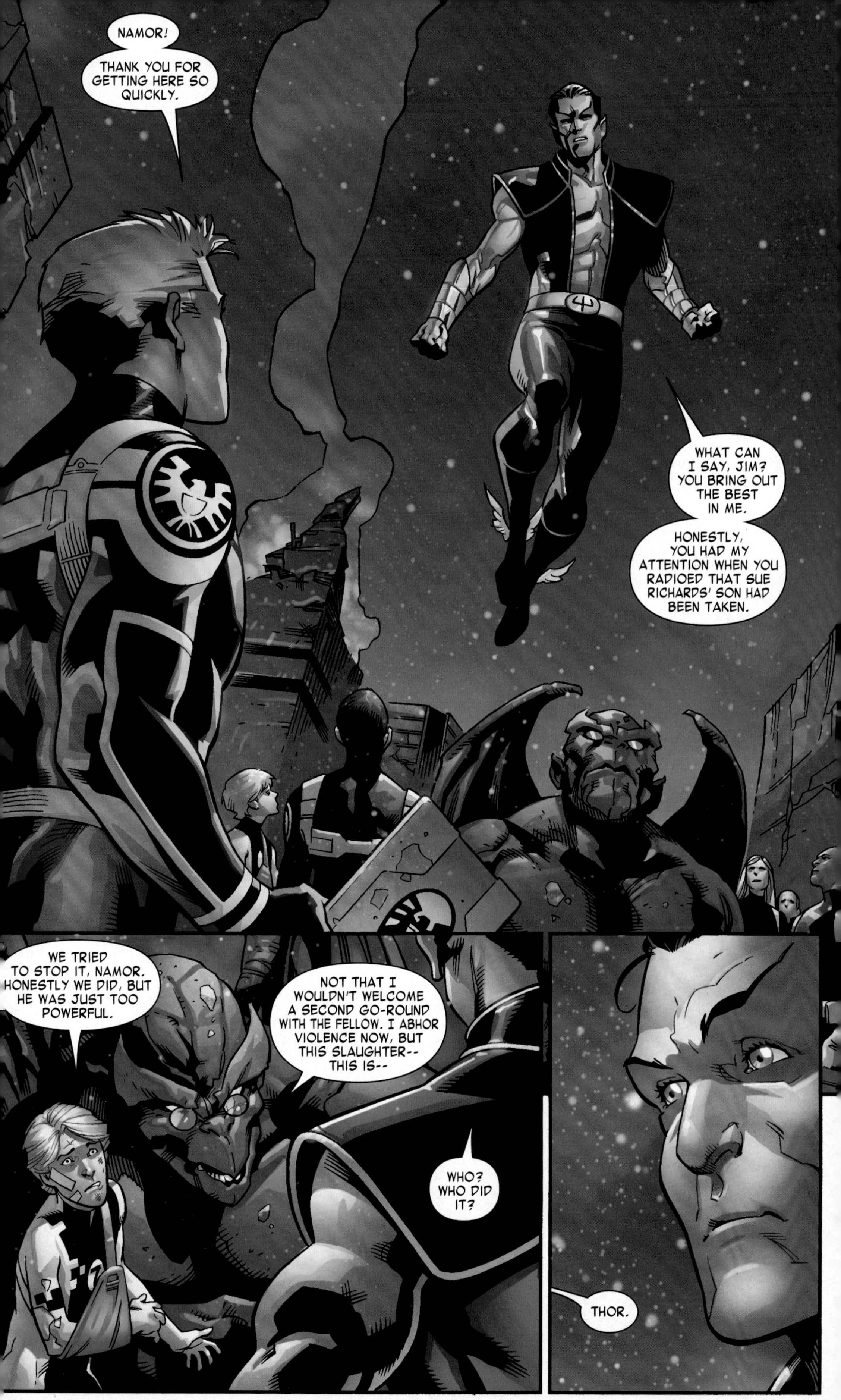
NAMOR!
THANK YOU FOR GETTING HERE SO QUICKLY.
WHAT CAN I SAY, JIM? YOU BRING OUT THE BEST IN ME.
HONESTLY, YOU HAD MY ATTENTION WHEN YOU RADIOED THAT SUE RICHARDS' SON HAD BEEN TAKEN.
WE TRIED TO STOP IT, NAMOR. HONESTLY WE DID, BUT HE WAS JUST TOO POWERFUL.
NOT THAT I WOULDN'T WELCOME A SECOND GO-ROUND WITH THE FELLOW. I ABHOR VIOLENCE NOW, BUT THIS SLAUGHTER-- THIS IS--
WHO? WHO DID IT?
THOR.

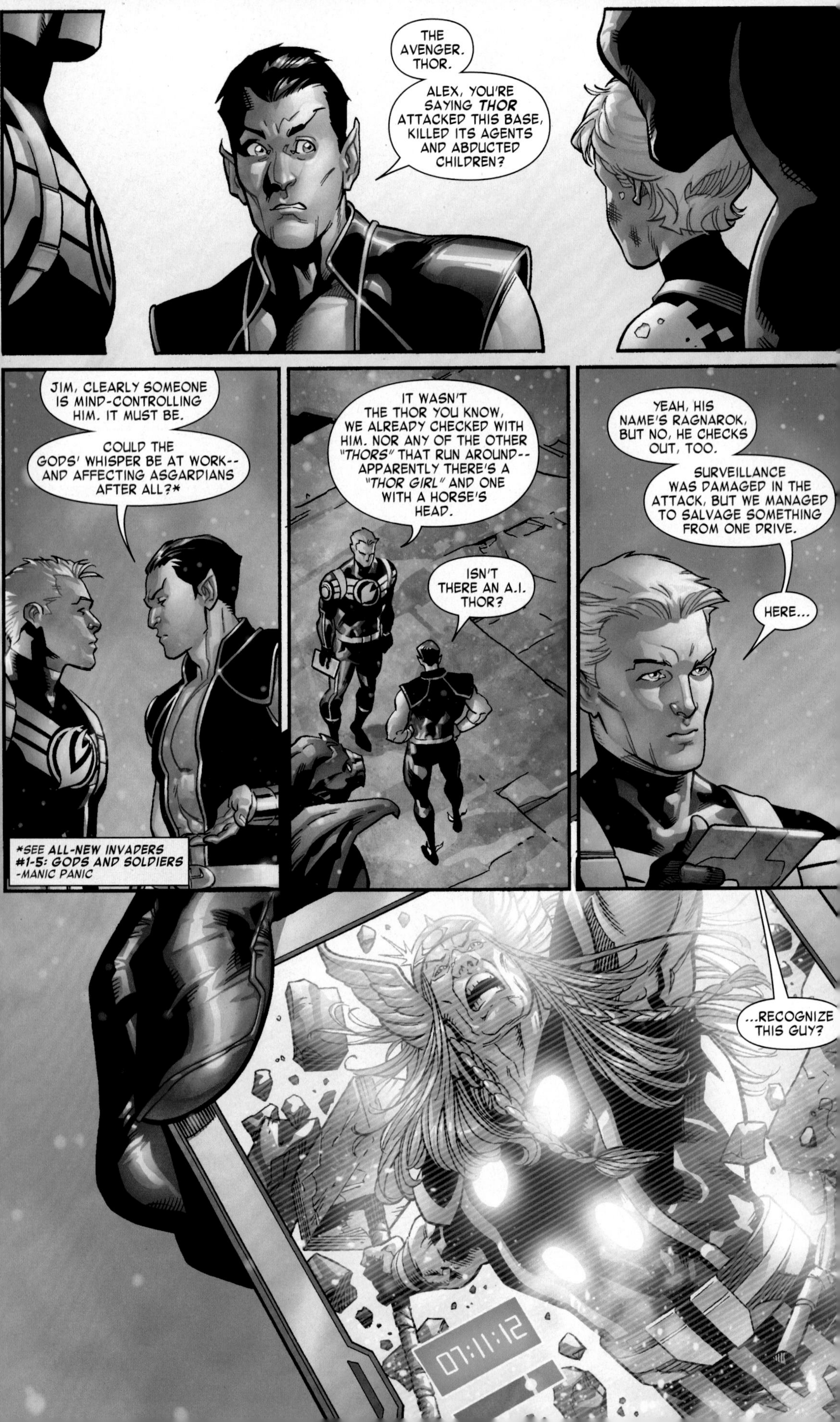

THE AVENGER. THOR.
ALEX, YOU'RE SAYING THOR ATTACKED THIS BASE, KILLED ITS AGENTS AND ABDUCTED CHILDREN?
JIM, CLEARLY SOMEONE IS MIND-CONTROLLING HIM. IT MUST BE.
COULD THE GODS' WHISPER BE AT WORK-- AND AFFECTING ASGARDIANS AFTER ALL?*
*SEE ALL-NEW INVADERS #1-5: GODS AND SOLDIERS -MANIC PANIC
IT WASN'T THE THOR YOU KNOW, WE ALREADY CHECKED WITH HIM. NOR ANY OF THE OTHER "THORS" THAT RUN AROUND-- APPARENTLY THERE'S A "THOR GIRL" AND ONE WITH A HORSE'S HEAD.
ISN'T THERE AN A.I. THOR?
YEAH, HIS NAME'S RAGNAROK, BUT NO, HE CHECKS OUT, TOO.
SURVEILLANCE WAS DAMAGED IN THE ATTACK, BUT WE MANAGED TO SALVAGE SOMETHING FROM ONE DRIVE.
HERE...
...RECOGNIZE THIS GUY?
07:11:12

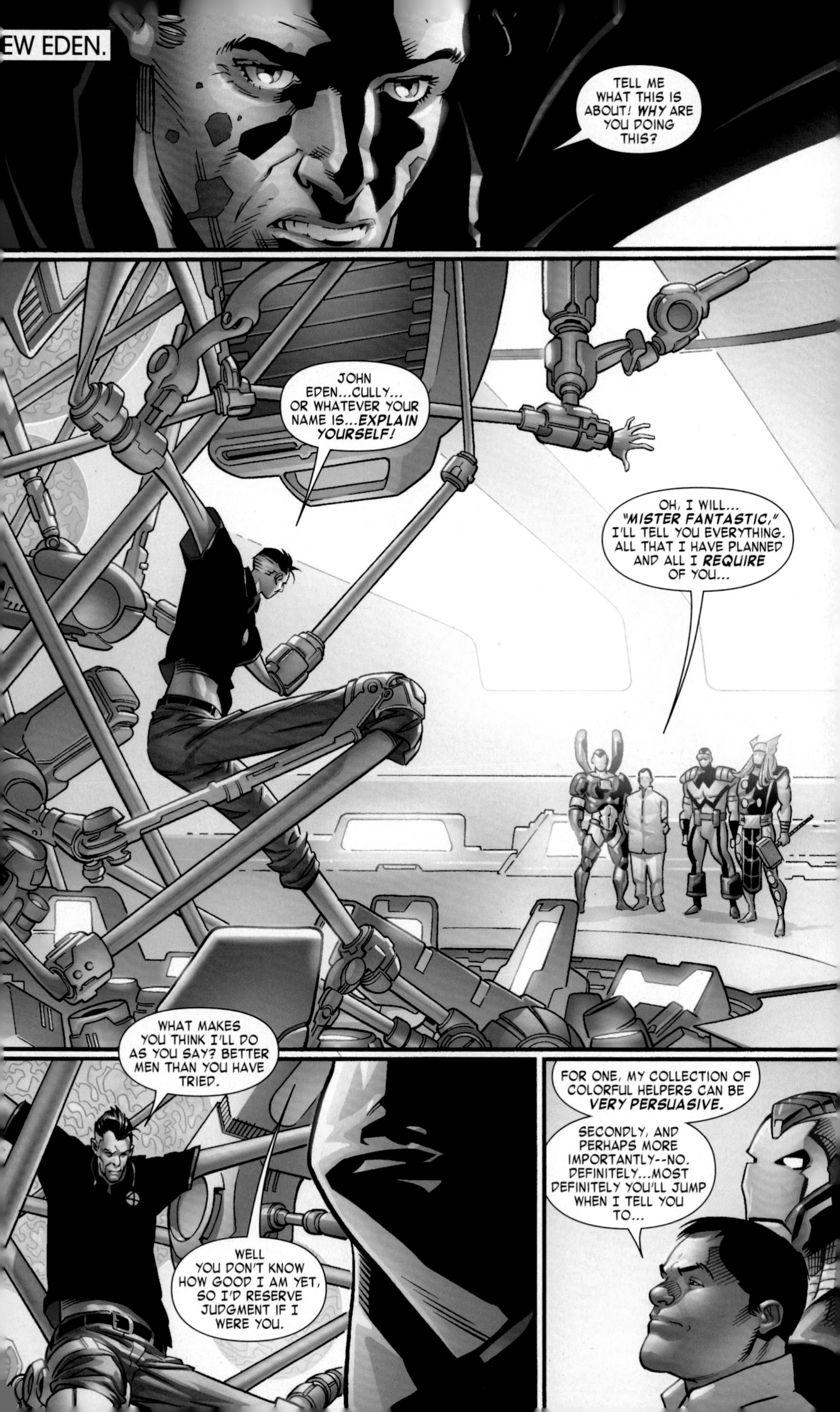
EW EDEN.
TELL ME WHAT THIS IS ABOUT! WHY ARE YOU DOING THIS?
JOHN EDEN...CULLY... OR WHATEVER YOUR NAME IS...EXPLAIN YOURSELF!
OH, I WILL... "MISTER FANTASTIC," I'LL TELL YOU EVERYTHING. ALL THAT I HAVE PLANNED AND ALL I REQUIRE OF YOU...
WHAT MAKES YOU THINK I'LL DO AS YOU SAY? BETTER MEN THAN YOU HAVE TRIED.
WELL YOU DON'T KNOW HOW GOOD I AM YET, SO I'D RESERVE JUDGMENT IF I WERE YOU.
FOR ONE, MY COLLECTION OF COLORFUL HELPERS CAN BE VERY PERSUASIVE.
SECONDLY, AND PERHAPS MORE IMPORTANTLY--NO. DEFINITELY...MOST DEFINITELY YOU'LL JUMP WHEN I TELL YOU TO...

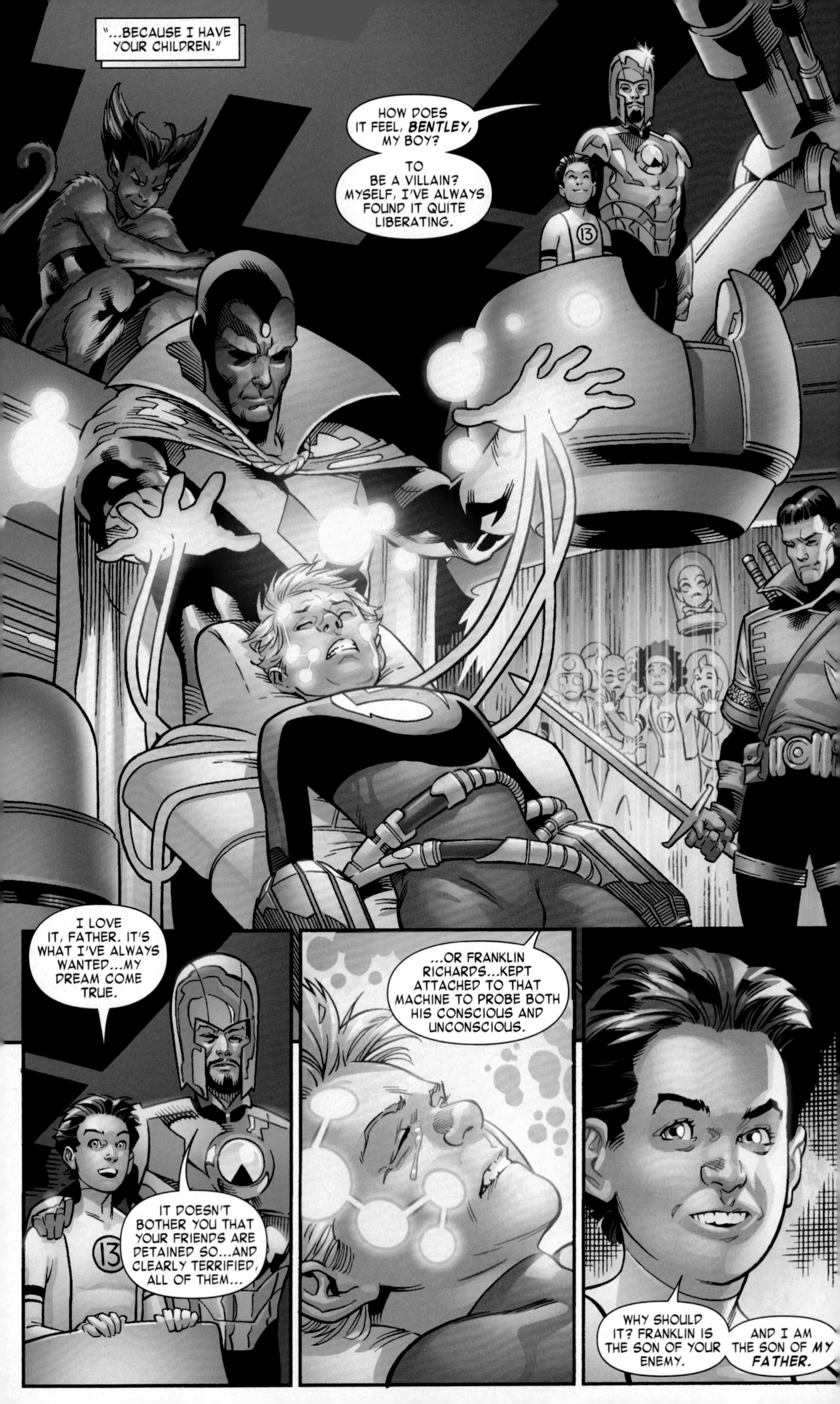
"...BECAUSE I HAVE YOUR CHILDREN."
HOW DOES IT FEEL, BENTLEY, MY BOY?
TO BE A VILLAIN? MYSELF, I'VE ALWAYS FOUND IT QUITE LIBERATING.
I LOVE IT, FATHER. IT'S WHAT I'VE ALWAYS WANTED...MY DREAM COME TRUE.
IT DOESN'T BOTHER YOU THAT YOUR FRIENDS ARE DETAINED SO...AND CLEARLY TERRIFIED, ALL OF THEM...
...OR FRANKLIN RICHARDS...KEPT ATTACHED TO THAT MACHINE TO PROBE BOTH HIS CONSCIOUS AND UNCONSCIOUS.
WHY SHOULD IT? FRANKLIN IS THE SON OF YOUR ENEMY.
AND I AM THE SON OF MY FATHER.

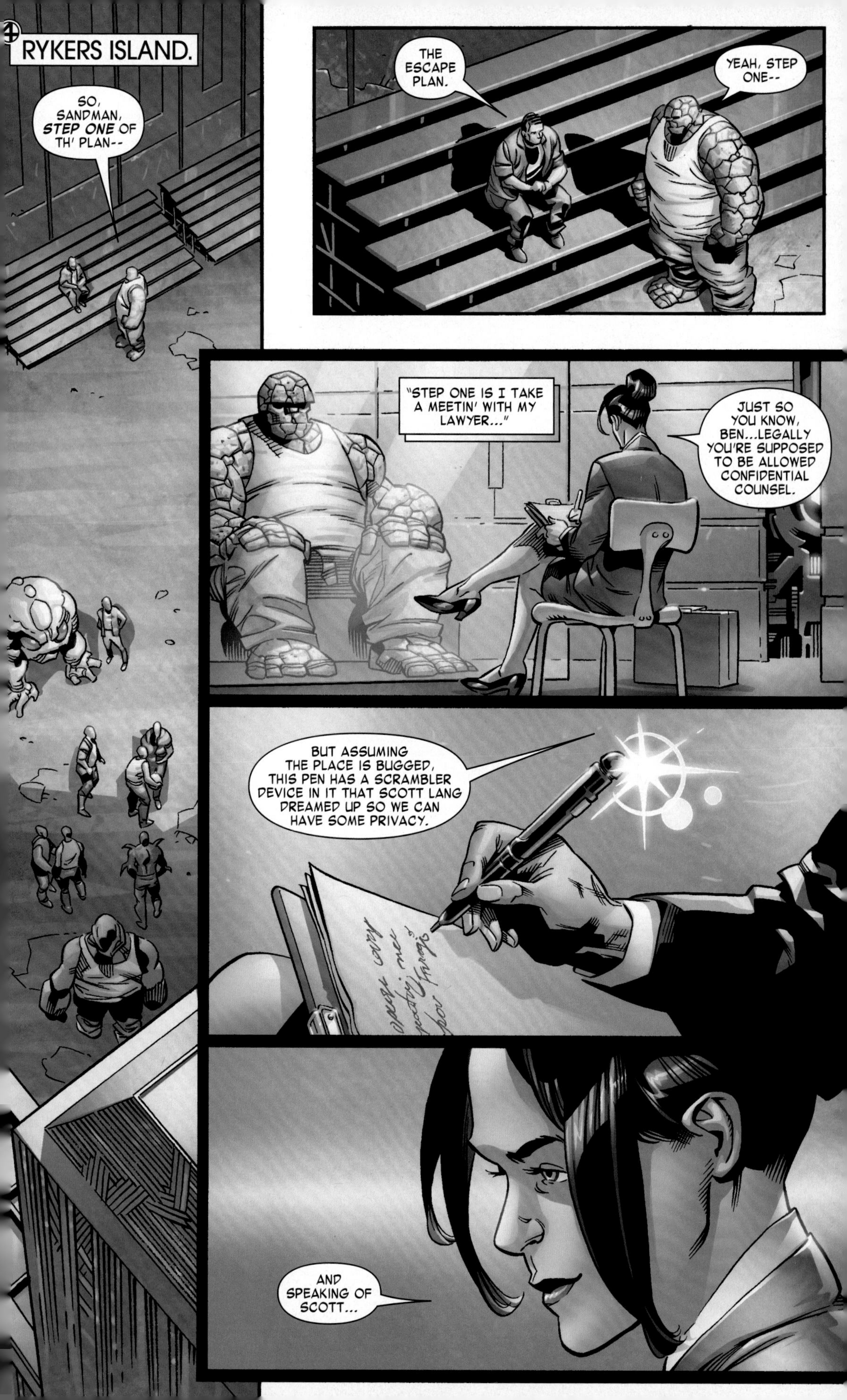
RYKERS ISLAND.
SO, SANDMAN, STEP ONE OF TH' PLAN--
THE ESCAPE PLAN.
YEAH, STEP ONE--
"STEP ONE IS I TAKE A MEETIN' WITH MY LAWYER..."
JUST SO YOU KNOW, BEN...LEGALLY YOU'RE SUPPOSED TO BE ALLOWED CONFIDENTIAL COUNSEL.
BUT ASSUMING THE PLACE IS BUGGED, THIS PEN HAS A SCRAMBLER DEVICE IN IT THAT SCOTT LANG DREAMED UP SO WE CAN HAVE SOME PRIVACY.
AND SPEAKING OF SCOTT...

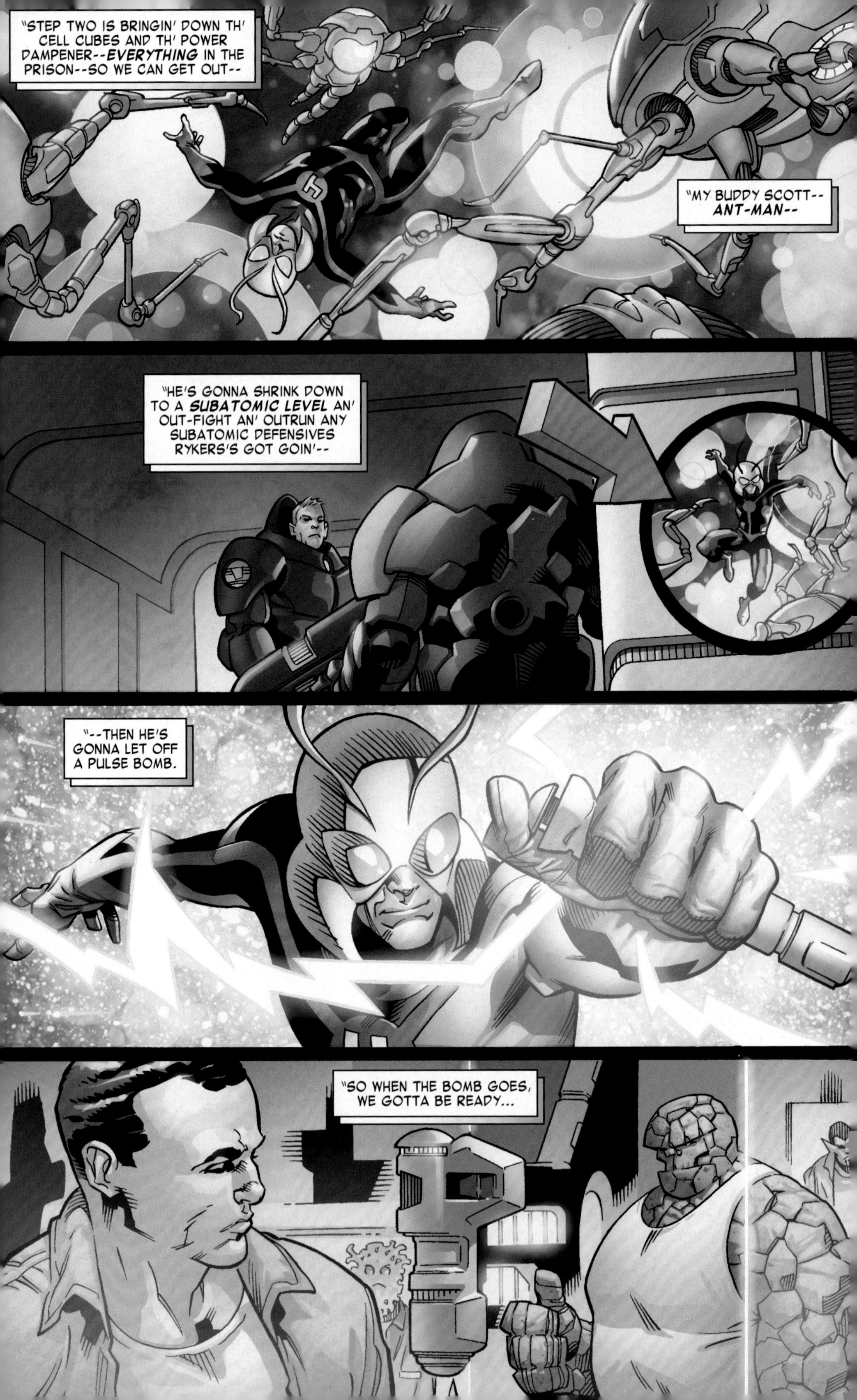
"STEP TWO IS BRINGIN' DOWN TH' CELL CUBES AND TH' POWER DAMPENER--*EVERYTHING* IN THE PRISON--SO WE CAN GET OUT--
"MY BUDDY SCOTT-- *ANT-MAN*--
"HE'S GONNA SHRINK DOWN TO A *SUBATOMIC LEVEL* AN' OUT-FIGHT AN' OUTRUN ANY SUBATOMIC DEFENSIVES RYKERS'S GOT GOIN'--
"--THEN HE'S GONNA LET OFF A PULSE BOMB.
"SO WHEN THE BOMB GOES, WE GOTTA BE READY...

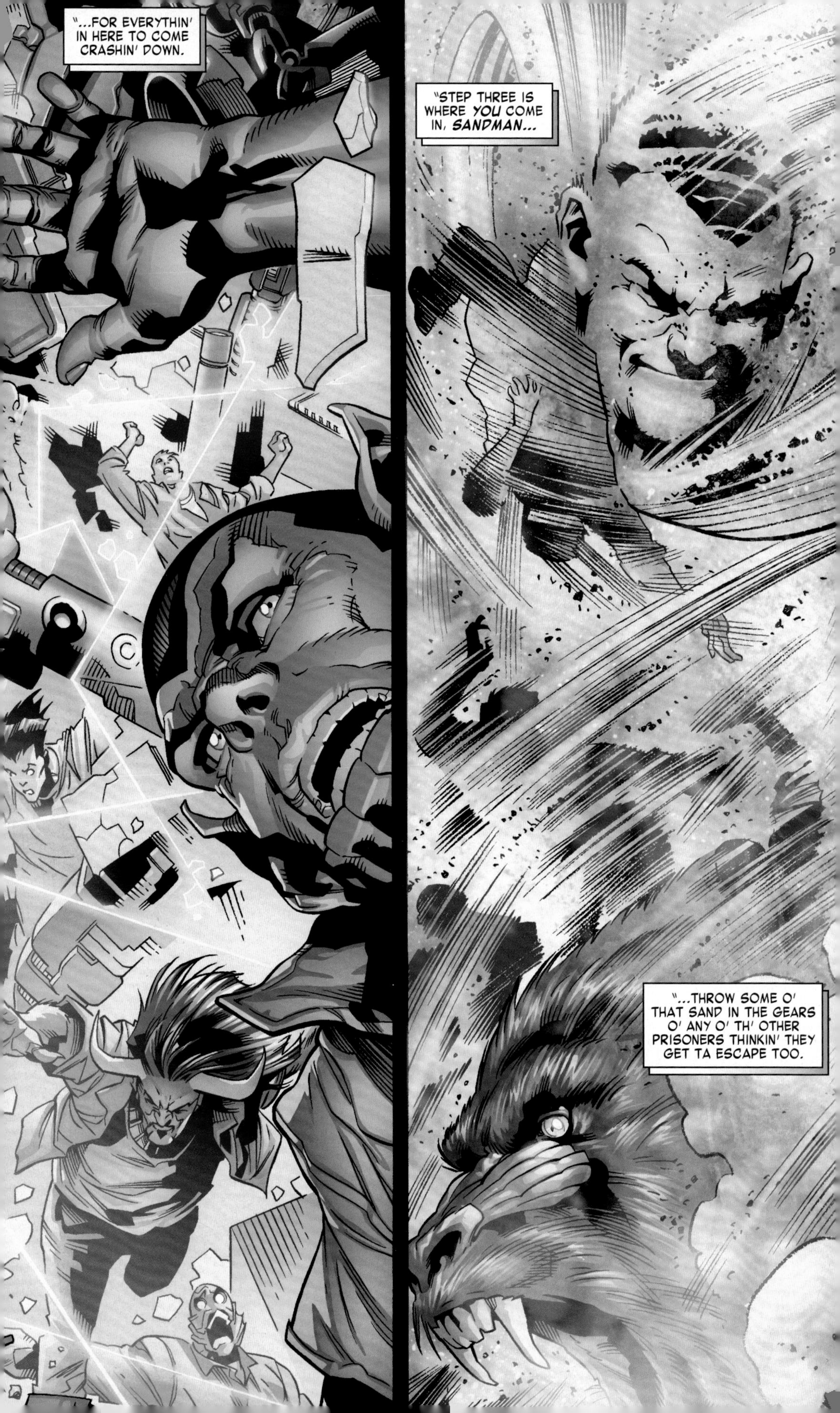
"...FOR EVERYTHIN' IN HERE TO COME CRASHIN' DOWN.
"STEP THREE IS WHERE *YOU* COME IN, *SANDMAN*...
"...THROW SOME O' THAT SAND IN THE GEARS O' ANY O' TH' OTHER PRISONERS THINKIN' THEY GET TA ESCAPE TOO.

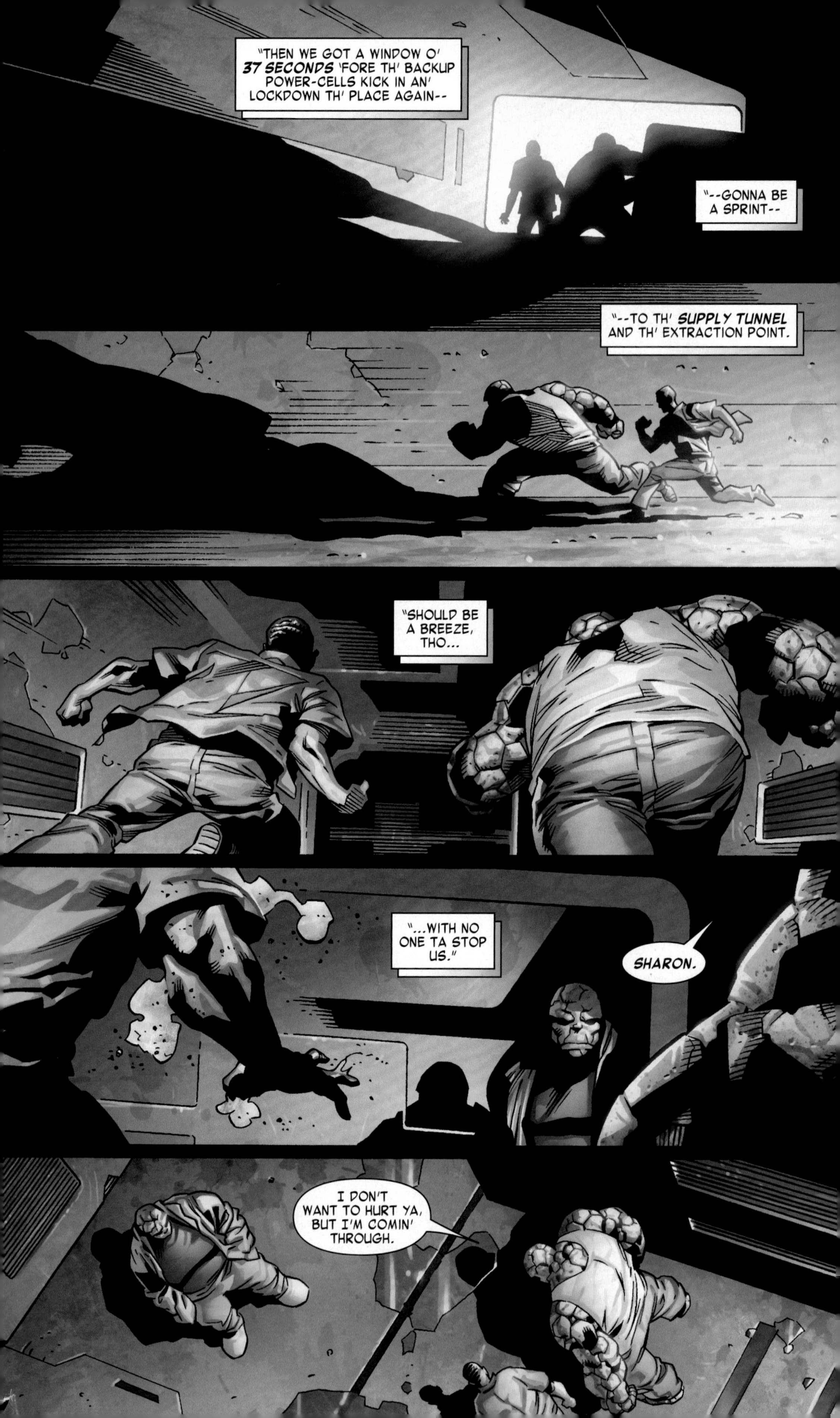
"THEN WE GOT A WINDOW O' 37 SECONDS 'FORE TH' BACKUP POWER-CELLS KICK IN AN' LOCKDOWN TH' PLACE AGAIN--
"--GONNA BE A SPRINT--
"--TO TH' SUPPLY TUNNEL AND TH' EXTRACTION POINT.
"SHOULD BE A BREEZE, THO...
"...WITH NO ONE TA STOP US."
SHARON.
I DON'T WANT TO HURT YA, BUT I'M COMIN' THROUGH.

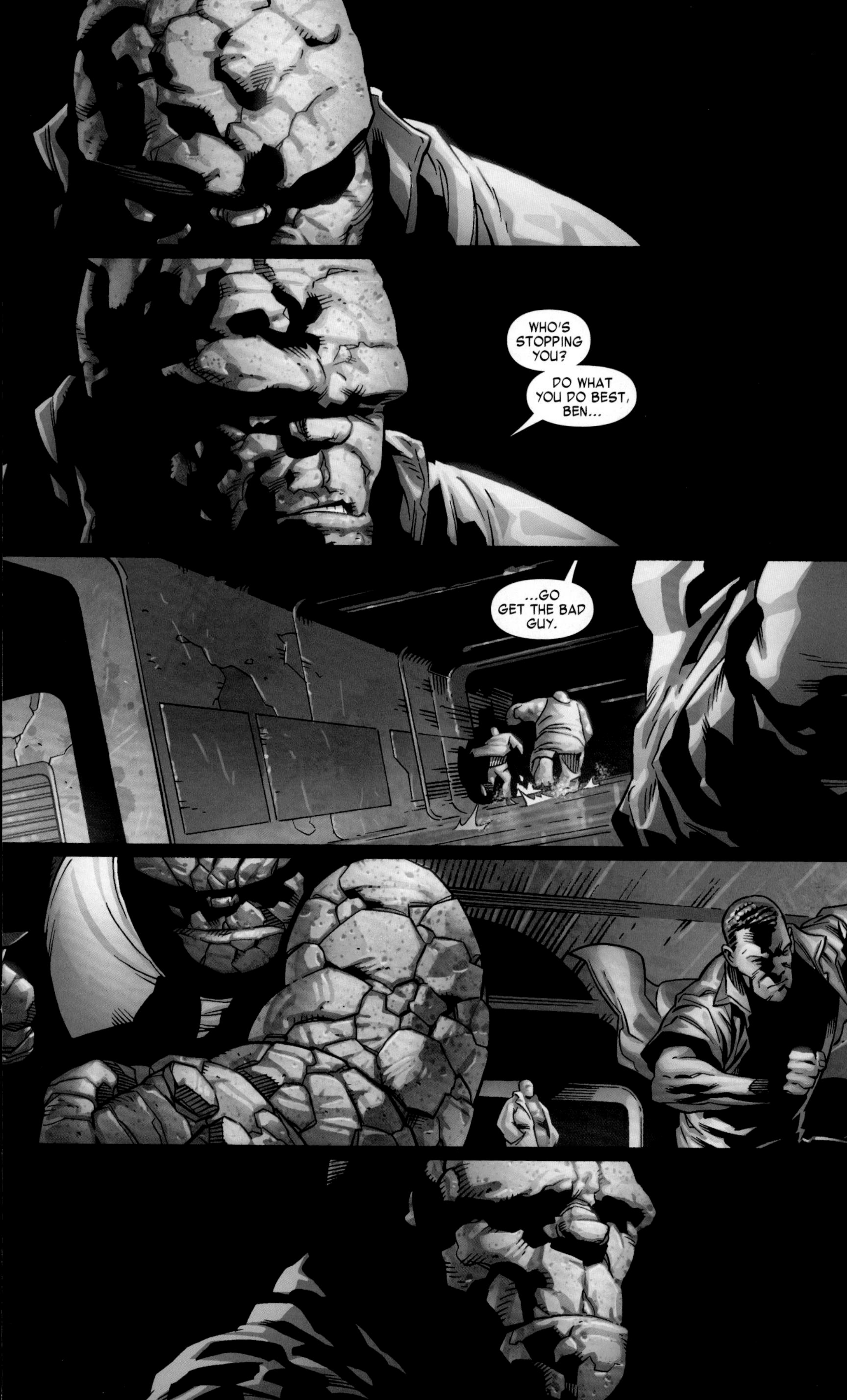
WHO'S STOPPING YOU?
DO WHAT YOU DO BEST, BEN...
...GO GET THE BAD GUY.

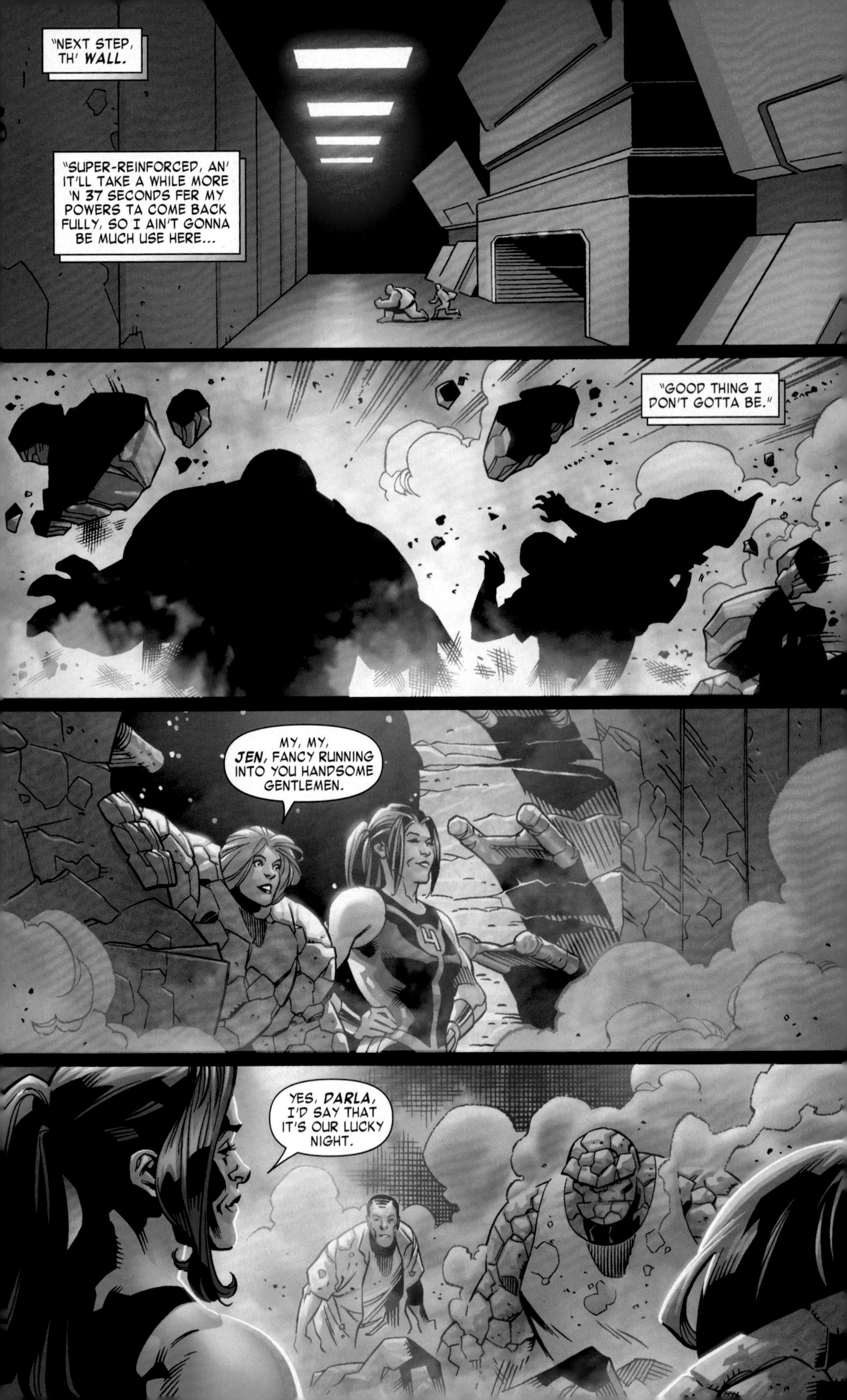
"NEXT STEP, TH' WALL.
"SUPER-REINFORCED, AN' IT'LL TAKE A WHILE MORE 'N 37 SECONDS FER MY POWERS TA COME BACK FULLY, SO I AIN'T GONNA BE MUCH USE HERE...
"GOOD THING I DON'T GOTTA BE."
MY, MY, JEN, FANCY RUNNING INTO YOU HANDSOME GENTLEMEN.
YES, DARLA, I'D SAY THAT IT'S OUR LUCKY NIGHT.

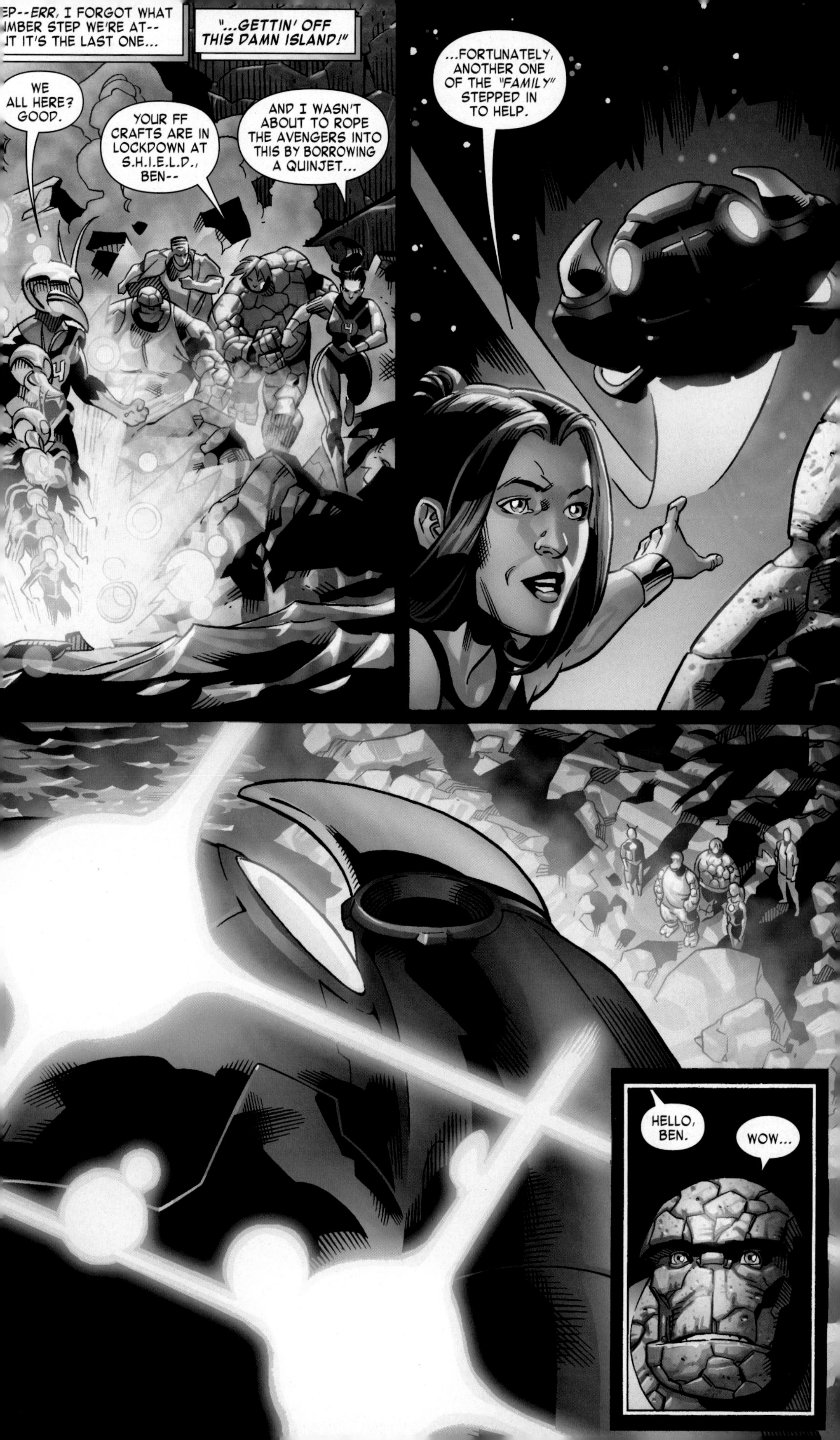

EP--ERR, I FORGOT WHAT
IMBER STEP WE'RE AT--
IT IT'S THE LAST ONE...
"...GETTIN' OFF THIS DAMN ISLAND!"
WE ALL HERE? GOOD.
YOUR FF CRAFTS ARE IN LOCKDOWN AT S.H.I.E.L.D., BEN--
AND I WASN'T ABOUT TO ROPE THE AVENGERS INTO THIS BY BORROWING A QUINJET...
...FORTUNATELY, ANOTHER ONE OF THE "FAMILY" STEPPED IN TO HELP.
HELLO, BEN.
WOW...

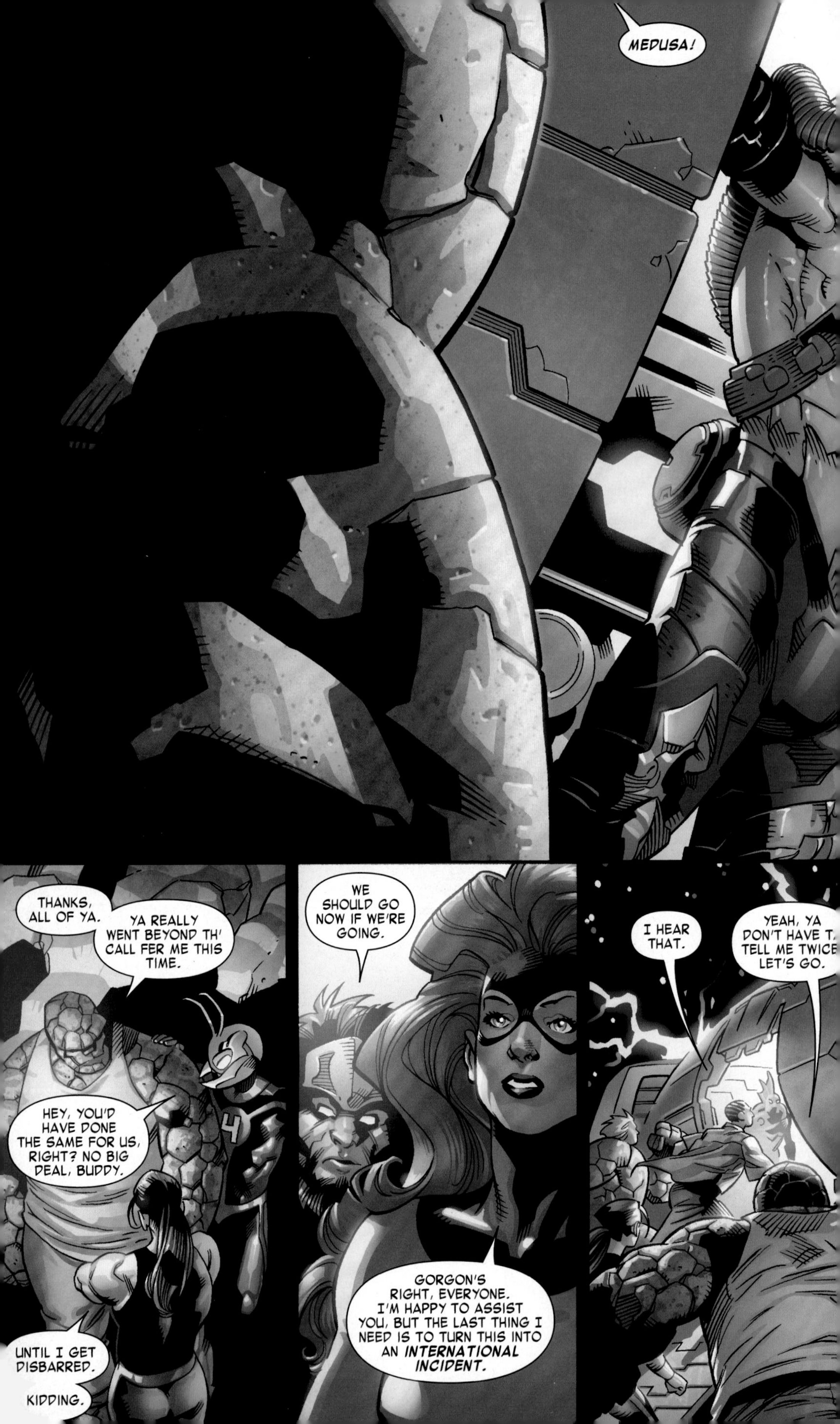
MEDUSA!
THANKS, ALL OF YA.
YA REALLY WENT BEYOND TH' CALL FER ME THIS TIME.
HEY, YOU'D HAVE DONE THE SAME FOR US, RIGHT? NO BIG DEAL, BUDDY.
UNTIL I GET DISBARRED.
KIDDING.
WE SHOULD GO NOW IF WE'RE GOING.
GORGON'S RIGHT, EVERYONE. I'M HAPPY TO ASSIST YOU, BUT THE LAST THING I NEED IS TO TURN THIS INTO AN *INTERNATIONAL INCIDENT*.
I HEAR THAT.
YEAH, YA DON'T HAVE T' TELL ME TWICE. LET'S GO.

I'M GLAD THAT I CAN HELP YOU.

"AND THAT'S THE PLAN."

"ARE YOU KIDDING ME? IT'LL *NEVER* WORK."

"SO, YOU DON'T WANT IN ON IT?"

"NAH, DIDN'T SAY THAT.

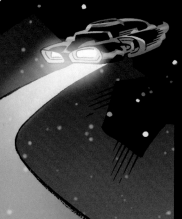

"WHAT'S THE WORST THEY CAN DO IF IT FAILS? SEND ME TO PRISON?"

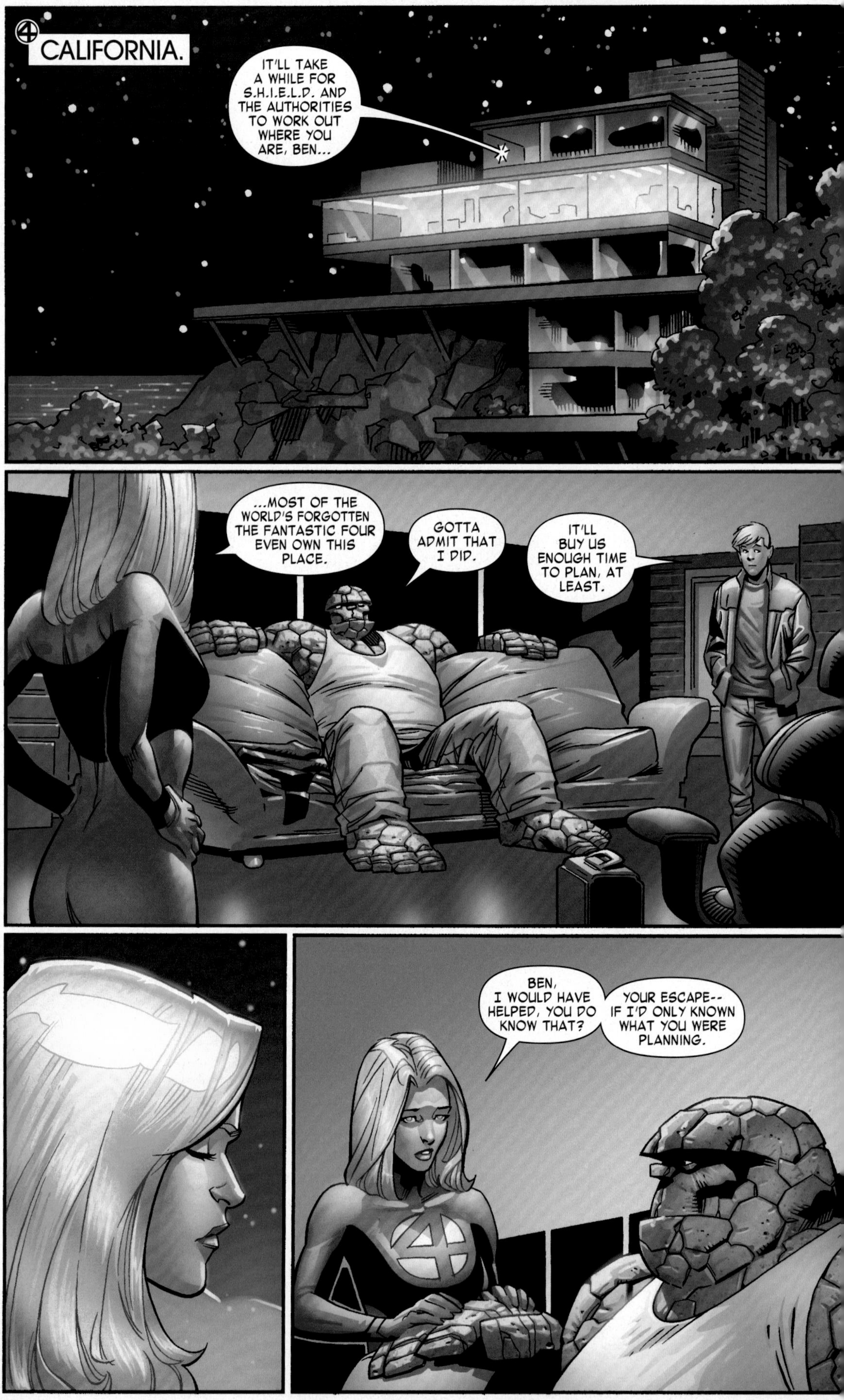
CALIFORNIA.
IT'LL TAKE A WHILE FOR S.H.I.E.L.D. AND THE AUTHORITIES TO WORK OUT WHERE YOU ARE, BEN...
...MOST OF THE WORLD'S FORGOTTEN THE FANTASTIC FOUR EVEN OWN THIS PLACE.
GOTTA ADMIT THAT I DID.
IT'LL BUY US ENOUGH TIME TO PLAN, AT LEAST.
BEN, I WOULD HAVE HELPED, YOU DO KNOW THAT?
YOUR ESCAPE-- IF I'D ONLY KNOWN WHAT YOU WERE PLANNING.

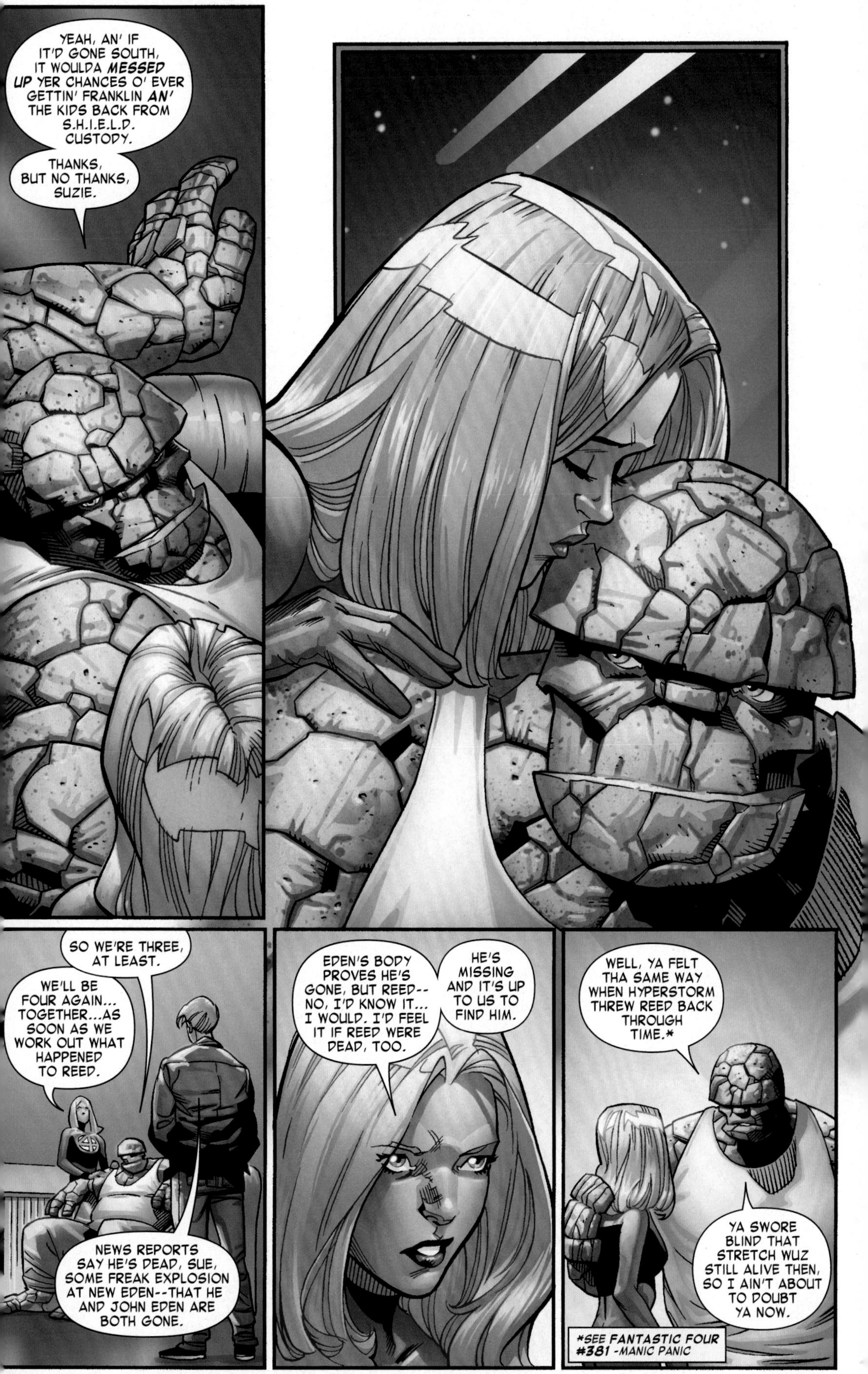

YEAH, AN' IF IT'D GONE SOUTH, IT WOULDA MESSED UP YER CHANCES O' EVER GETTIN' FRANKLIN AN' THE KIDS BACK FROM S.H.I.E.L.D. CUSTODY.
THANKS, BUT NO THANKS, SUZIE.
SO WE'RE THREE, AT LEAST.
WE'LL BE FOUR AGAIN... TOGETHER...AS SOON AS WE WORK OUT WHAT HAPPENED TO REED.
NEWS REPORTS SAY HE'S DEAD, SUE, SOME FREAK EXPLOSION AT NEW EDEN--THAT HE AND JOHN EDEN ARE BOTH GONE.
EDEN'S BODY PROVES HE'S GONE, BUT REED--NO, I'D KNOW IT... I WOULD. I'D FEEL IT IF REED WERE DEAD, TOO.
HE'S MISSING AND IT'S UP TO US TO FIND HIM.
WELL, YA FELT THA SAME WAY WHEN HYPERSTORM THREW REED BACK THROUGH TIME.*
YA SWORE BLIND THAT STRETCH WUZ STILL ALIVE THEN, SO I AIN'T ABOUT TO DOUBT YA NOW.
*SEE FANTASTIC FOUR #381 -MANIC PANIC

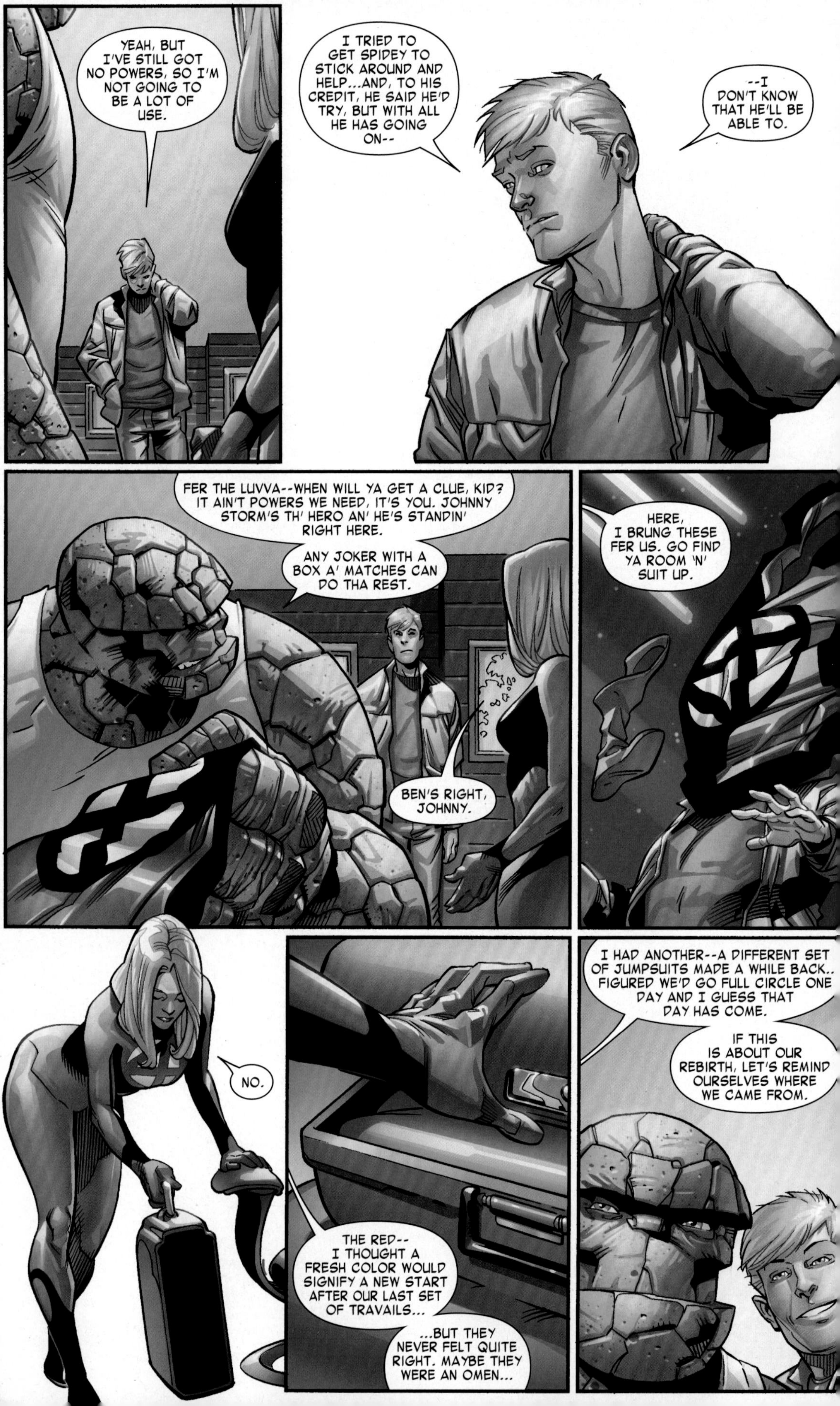
YEAH, BUT I'VE STILL GOT NO POWERS, SO I'M NOT GOING TO BE A LOT OF USE.
I TRIED TO GET SPIDEY TO STICK AROUND AND HELP...AND, TO HIS CREDIT, HE SAID HE'D TRY, BUT WITH ALL HE HAS GOING ON--
--I DON'T KNOW THAT HE'LL BE ABLE TO.
FER THE LUVVA--WHEN WILL YA GET A CLUE, KID? IT AIN'T POWERS WE NEED, IT'S YOU. JOHNNY STORM'S TH' HERO AN' HE'S STANDIN' RIGHT HERE.
ANY JOKER WITH A BOX A' MATCHES CAN DO THA REST.
BEN'S RIGHT, JOHNNY.
HERE, I BRUNG THESE FER US. GO FIND YA ROOM 'N' SUIT UP.
NO.
THE RED-- I THOUGHT A FRESH COLOR WOULD SIGNIFY A NEW START AFTER OUR LAST SET OF TRAVAILS...
...BUT THEY NEVER FELT QUITE RIGHT. MAYBE THEY WERE AN OMEN...
I HAD ANOTHER--A DIFFERENT SET OF JUMPSUITS MADE A WHILE BACK.. FIGURED WE'D GO FULL CIRCLE ONE DAY AND I GUESS THAT DAY HAS COME.
IF THIS IS ABOUT OUR REBIRTH, LET'S REMIND OURSELVES WHERE WE CAME FROM.

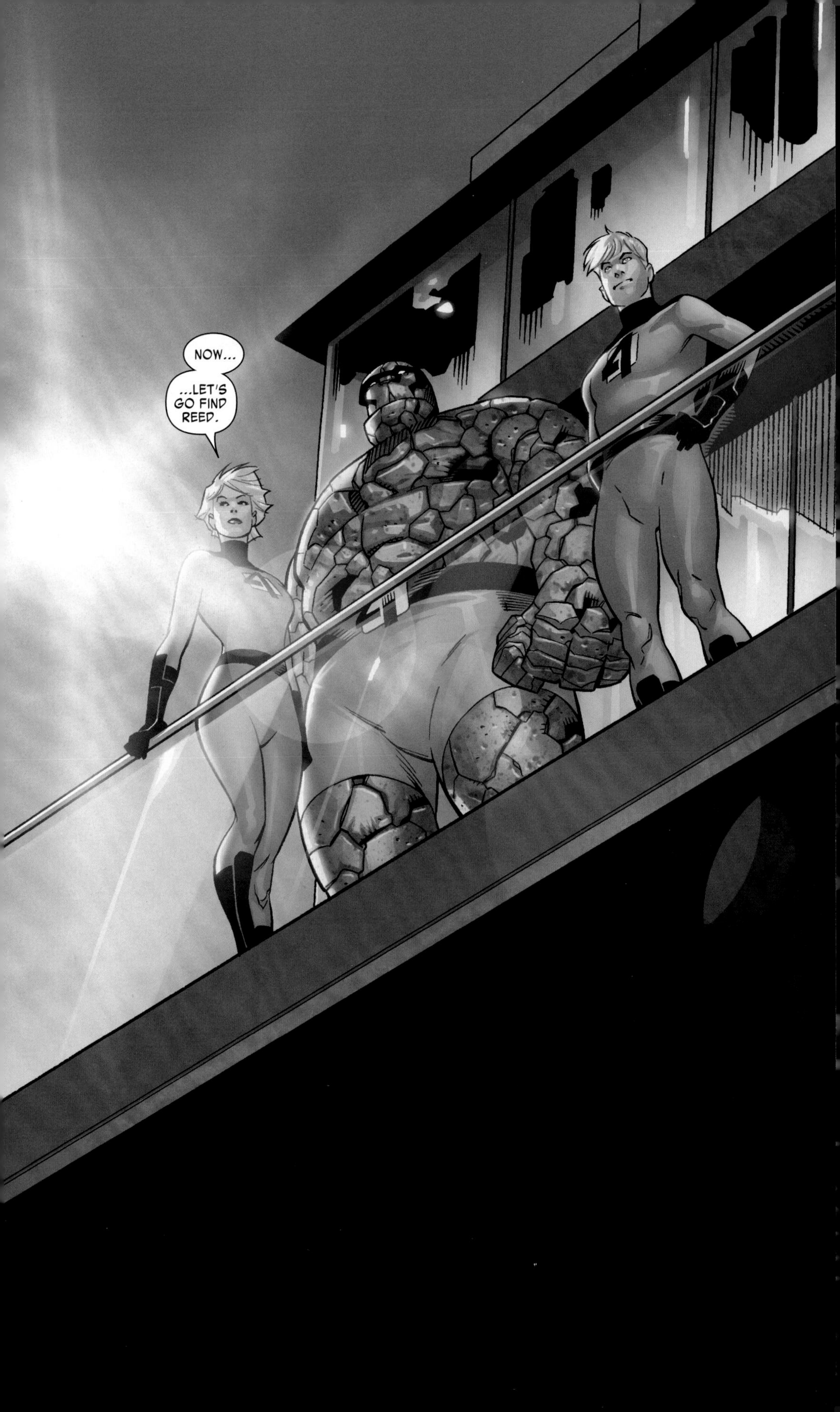
NOW...
...LET'S GO FIND REED.

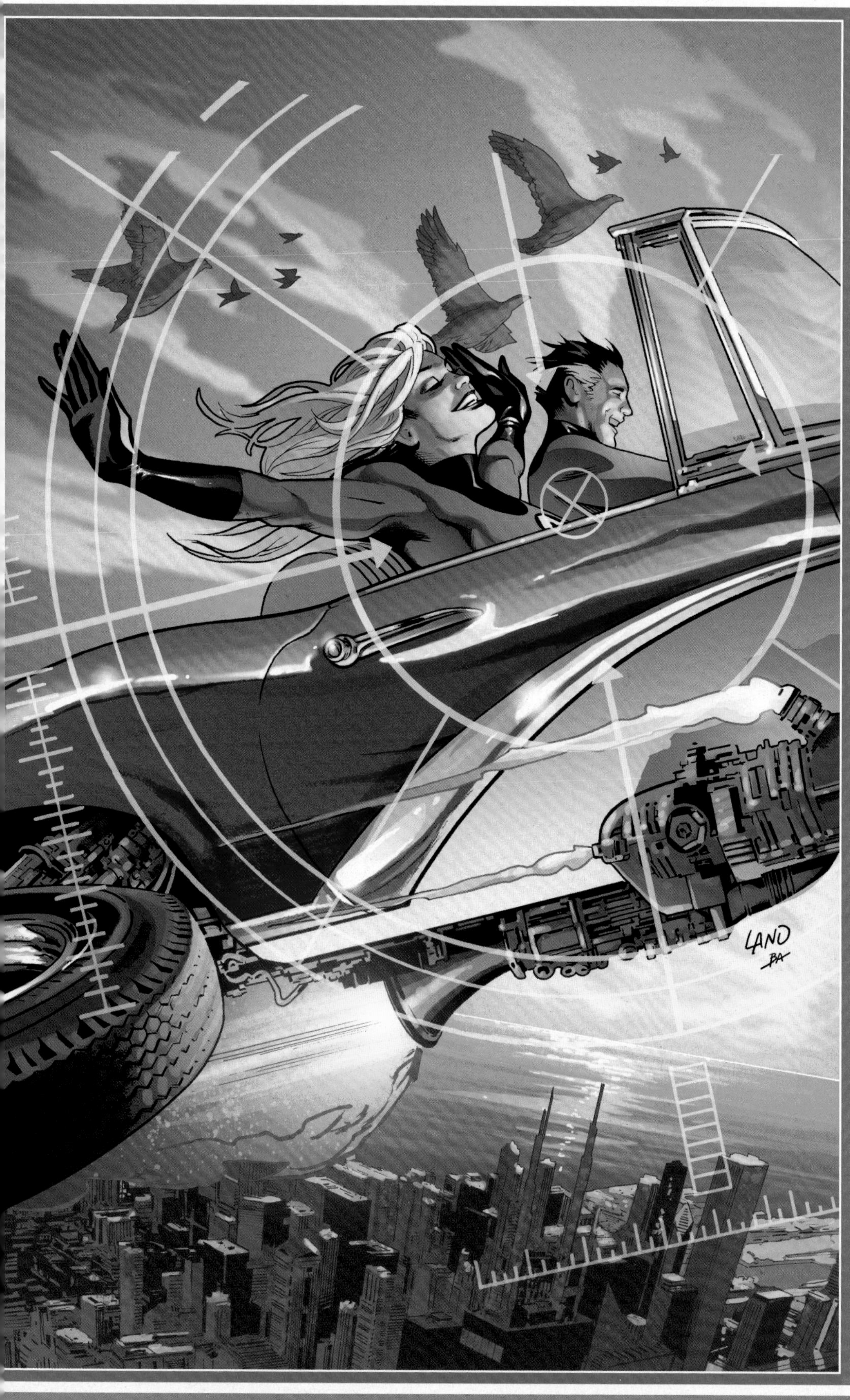
LAND
BA

FOURTEEN

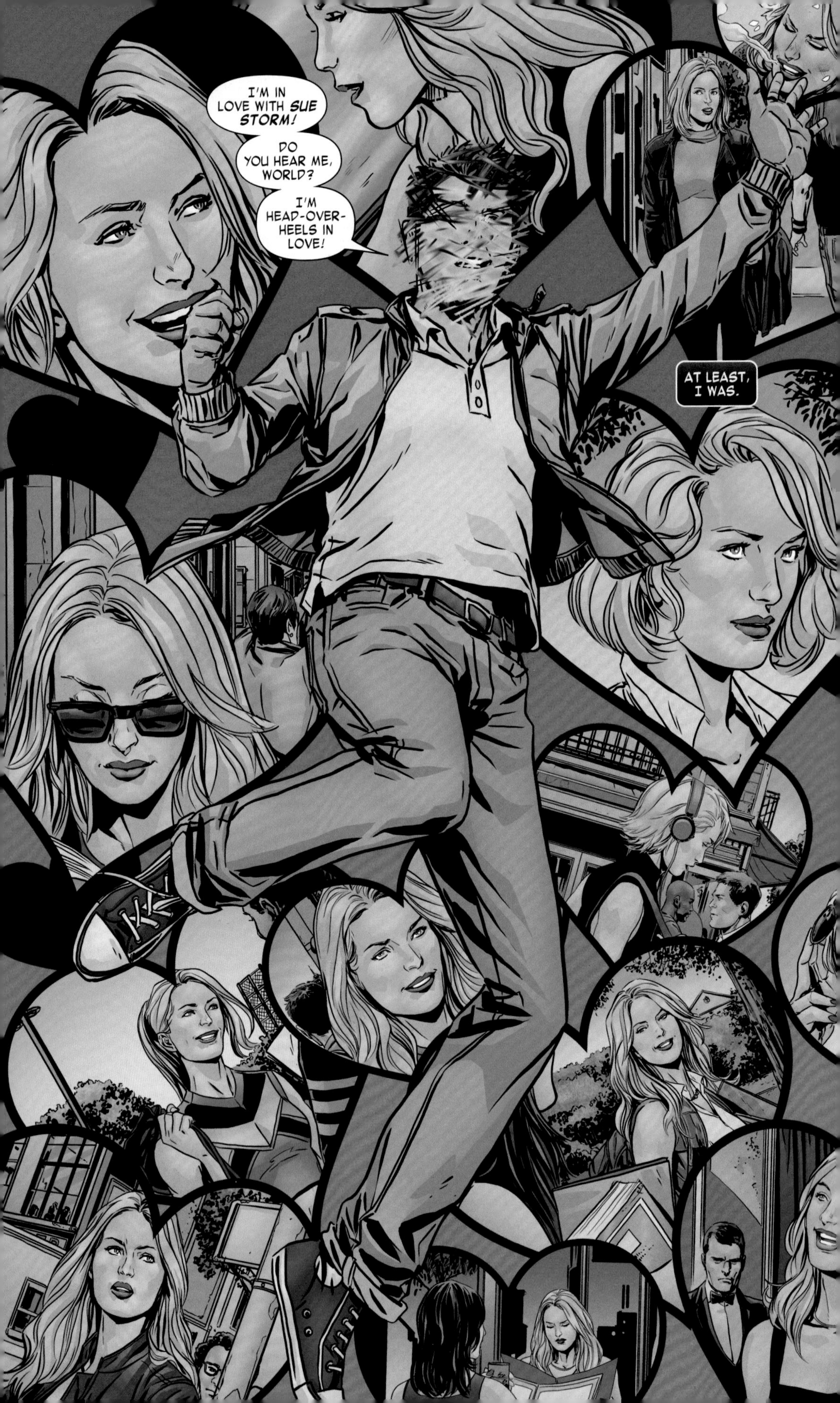

I'M IN LOVE WITH SUE STORM!
DO YOU HEAR ME, WORLD?
I'M HEAD-OVER-HEELS IN LOVE!
AT LEAST, I WAS.

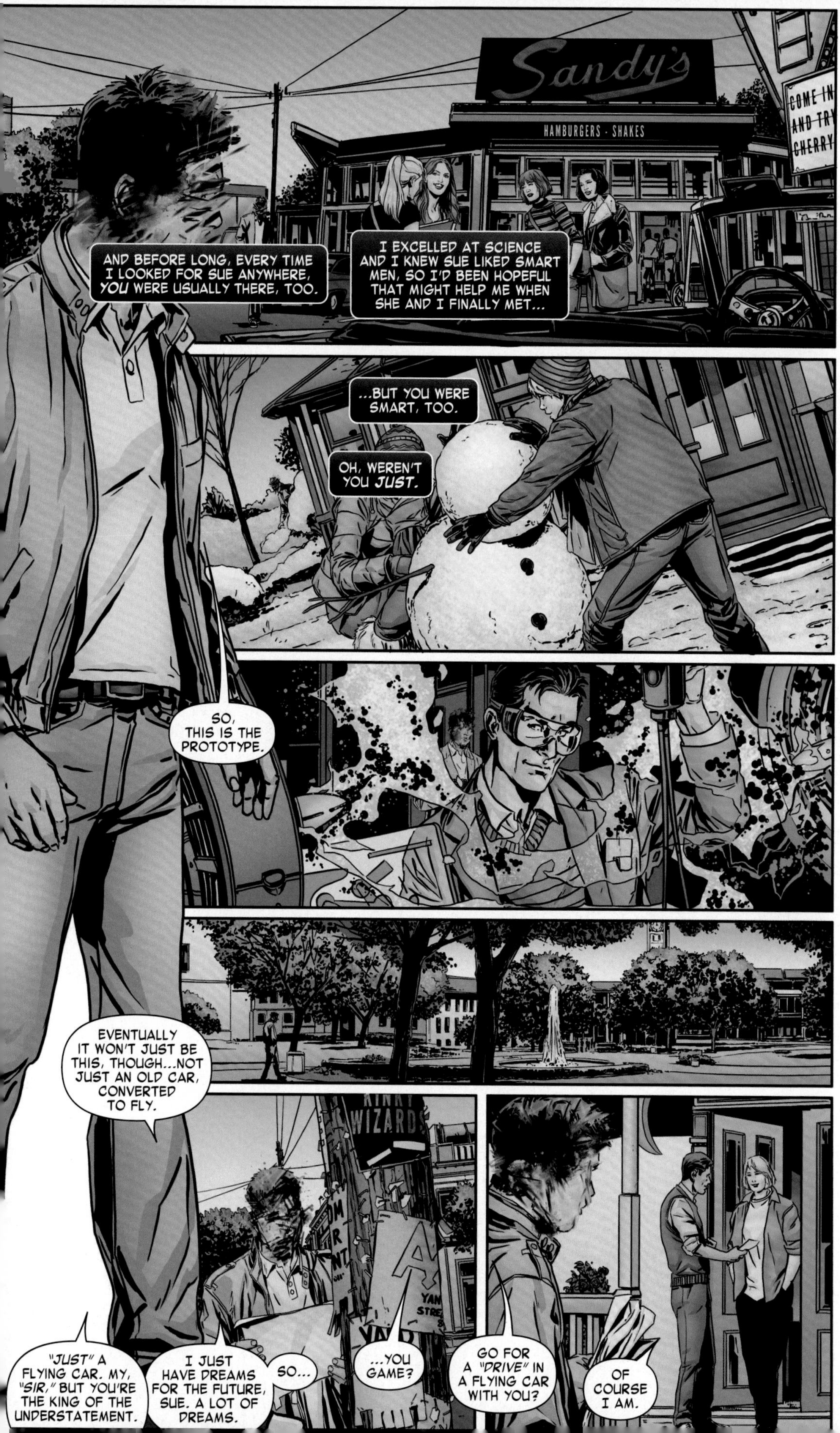
Sandy's
HAMBURGERS - SHAKES
COME IN AND TRY CHERRY
AND BEFORE LONG, EVERY TIME I LOOKED FOR SUE ANYWHERE, *YOU* WERE USUALLY THERE, TOO.
I EXCELLED AT SCIENCE AND I KNEW SUE LIKED SMART MEN, SO I'D BEEN HOPEFUL THAT MIGHT HELP ME WHEN SHE AND I FINALLY MET...
...BUT YOU WERE SMART, TOO.
OH, WEREN'T YOU *JUST.*
SO, THIS IS THE PROTOTYPE.
EVENTUALLY IT WON'T JUST BE THIS, THOUGH...NOT JUST AN OLD CAR, CONVERTED TO FLY.
WIZARDS
"*JUST*" A FLYING CAR. MY, "*SIR,*" BUT YOU'RE THE KING OF THE UNDERSTATEMENT.
I JUST HAVE DREAMS FOR THE FUTURE, SUE. A LOT OF DREAMS.
SO...
...YOU GAME?
GO FOR A "*DRIVE*" IN A FLYING CAR WITH YOU?
OF COURSE I AM.

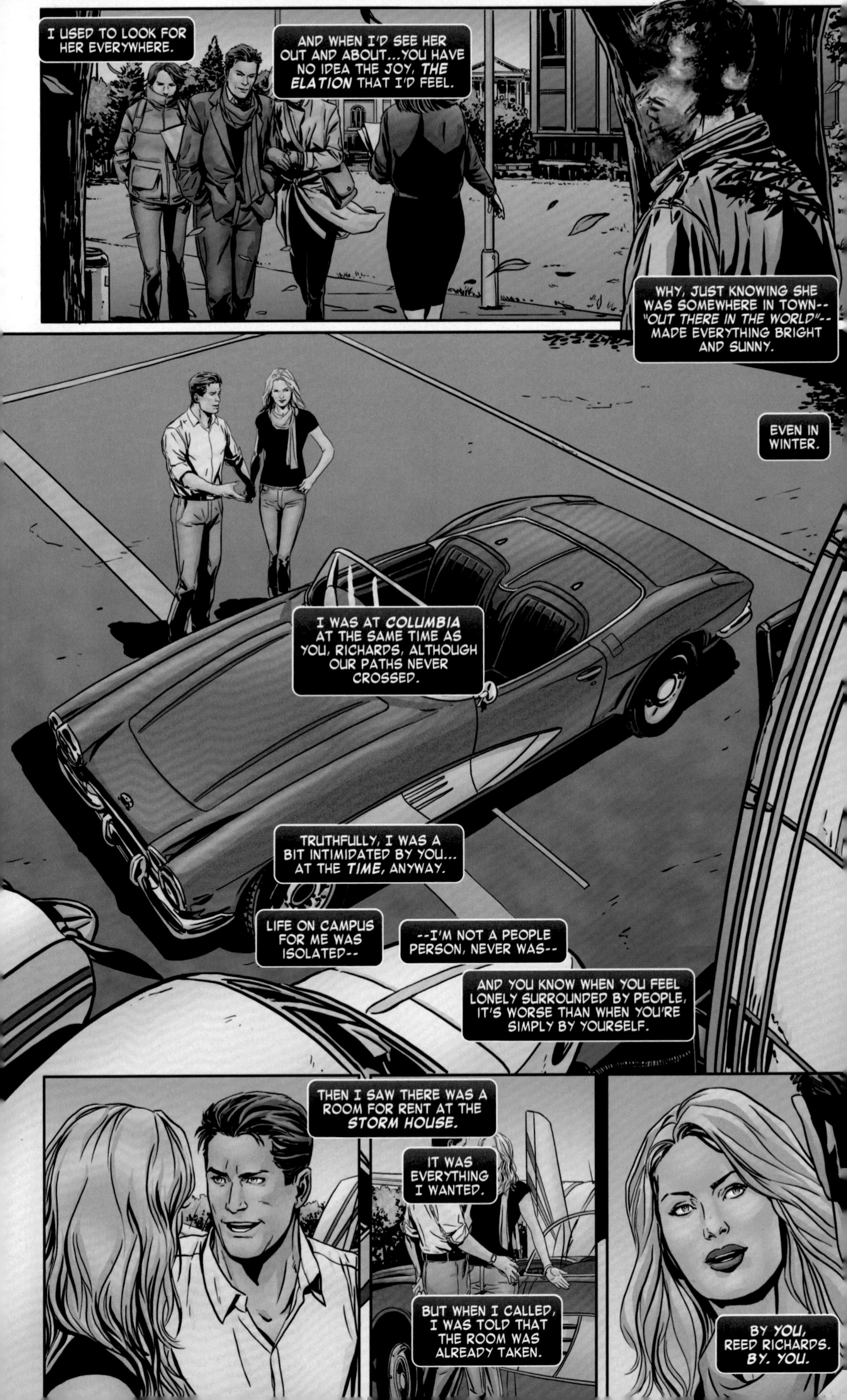

I USED TO LOOK FOR HER EVERYWHERE.
AND WHEN I'D SEE HER OUT AND ABOUT...YOU HAVE NO IDEA THE JOY, THE ELATION THAT I'D FEEL.
WHY, JUST KNOWING SHE WAS SOMEWHERE IN TOWN-- "OUT THERE IN THE WORLD"-- MADE EVERYTHING BRIGHT AND SUNNY.
EVEN IN WINTER.
I WAS AT COLUMBIA AT THE SAME TIME AS YOU, RICHARDS, ALTHOUGH OUR PATHS NEVER CROSSED.
TRUTHFULLY, I WAS A BIT INTIMIDATED BY YOU... AT THE TIME, ANYWAY.
LIFE ON CAMPUS FOR ME WAS ISOLATED--
--I'M NOT A PEOPLE PERSON, NEVER WAS--
AND YOU KNOW WHEN YOU FEEL LONELY SURROUNDED BY PEOPLE, IT'S WORSE THAN WHEN YOU'RE SIMPLY BY YOURSELF.
THEN I SAW THERE WAS A ROOM FOR RENT AT THE STORM HOUSE.
IT WAS EVERYTHING I WANTED.
BUT WHEN I CALLED, I WAS TOLD THAT THE ROOM WAS ALREADY TAKEN.
BY YOU, REED RICHARDS. BY. YOU.

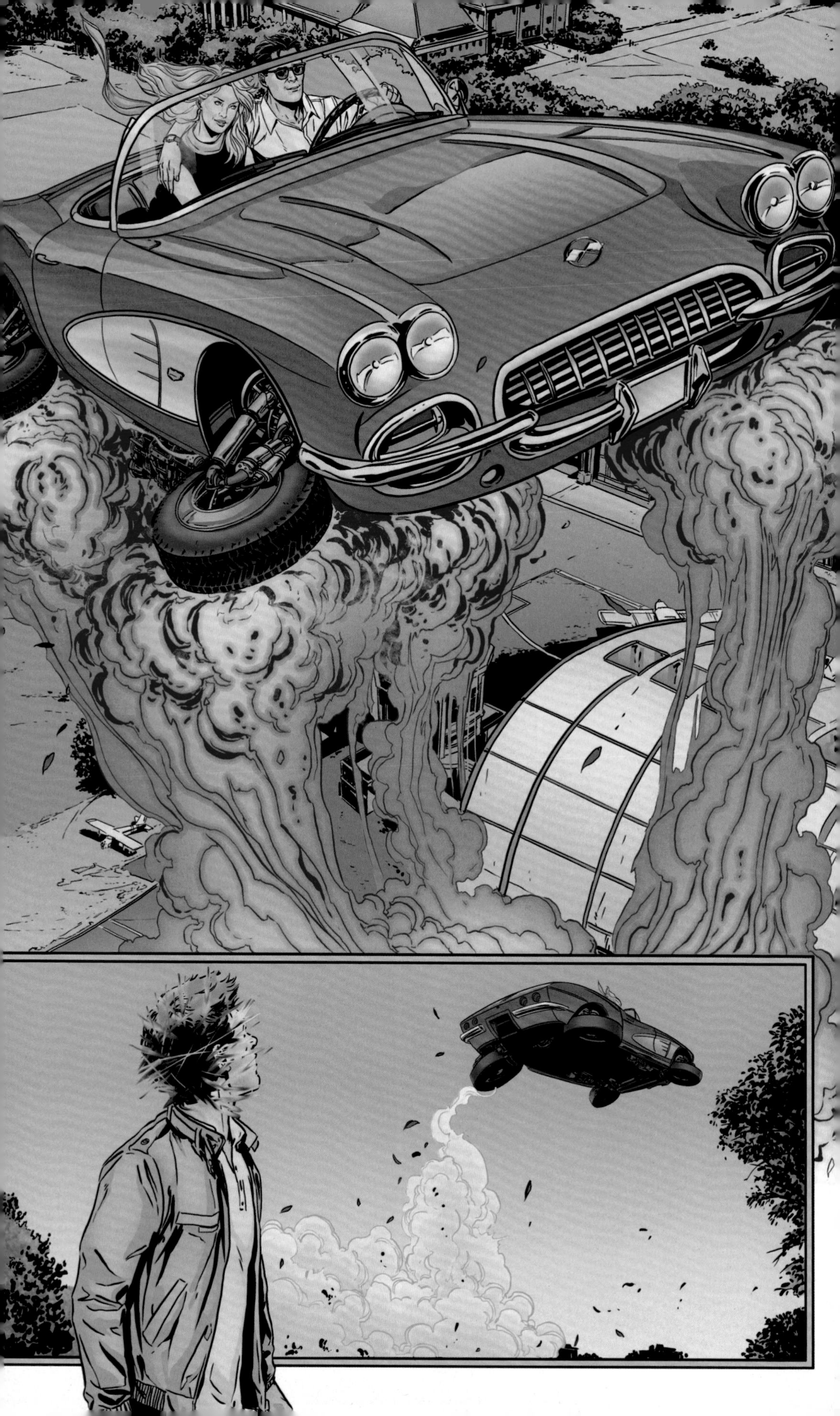

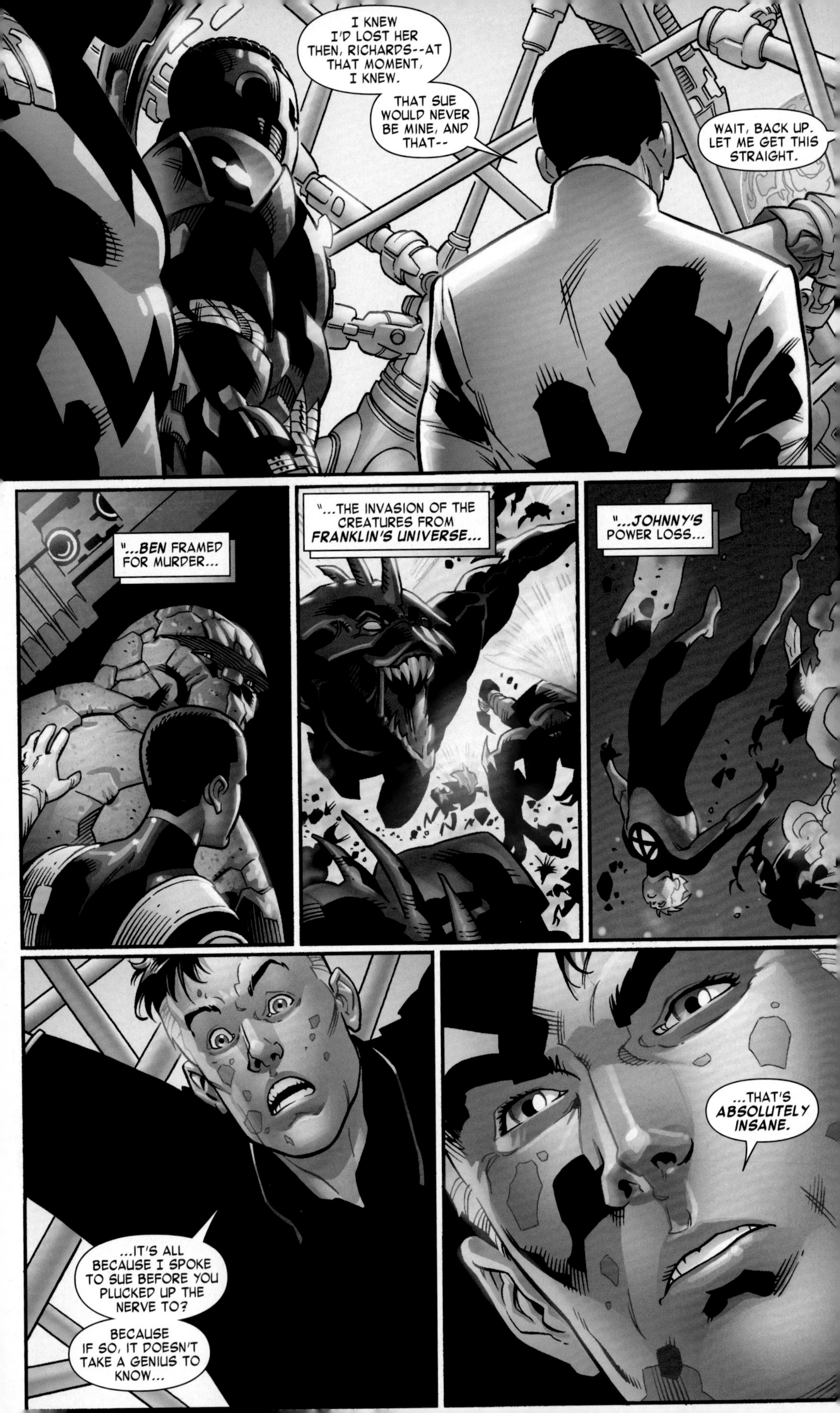
I KNEW I'D LOST HER THEN, RICHARDS--AT THAT MOMENT, I KNEW.
THAT SUE WOULD NEVER BE MINE, AND THAT--
WAIT, BACK UP. LET ME GET THIS STRAIGHT.
"...BEN FRAMED FOR MURDER...
"...THE INVASION OF THE CREATURES FROM FRANKLIN'S UNIVERSE...
"...JOHNNY'S POWER LOSS...
...IT'S ALL BECAUSE I SPOKE TO SUE BEFORE YOU PLUCKED UP THE NERVE TO?
BECAUSE IF SO, IT DOESN'T TAKE A GENIUS TO KNOW...
...THAT'S ABSOLUTELY INSANE.

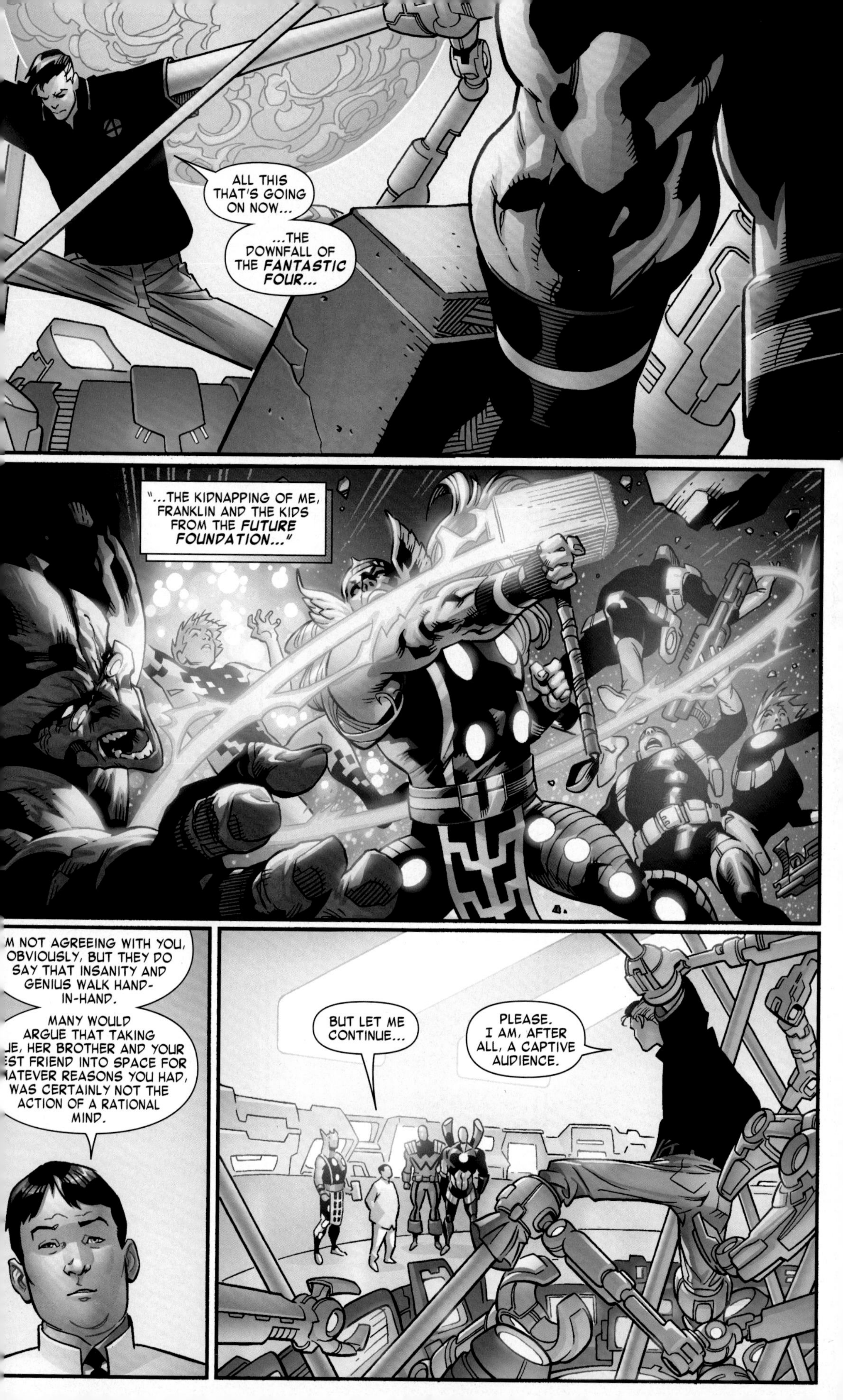
ALL THIS THAT'S GOING ON NOW...
...THE DOWNFALL OF THE FANTASTIC FOUR...
"...THE KIDNAPPING OF ME, FRANKLIN AND THE KIDS FROM THE FUTURE FOUNDATION..."
M NOT AGREEING WITH YOU, OBVIOUSLY, BUT THEY DO SAY THAT INSANITY AND GENIUS WALK HAND-IN-HAND.
MANY WOULD ARGUE THAT TAKING JE, HER BROTHER AND YOUR EST FRIEND INTO SPACE FOR HATEVER REASONS YOU HAD, WAS CERTAINLY NOT THE ACTION OF A RATIONAL MIND.
BUT LET ME CONTINUE...
PLEASE. I AM, AFTER ALL, A CAPTIVE AUDIENCE.

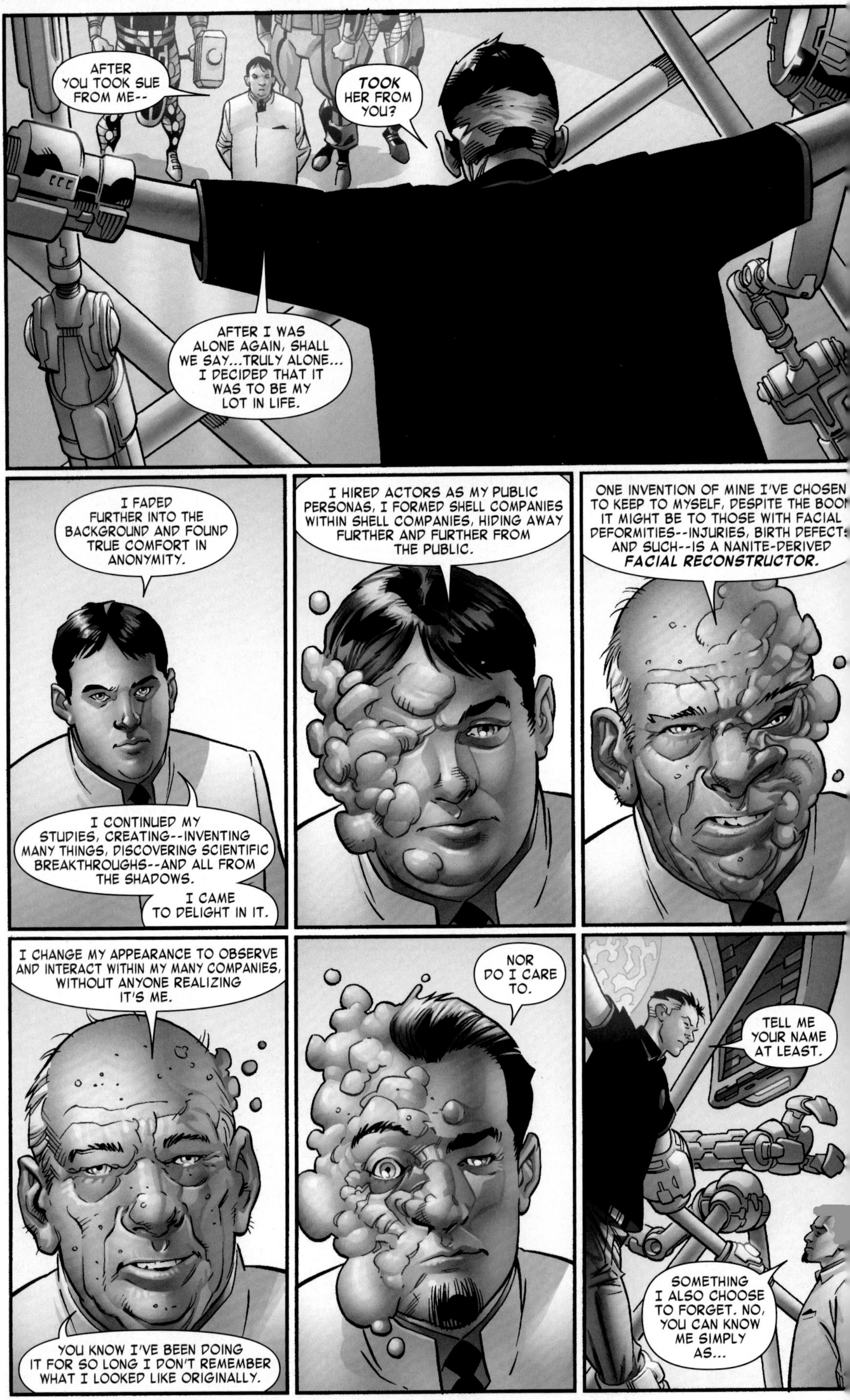
AFTER YOU TOOK SUE FROM ME--
TOOK HER FROM YOU?
AFTER I WAS ALONE AGAIN, SHALL WE SAY...TRULY ALONE... I DECIDED THAT IT WAS TO BE MY LOT IN LIFE.
I FADED FURTHER INTO THE BACKGROUND AND FOUND TRUE COMFORT IN ANONYMITY.
I CONTINUED MY STUDIES, CREATING--INVENTING MANY THINGS, DISCOVERING SCIENTIFIC BREAKTHROUGHS--AND ALL FROM THE SHADOWS.
I CAME TO DELIGHT IN IT.
I HIRED ACTORS AS MY PUBLIC PERSONAS, I FORMED SHELL COMPANIES WITHIN SHELL COMPANIES, HIDING AWAY FURTHER AND FURTHER FROM THE PUBLIC.
ONE INVENTION OF MINE I'VE CHOSEN TO KEEP TO MYSELF, DESPITE THE BOON IT MIGHT BE TO THOSE WITH FACIAL DEFORMITIES--INJURIES, BIRTH DEFECTS AND SUCH--IS A NANITE-DERIVED FACIAL RECONSTRUCTOR.
I CHANGE MY APPEARANCE TO OBSERVE AND INTERACT WITHIN MY MANY COMPANIES, WITHOUT ANYONE REALIZING IT'S ME.
YOU KNOW I'VE BEEN DOING IT FOR SO LONG I DON'T REMEMBER WHAT I LOOKED LIKE ORIGINALLY.
NOR DO I CARE TO.
TELL ME YOUR NAME AT LEAST.
SOMETHING I ALSO CHOOSE TO FORGET. NO, YOU CAN KNOW ME SIMPLY AS...

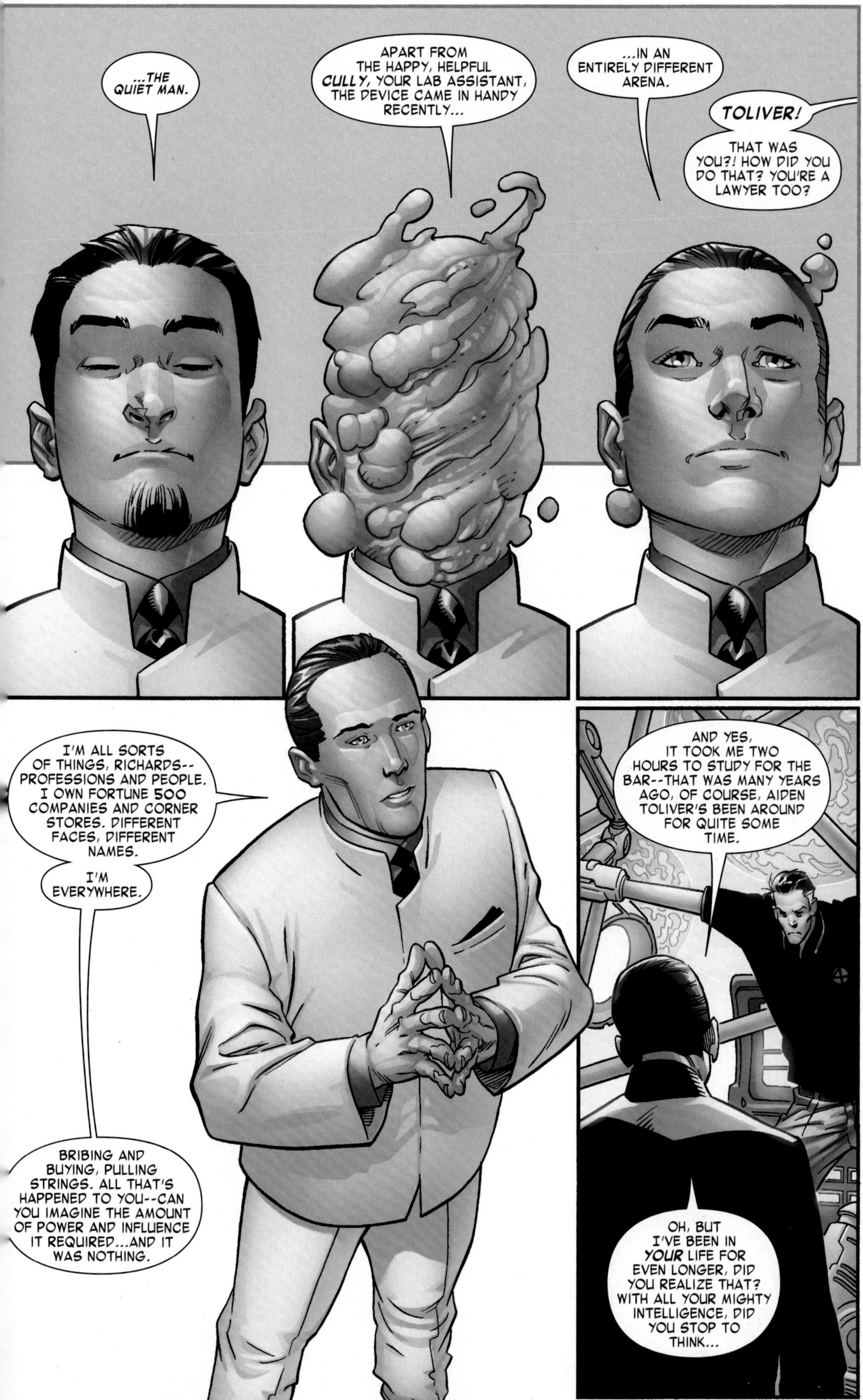
...THE QUIET MAN.
APART FROM THE HAPPY, HELPFUL CULLY, YOUR LAB ASSISTANT, THE DEVICE CAME IN HANDY RECENTLY...
...IN AN ENTIRELY DIFFERENT ARENA.
TOLIVER!
THAT WAS YOU?! HOW DID YOU DO THAT? YOU'RE A LAWYER TOO?
I'M ALL SORTS OF THINGS, RICHARDS--PROFESSIONS AND PEOPLE. I OWN FORTUNE 500 COMPANIES AND CORNER STORES. DIFFERENT FACES, DIFFERENT NAMES.
I'M EVERYWHERE.
BRIBING AND BUYING, PULLING STRINGS. ALL THAT'S HAPPENED TO YOU--CAN YOU IMAGINE THE AMOUNT OF POWER AND INFLUENCE IT REQUIRED...AND IT WAS NOTHING.
AND YES, IT TOOK ME TWO HOURS TO STUDY FOR THE BAR--THAT WAS MANY YEARS AGO, OF COURSE, AIDEN TOLIVER'S BEEN AROUND FOR QUITE SOME TIME.
OH, BUT I'VE BEEN IN YOUR LIFE FOR EVEN LONGER, DID YOU REALIZE THAT? WITH ALL YOUR MIGHTY INTELLIGENCE, DID YOU STOP TO THINK...

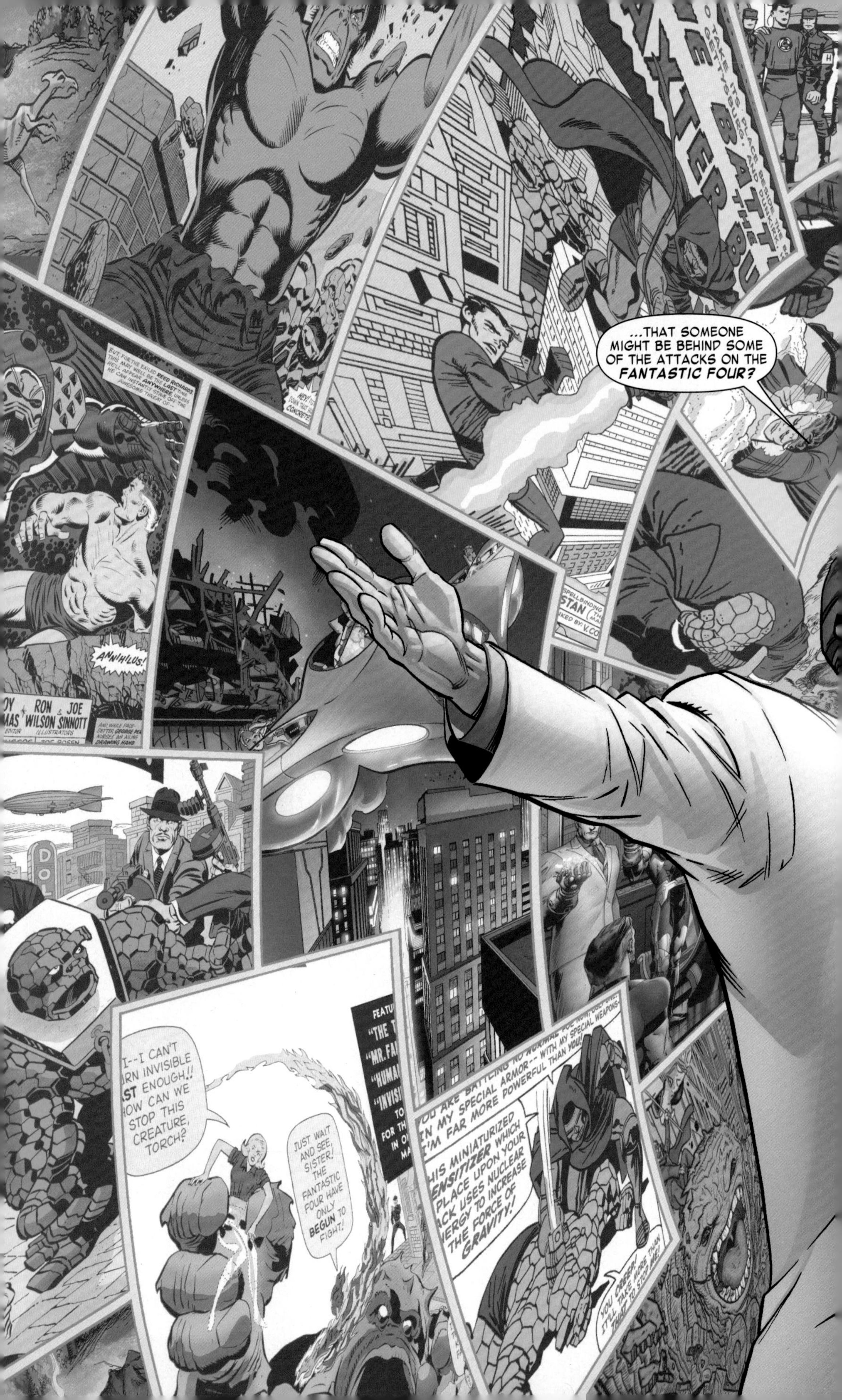

...THAT SOMEONE MIGHT BE BEHIND SOME OF THE ATTACKS ON THE FANTASTIC FOUR?
ANNIHILUS!
RON WILSON
JOE SINNOTT
ILLUSTRATORS
STOP THIS CREATURE, TORCH?
JUST WAIT AND SEE, SISTER! THE FANTASTIC FOUR HAVE ONLY BEGUN TO FIGHT!
PLACE UPON YOUR
THE FORCE OF GRAVITY!

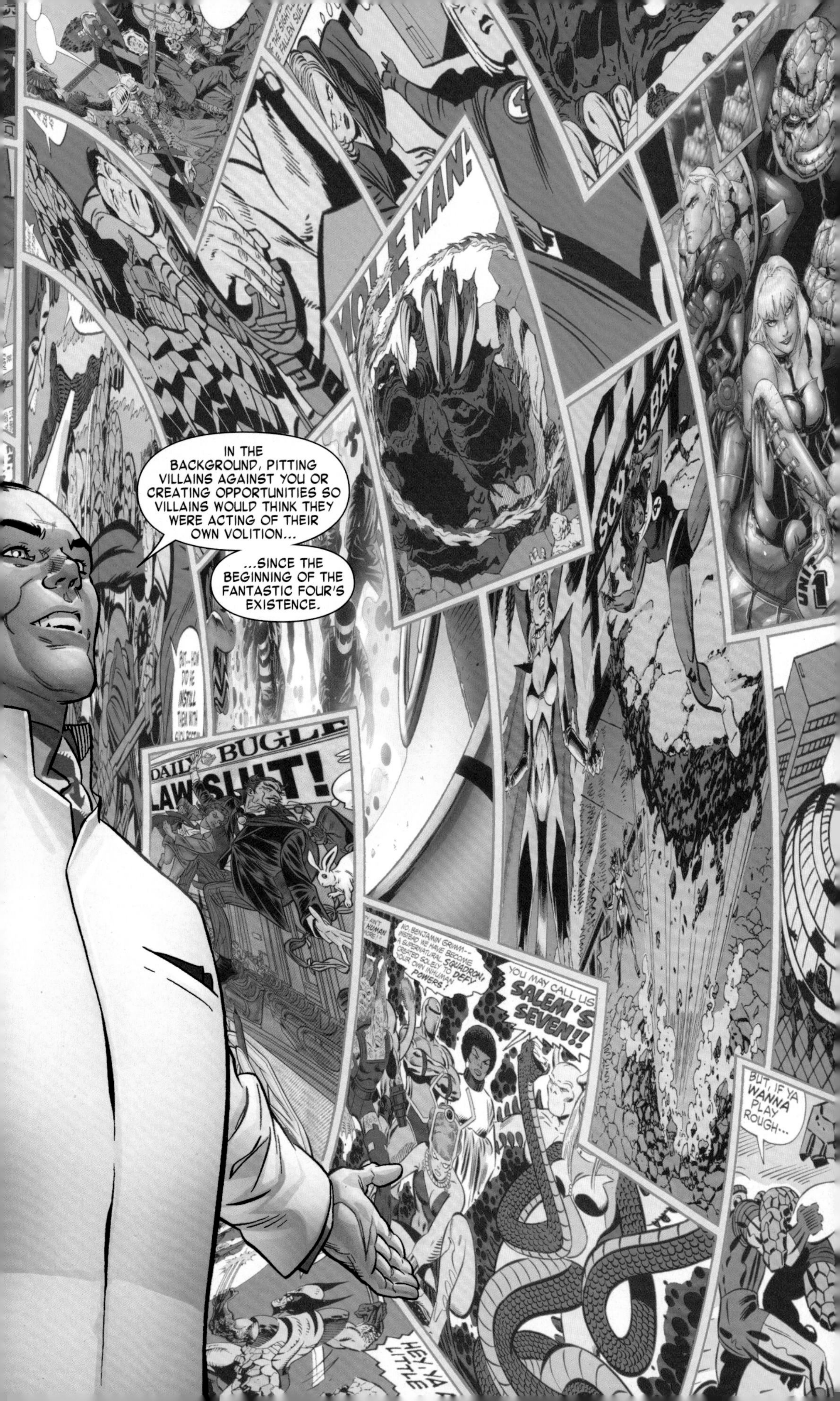
IN THE BACKGROUND, PITTING VILLAINS AGAINST YOU OR CREATING OPPORTUNITIES SO VILLAINS WOULD THINK THEY WERE ACTING OF THEIR OWN VOLITION...
...SINCE THE BEGINNING OF THE FANTASTIC FOUR'S EXISTENCE.
DAILY BUGLE
LAWSUIT!
NO, BENJAMIN GRIMM-- INSTEAD WE HAVE BECOME A SUPERNATURAL SQUADRON, CREATED SOLELY TO DEFY YOUR OWN INHUMAN POWERS!
YOU MAY CALL US SALEM'S SEVEN!!
BUT, IF YA WANNA PLAY ROUGH...
HEY, YA LITTLE

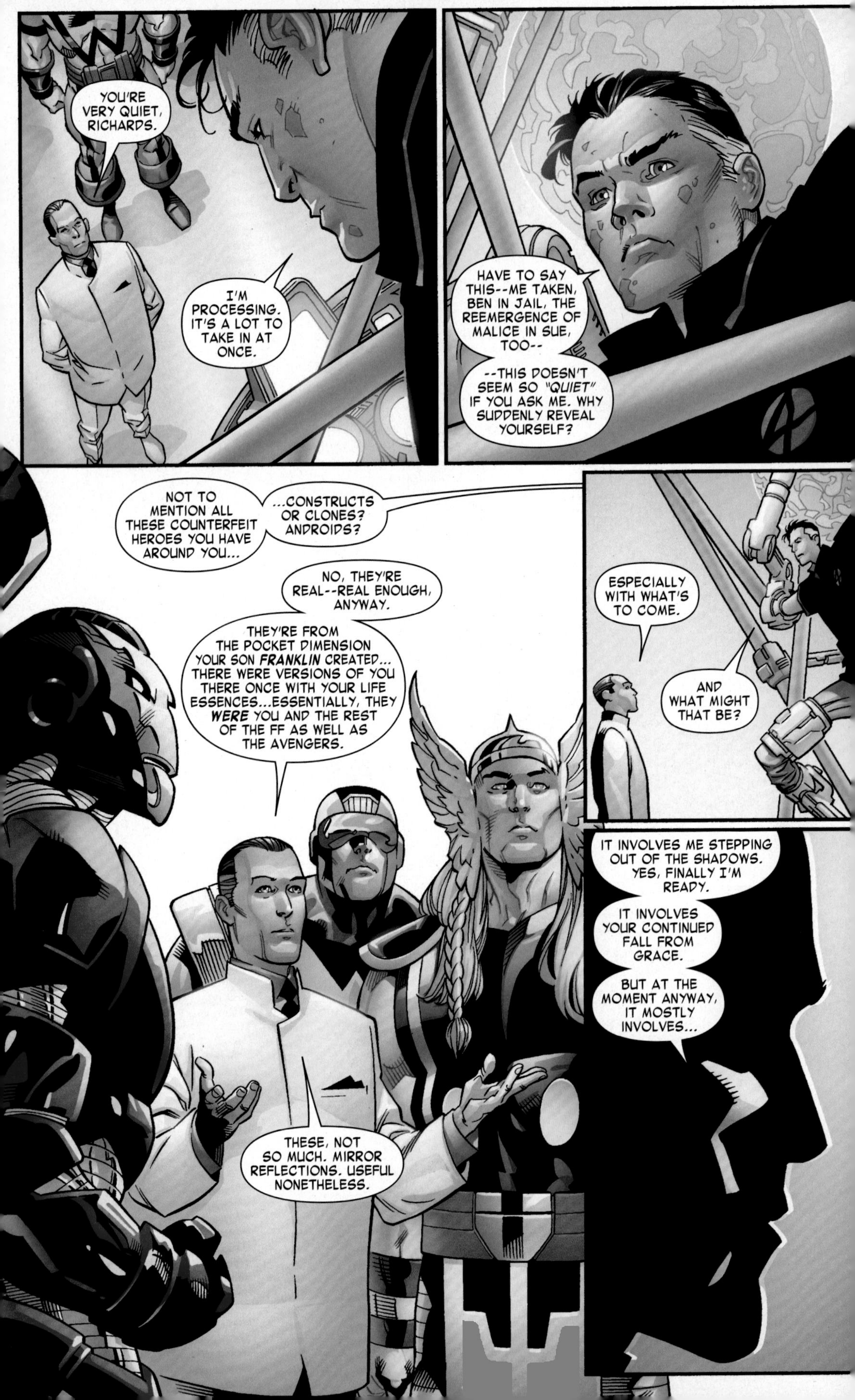
YOU'RE VERY QUIET, RICHARDS.
I'M PROCESSING. IT'S A LOT TO TAKE IN AT ONCE.
HAVE TO SAY THIS--ME TAKEN, BEN IN JAIL, THE REEMERGENCE OF MALICE IN SUE, TOO--
--THIS DOESN'T SEEM SO "QUIET" IF YOU ASK ME. WHY SUDDENLY REVEAL YOURSELF?
NOT TO MENTION ALL THESE COUNTERFEIT HEROES YOU HAVE AROUND YOU...
...CONSTRUCTS OR CLONES? ANDROIDS?
NO, THEY'RE REAL--REAL ENOUGH, ANYWAY.
THEY'RE FROM THE POCKET DIMENSION YOUR SON FRANKLIN CREATED... THERE WERE VERSIONS OF YOU THERE ONCE WITH YOUR LIFE ESSENCES...ESSENTIALLY, THEY WERE YOU AND THE REST OF THE FF AS WELL AS THE AVENGERS.
THESE, NOT SO MUCH. MIRROR REFLECTIONS. USEFUL NONETHELESS.
ESPECIALLY WITH WHAT'S TO COME.
AND WHAT MIGHT THAT BE?
IT INVOLVES ME STEPPING OUT OF THE SHADOWS. YES, FINALLY I'M READY.
IT INVOLVES YOUR CONTINUED FALL FROM GRACE.
BUT AT THE MOMENT ANYWAY, IT MOSTLY INVOLVES...

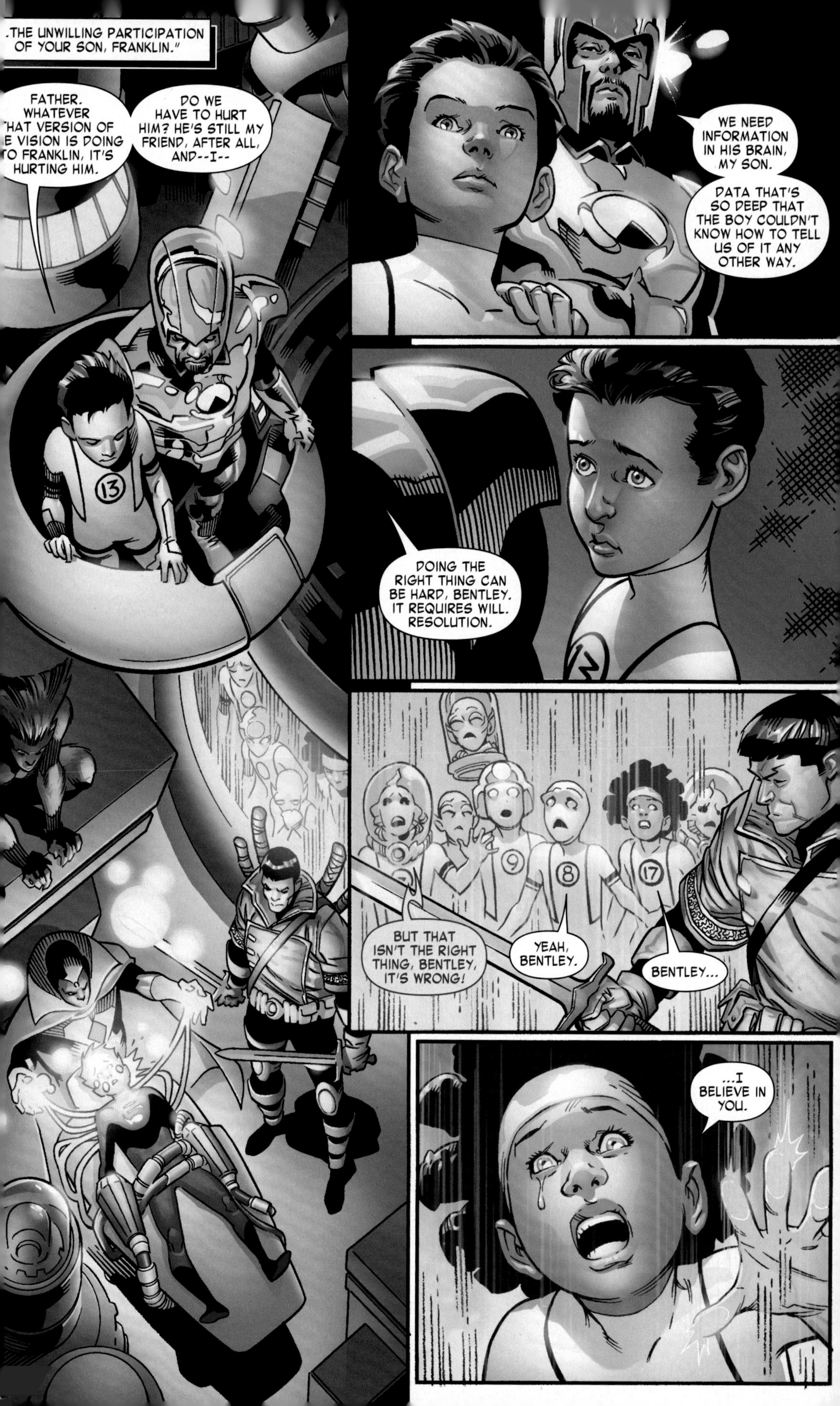

...THE UNWILLING PARTICIPATION OF YOUR SON, FRANKLIN."
FATHER. WHATEVER THAT VERSION OF E VISION IS DOING TO FRANKLIN, IT'S HURTING HIM.
DO WE HAVE TO HURT HIM? HE'S STILL MY FRIEND, AFTER ALL, AND--I--
WE NEED INFORMATION IN HIS BRAIN, MY SON.
DATA THAT'S SO DEEP THAT THE BOY COULDN'T KNOW HOW TO TELL US OF IT ANY OTHER WAY.
DOING THE RIGHT THING CAN BE HARD, BENTLEY. IT REQUIRES WILL. RESOLUTION.
BUT THAT ISN'T THE RIGHT THING, BENTLEY, IT'S WRONG!
YEAH, BENTLEY.
BENTLEY...
...I BELIEVE IN YOU.

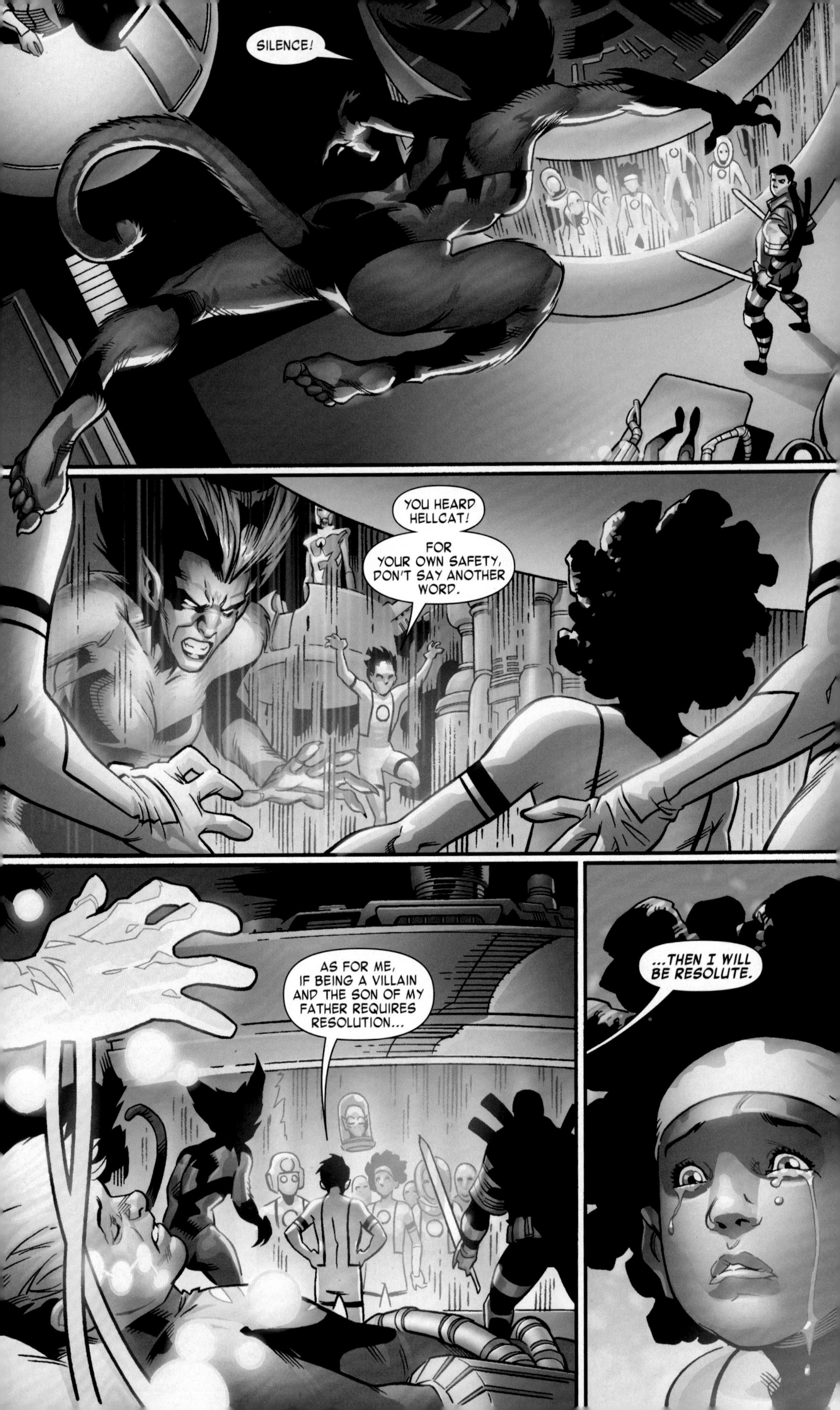
SILENCE!
YOU HEARD HELLCAT!
FOR YOUR OWN SAFETY, DON'T SAY ANOTHER WORD.
AS FOR ME, IF BEING A VILLAIN AND THE SON OF MY FATHER REQUIRES RESOLUTION...
...THEN I WILL BE RESOLUTE.

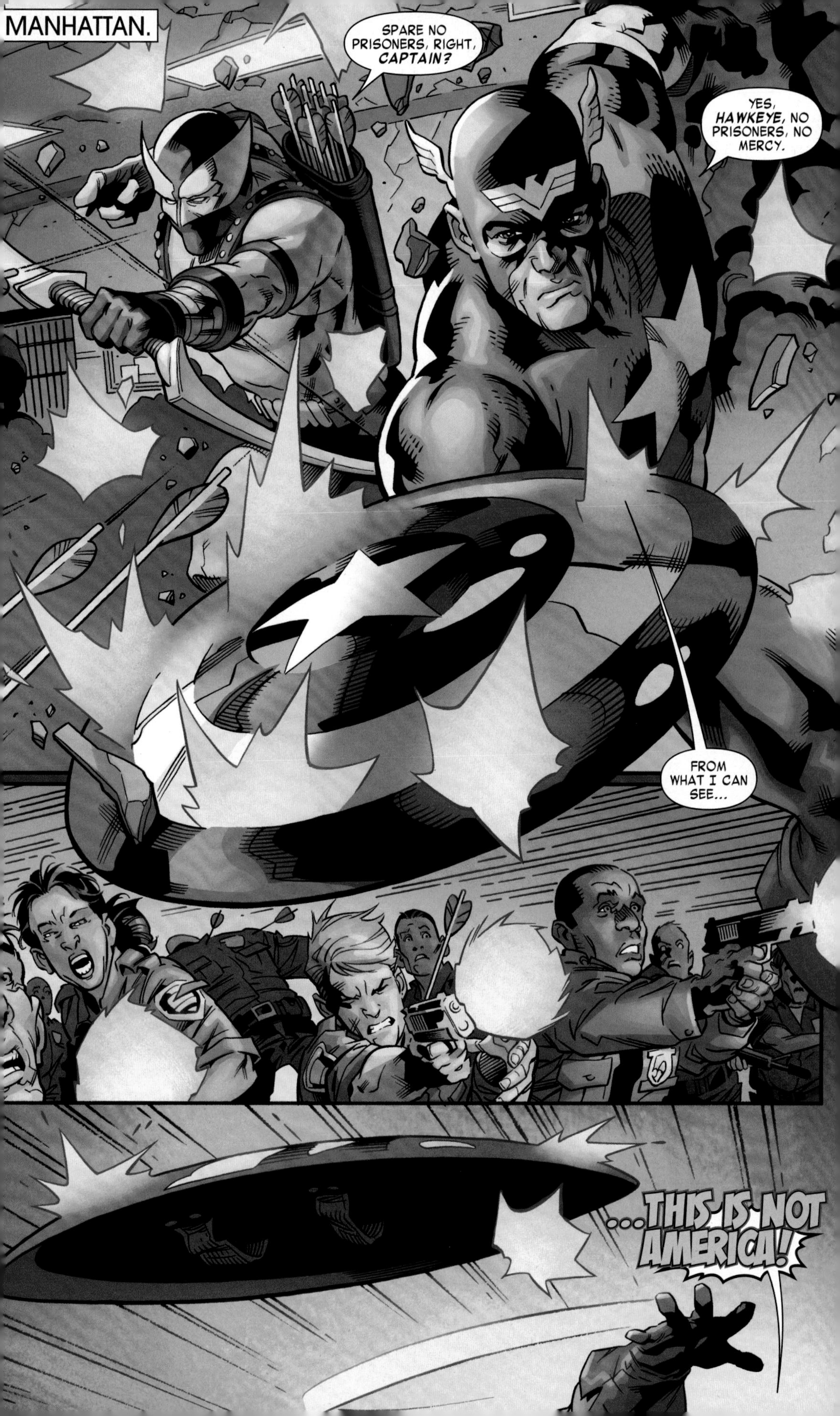

MANHATTAN.
SPARE NO PRISONERS, RIGHT, CAPTAIN?
YES, HAWKEYE, NO PRISONERS, NO MERCY.
FROM WHAT I CAN SEE...
...THIS IS NOT AMERICA!

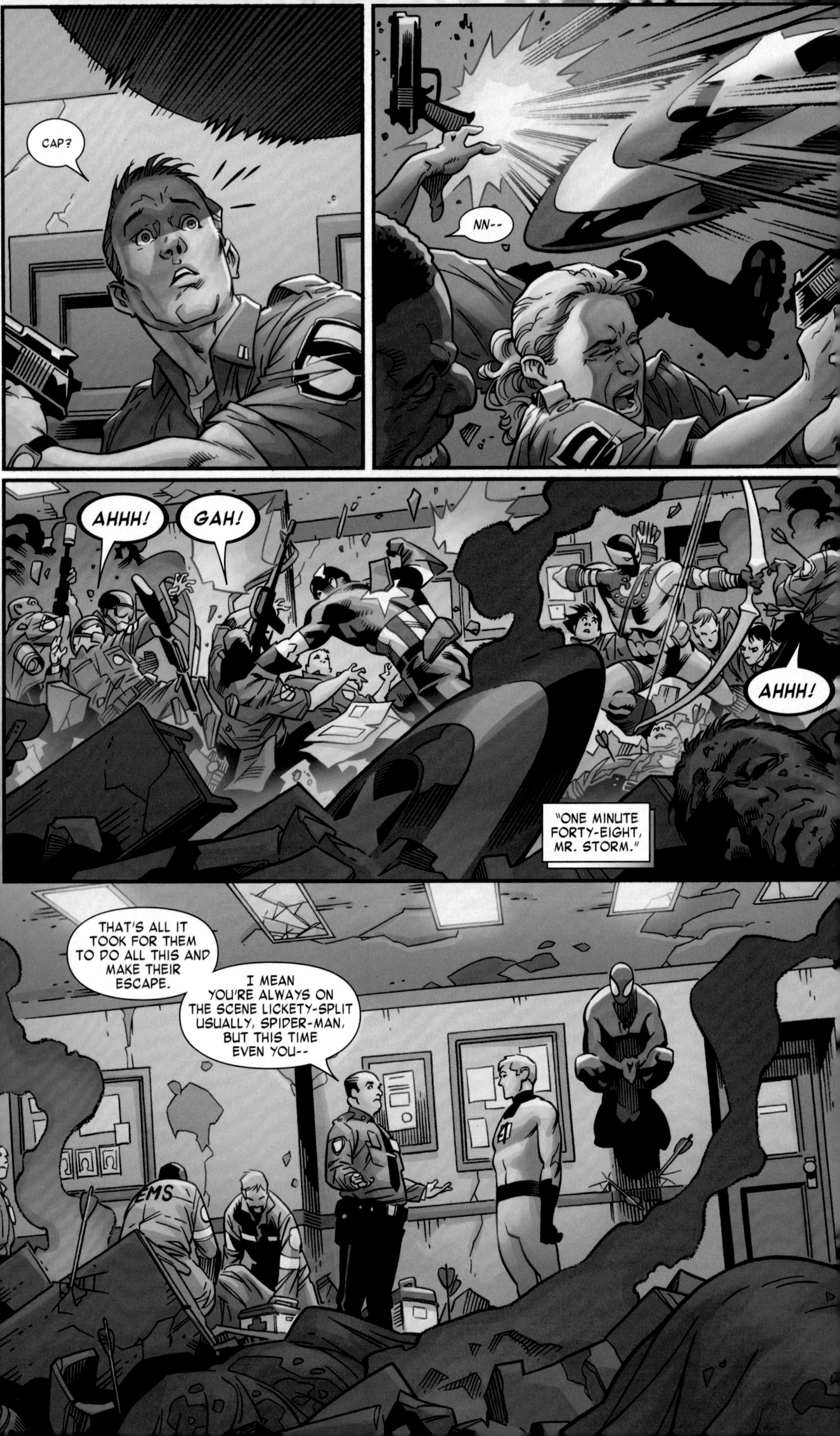
CAP?
NN--
AHHH!
GAH!
AHHH!
"ONE MINUTE FORTY-EIGHT, MR. STORM."
THAT'S ALL IT TOOK FOR THEM TO DO ALL THIS AND MAKE THEIR ESCAPE.
I MEAN YOU'RE ALWAYS ON THE SCENE LICKETY-SPLIT USUALLY, SPIDER-MAN, BUT THIS TIME EVEN YOU--
EMS

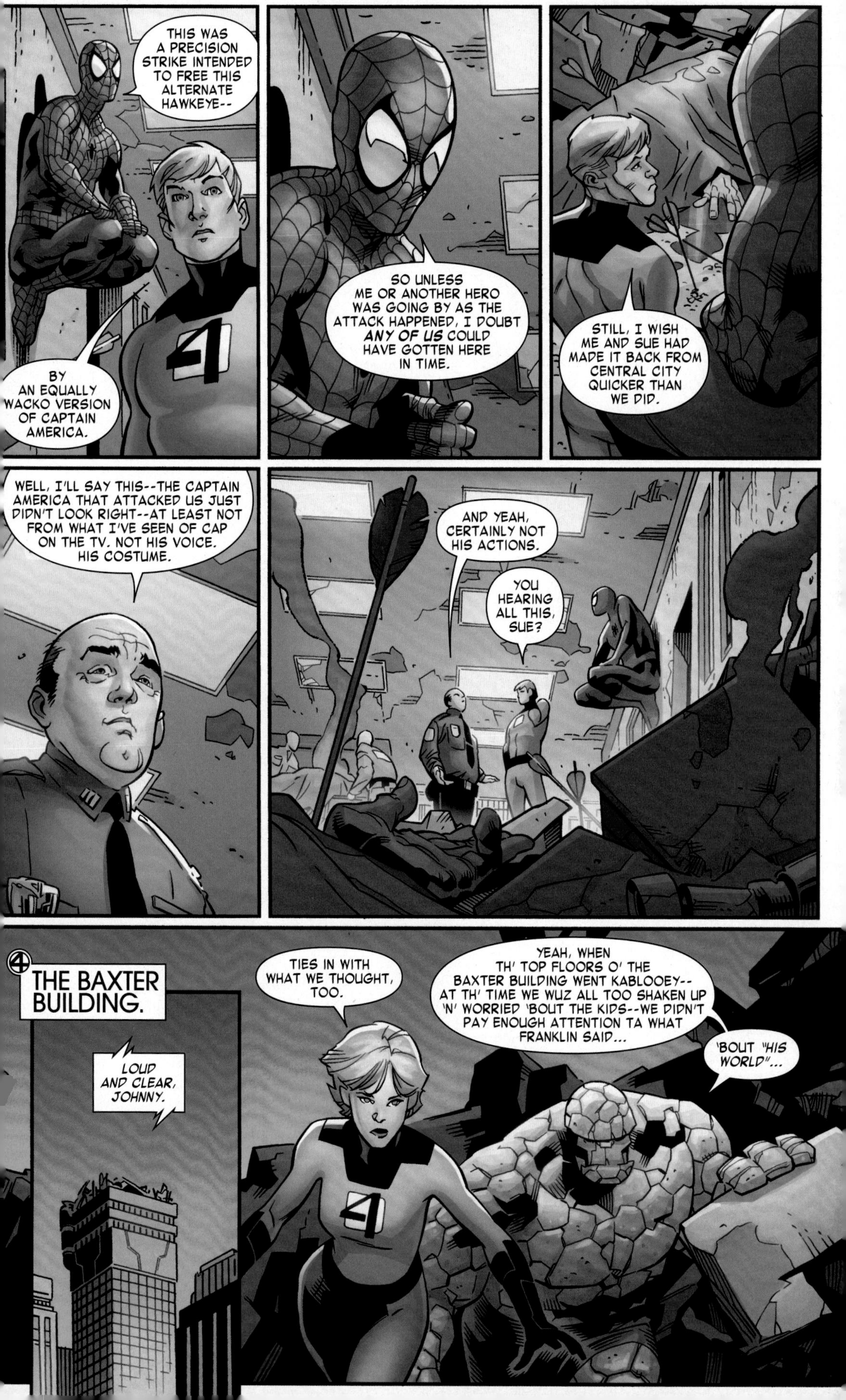
THIS WAS A PRECISION STRIKE INTENDED TO FREE THIS ALTERNATE HAWKEYE--
BY AN EQUALLY WACKO VERSION OF CAPTAIN AMERICA.
SO UNLESS ME OR ANOTHER HERO WAS GOING BY AS THE ATTACK HAPPENED, I DOUBT ANY OF US COULD HAVE GOTTEN HERE IN TIME.
STILL, I WISH ME AND SUE HAD MADE IT BACK FROM CENTRAL CITY QUICKER THAN WE DID.
WELL, I'LL SAY THIS--THE CAPTAIN AMERICA THAT ATTACKED US JUST DIDN'T LOOK RIGHT--AT LEAST NOT FROM WHAT I'VE SEEN OF CAP ON THE TV. NOT HIS VOICE. HIS COSTUME.
AND YEAH, CERTAINLY NOT HIS ACTIONS.
YOU HEARING ALL THIS, SUE?
THE BAXTER BUILDING.
LOUD AND CLEAR, JOHNNY.
TIES IN WITH WHAT WE THOUGHT, TOO.
YEAH, WHEN TH' TOP FLOORS O' THE BAXTER BUILDING WENT KABLOOEY--AT TH' TIME WE WUZ ALL TOO SHAKEN UP 'N' WORRIED 'BOUT THE KIDS--WE DIDN'T PAY ENOUGH ATTENTION TA WHAT FRANKLIN SAID...
'BOUT "HIS WORLD"...

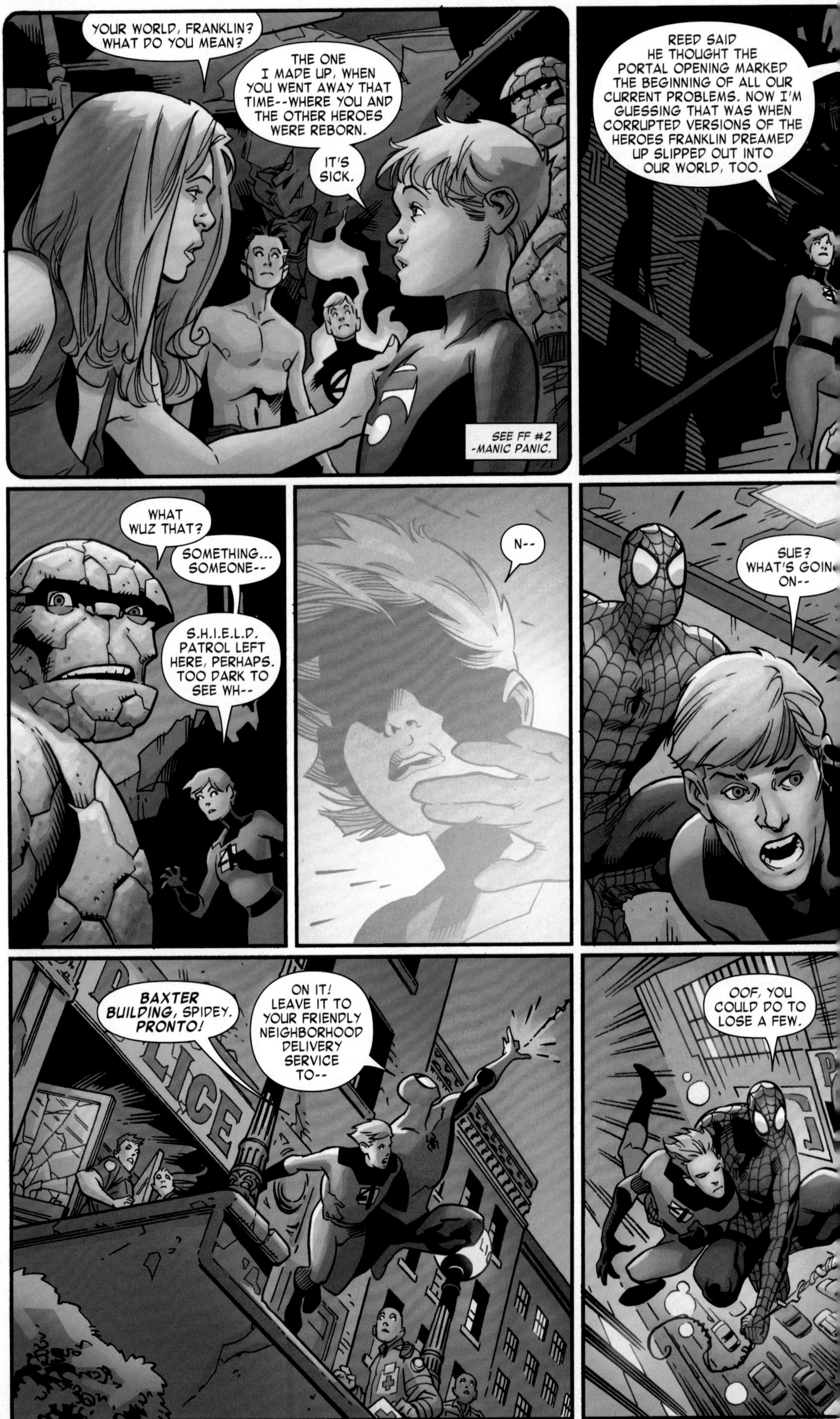
YOUR WORLD, FRANKLIN? WHAT DO YOU MEAN?
THE ONE I MADE UP, WHEN YOU WENT AWAY THAT TIME--WHERE YOU AND THE OTHER HEROES WERE REBORN.
IT'S SICK.
SEE FF #2 -MANIC PANIC.
REED SAID HE THOUGHT THE PORTAL OPENING MARKED THE BEGINNING OF ALL OUR CURRENT PROBLEMS. NOW I'M GUESSING THAT WAS WHEN CORRUPTED VERSIONS OF THE HEROES FRANKLIN DREAMED UP SLIPPED OUT INTO OUR WORLD, TOO.
WHAT WUZ THAT?
SOMETHING... SOMEONE--
S.H.I.E.L.D. PATROL LEFT HERE, PERHAPS. TOO DARK TO SEE WH--
N--
SUE? WHAT'S GOIN ON--
BAXTER BUILDING, SPIDEY. PRONTO!
ON IT! LEAVE IT TO YOUR FRIENDLY NEIGHBORHOOD DELIVERY SERVICE TO--
OOF, YOU COULD DO TO LOSE A FEW.

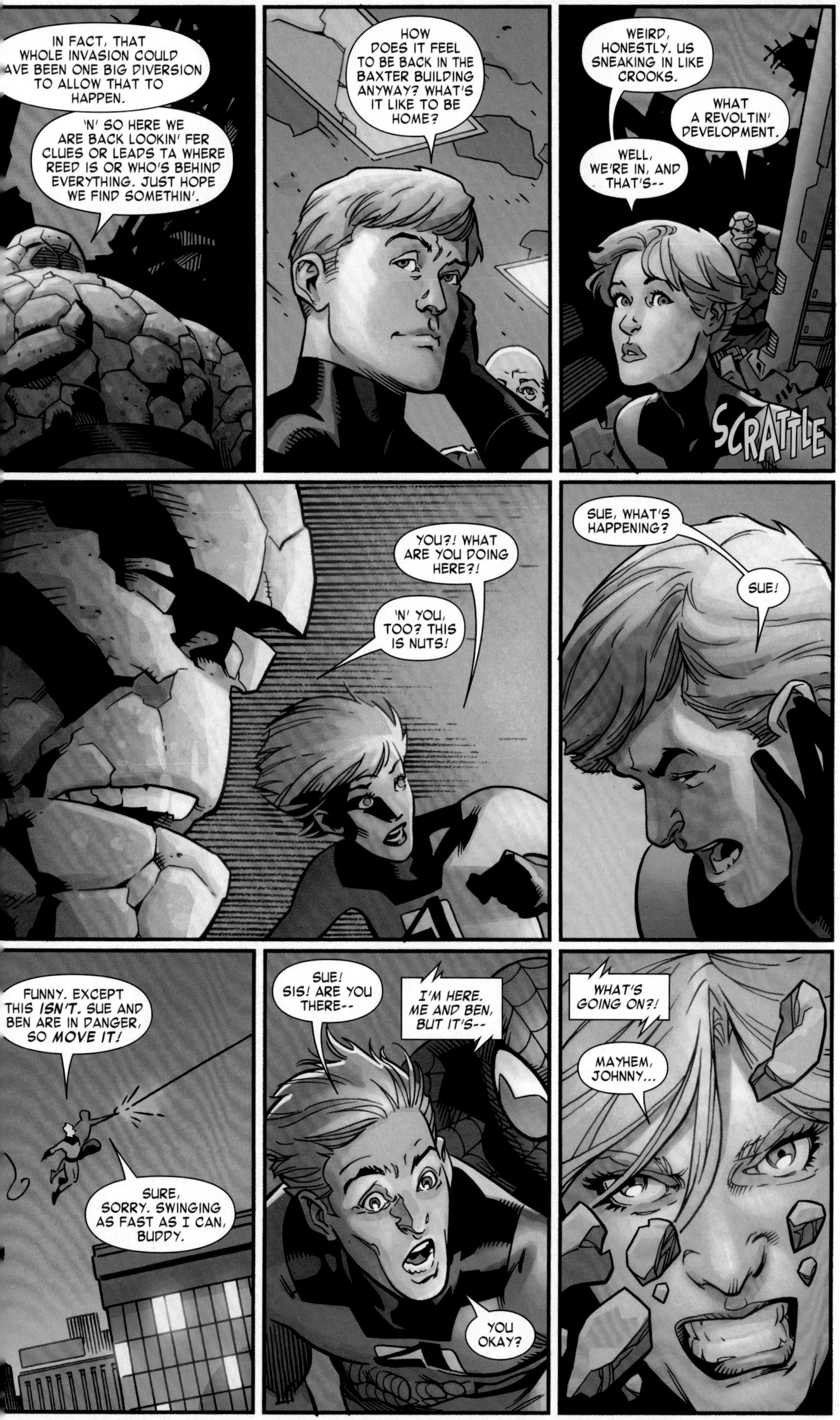

IN FACT, THAT WHOLE INVASION COULD AVE BEEN ONE BIG DIVERSION TO ALLOW THAT TO HAPPEN.
'N' SO HERE WE ARE BACK LOOKIN' FER CLUES OR LEADS TA WHERE REED IS OR WHO'S BEHIND EVERYTHING. JUST HOPE WE FIND SOMETHIN'.
HOW DOES IT FEEL TO BE BACK IN THE BAXTER BUILDING ANYWAY? WHAT'S IT LIKE TO BE HOME?
WEIRD, HONESTLY. US SNEAKING IN LIKE CROOKS.
WHAT A REVOLTIN' DEVELOPMENT.
WELL, WE'RE IN, AND THAT'S--
SCRATTLE
YOU?! WHAT ARE YOU DOING HERE?!
'N' YOU, TOO? THIS IS NUTS!
SUE, WHAT'S HAPPENING?
SUE!
FUNNY. EXCEPT THIS *ISN'T.* SUE AND BEN ARE IN DANGER, SO *MOVE IT!*
SURE, SORRY. SWINGING AS FAST AS I CAN, BUDDY.
SUE! SIS! ARE YOU THERE--
I'M HERE. ME AND BEN, BUT IT'S--
YOU OKAY?
WHAT'S GOING ON?!
MAYHEM, JOHNNY...

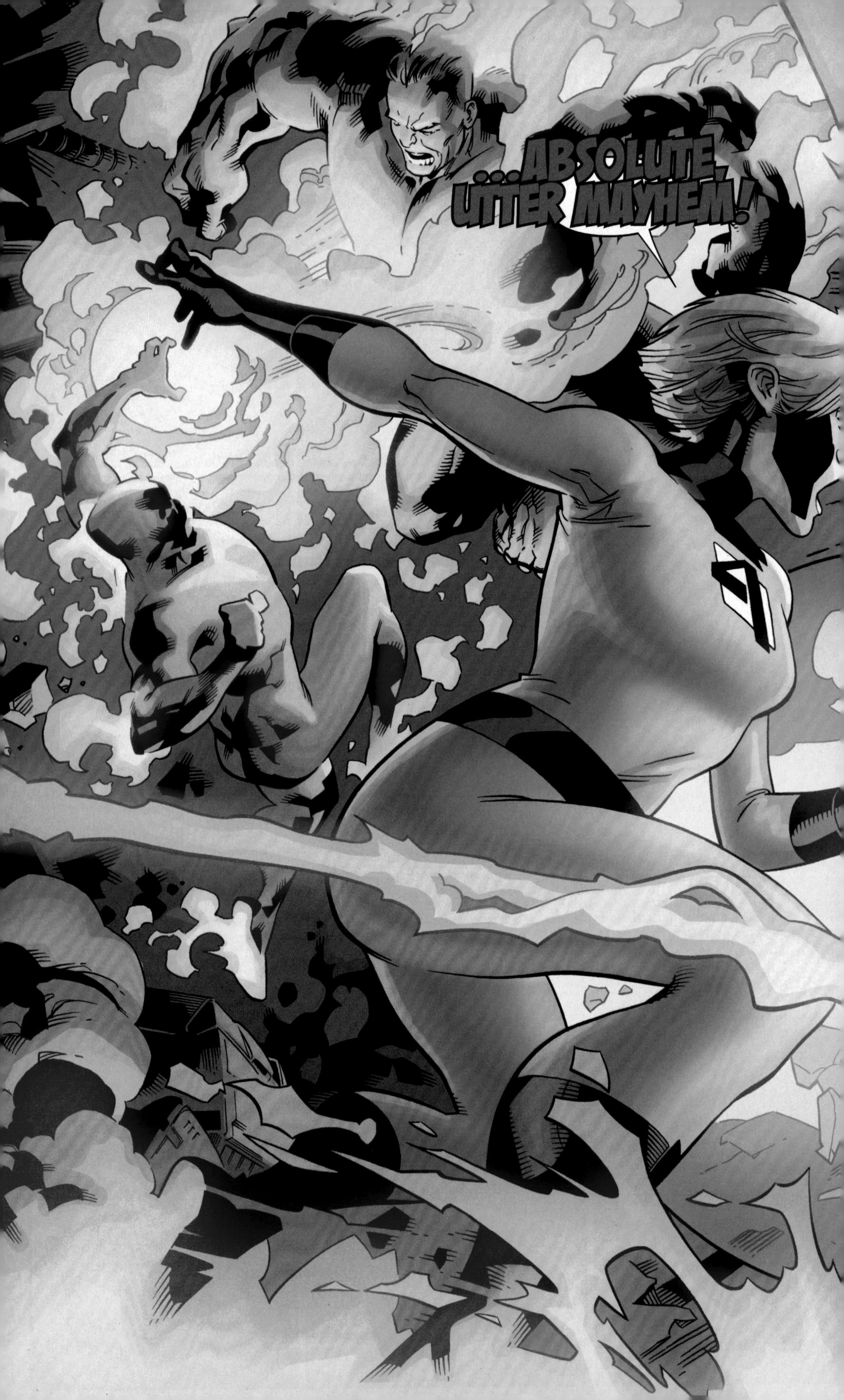
...ABSOLUTE, UTTER MAYHEM!

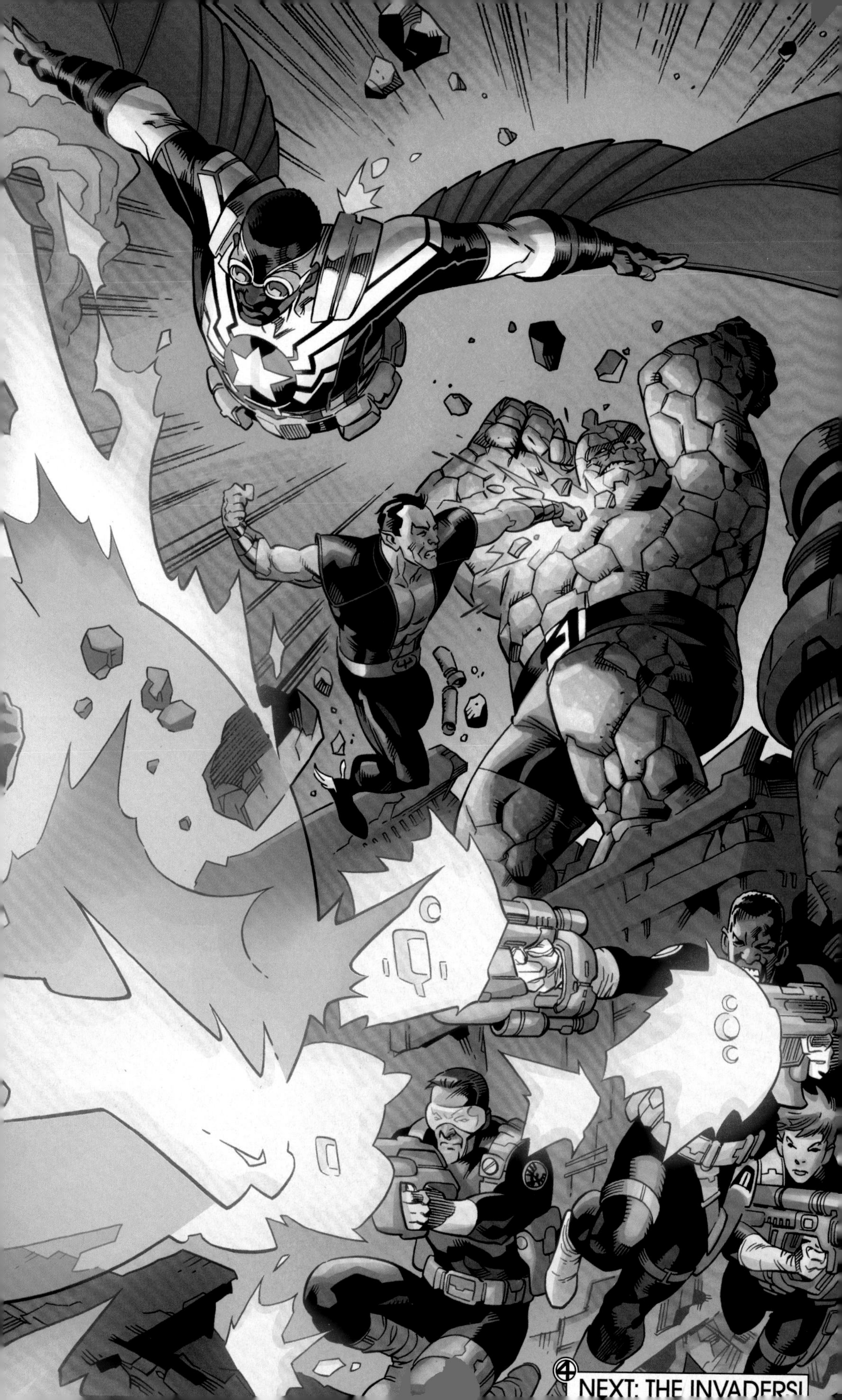
NEXT: THE INVADERS!

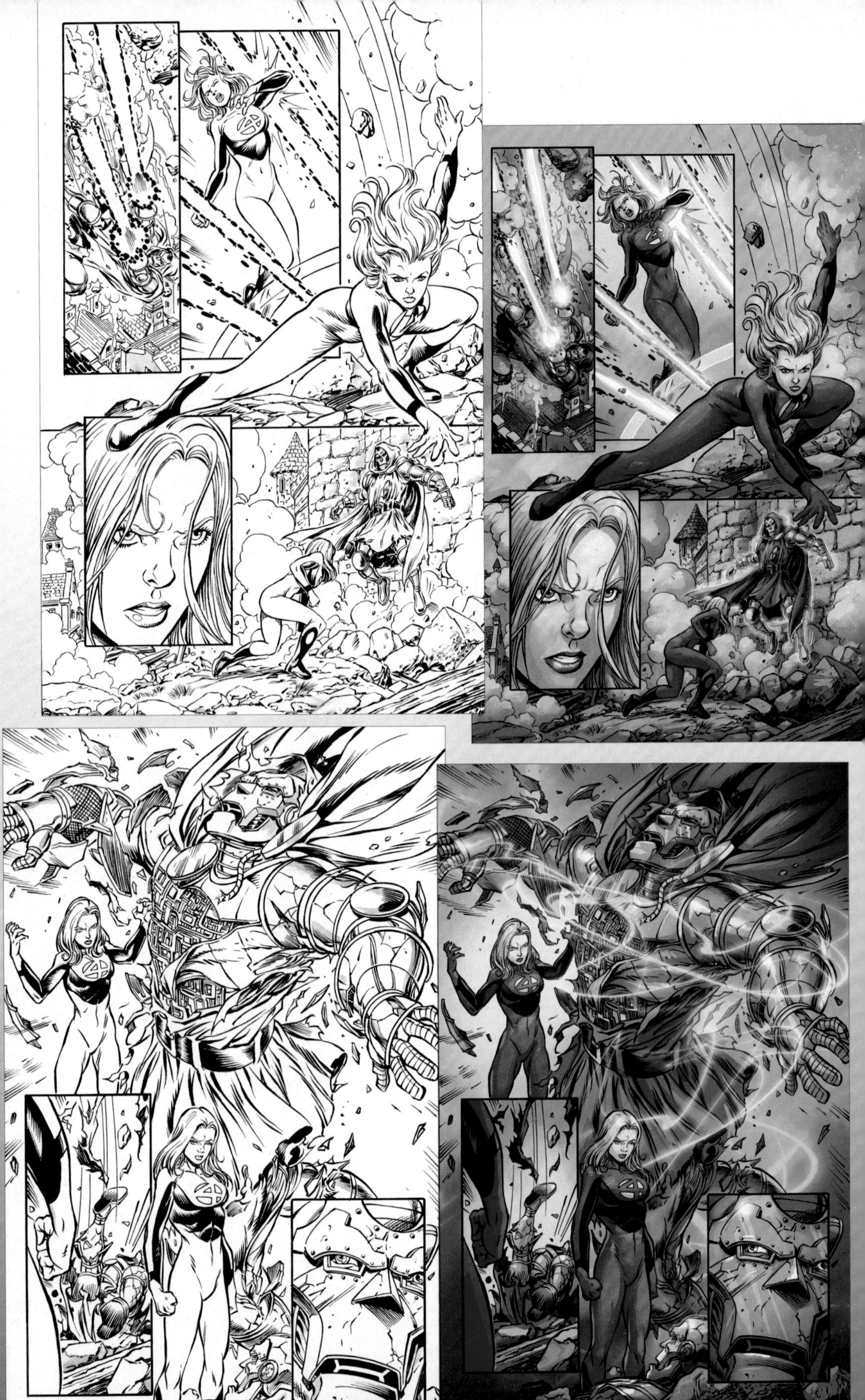

Annual #1 pages 26-27 art by Grummett, Palmer & Charalampidis